# The Subject Is writing

# The Subject Is writing

## Essays by Teachers and Students

### Second Edition

Edited by

**Wendy Bishop**

Boynton/Cook Publishers
HEINEMANN
Portsmouth, NH

Boynton/Cook Publishers, Inc.
A subsidiary of Reed Elsevier Inc.
361 Hanover Street
Portsmouth, NH 03801-3912
http://www.boyntoncook.com
Offices and agents throughout the world.

Cataloging in Publication data is on file at the Library of Congress.
**ISBN: 0–86709–457–5**

Editor: Lisa Luedeke
Cover design: Darci Mehall, Aureo Design
Manufacturing: Louse Richardson
Printed in the United States of America on acid-free paper.
03 02 01 00 99 DA 1 2 3 4 5 6

# Contents

# Preface to the Second Edition

It has been a pleasure to prepare a second edition of *The Subject Is Writing*. To make sure this collection continues to respond to the needs of student writers, I surveyed readers of the first edition to ask how I could improve things. As a result of that survey, I commissioned several new essays. Unfortunately, due to space constraints, adding some essays meant that I had to retire some also, but their authors' voices—so essential in the first edition—remain with us in the epigraphs that open Parts I through V of this edition. Also new to this book is Part VI: Hint Sheets. These, you'll find, are classroom handouts and advice sheets that help you navigate the immediate action of your writing course: Use them; adapt them; write your own variations.

It was true for the first edition, and it's true for the second edition. This book is for you and your teachers. By gathering these essays together, I hope to invite you into an ongoing discussion and to illustrate an important premise: Writing is the subject of writing classes. Your voices, then, join the voices of student writers Audrey Brown and Joe Quatrone and your essays join the essays of writing teachers who share their insights with you here.

In journals, at conferences, and in department meetings, I often hear assertions that writing classes have no "content," especially when compared to literature classes or other classes in other disciplines where famous texts by famous authors are commonly under discussion. Those of us who write, who teach writing, and who love writing and reading a variety of texts know that the *contentless* claim is simply not true. Student texts are valuable texts.

Maxine Hairston (1986) believes, as I do, that "a writing course has its own content, and that is the students' and teachers' writing and the writing process itself" (188). I believe her statement fully because I know my second-best hours as a writer are spent talking to writers, researching writing, and responding to writing. My best hours as a writer, of course, are spent writing, since *talk about* will never substitute for *writing about*. It is clear that we learn to write better by attempting writing and thinking through writing.

I know that not everyone shares my enthusiasm for writing and talking about writing. Still, I feel that shared enthusiasm—that of committed writing teachers and freshly engaged writing students in this text—will offer you the encouragement to begin and continue your own journey as a writer. I'd like to think that you might learn, in our company and the company of your writing class, the lesson shared by poet Marvin Bell: "I always feel better when I write, when I go to my study out back under the wild cherry tree. It only takes

a few minutes before I say, 'Why didn't I come out here sooner?' It feels wonderful" (Murray 1990, 190)

Of course that wonderful feeling isn't easy to achieve, but I believe it is
worth pursuing. The writing teachers in this book are all trying to create a new
kind of writing classroom, one that makes students ask "Why didn't I come
sooner?" At the same time, in their essays they examine the institutional constraints that still exist to slow the development of better writing instruction.

You may be in a writing class because you were told you needed to be
there, and we still need to convince you to stay willingly. On the other hand,
you may have already discovered that writing has a special place in your life
because writing is *for* you as well as for those you write to. Toni Morrison
claims:

> Writing was the only work I did that was for myself and by myself. In the
> process, one exercises sovereignty in a special way. All sensibilities are
> engaged, sometimes simultaneously, sometimes sequentially. While I'm
> writing, all of my experience is vital and useful and possibly important.
> (Murray, 1990, 8)

In the writing classes described in these essays and created by you and
your peers and your teacher, writing is for you and for others, work you do
alone and work you do together, work that engages you and that authorizes
your view and your experiences, work that remains central to your sense of
self—important *work*.

The six parts of this book are not intended to restrict your reading; move
freely between them. Essayists in Part I—Writing to Invent and Imagine—ask
you to see writing as part of your lifelong journey. In these chapters you'll look
at ways to get started. You'll consider how you change over time as a writer.
You'll be offered ideas for using journals and be asked to examine some of
your writing habits that may or may not be supporting your writing practices.
In Part II—Invitations to Write—two essayists encourage you to develop topics based on your own life stories and to examine the culture(s) you inhabit;
two other essayists provide solid advice about optimizing your writing
processes and learning to revise in ways that allow you to move more deeply
and specifically into your writing subject(s).

In Part III—To the Writer—essayists share their understandings of forces
that affect college writing and writers. They examine the nature of contemporary writing classrooms and the process of change writers undergo as they
become college writers; they provide an introduction to the computer-based
writing classroom and examine current understandings of how writing and
reading processes and writers and readers work together. In Part IV—Behind
the Scenes—the essayists do just that: invite you to take an insider's look at
writing classrooms. Here, you explore issues of interest and concern to any
student writer. It might well be you who asks: What is a grade? What do you
mean respond to my peer's essay? Why are writing groups used? What if I

have trouble with this assignment (teacher, classroom)? Reading essays in this section, you'll learn you're not alone in raising such questions. You, your teacher, and your class can use these discussions to begin investigations of your own. In Part V—Figuring out the World, Figuring in the World—essayists encourage you to explore what it means to write. What do you value as a writer? What do teachers value in writing? Are they the same thing? Should they be? By reading and responding to the discussions in this section, you begin to address decision points of your own life: What will you write; how; in what style; and for whom? How do you see yourself as a writer, now and in the future? Finally, Part VI—Hint Sheets, new to this edition—offers you and your teacher practical advice for everyday writing classroom events and activities.

None of these authors offers you pat answers. None intends his or her view to be the only way to look at writing. But all are trying to share their commitment to writing.

The essays in this textbook were reviewed before publication in writing classrooms across the country. Students responded to the essay drafts, and suggested revisions to authors who then revised, trying to improve the essays in light of those suggestions. These are, then, not esoteric academic journal essays but, we hope, essays in the best sense, exploratory and earnest communications from writers to readers. And you'll notice that our essay writing—like your essay writing—takes many forms.

# Works Cited

Hairston, Maxine (1986). "Using Nonfiction Literature in the Composition Classroom." In B.T. Peterson (Ed.), *Convergences: Transactions in Reading and Writing*. Urbana, IL: National Council of Teachers of English. (pp. 179--188).

Murray, Donald M. (1990) *Shoptalk: Learning to Write with Writers*. Portsmouth, NH: Boynton/Cook Heinemann.

# Acknowledgments

John Updike wrote: "Writing well involves two gifts—the art of adding and the art of taking away. Of the two, the first is more important, since without it the second could not exist" (Murray 1990, 187).

Clearly *The Subject Is Writing* represents a group effort in the best sense. I want to thank all the essayists—in both editions—who added to this book by sharing their work. Bob Boynton and Peter Stillman supported the first edition through every draft and revision. The second edition would not exist without that initial enthusiasm and vision. This edition owes its life and energy to the interest and support of Lisa Luedeke and Robin Najar. Robin helped me survey teachers and students and Lisa has helped to shape the course of this book; she also answered all my e-mails! Many thanks to you both.

The following teachers and their writing students helped with the manuscript drafts: thanks to Susan Barron; Anne Bower; Roger Casey; Devan Cook; Gay Lynn Crossley; Beth Daniell; Kevin Davis; Kim Haimes-Korn; Rich Haswell; Ruth Johnson; Ann Kalinak; Carolyn Kremers; Pat MacEnulty; Michael McMahon; Ruth Mirtz; Dean Newman; Elsie Rogers; Mary Jane Ryals; Jim Strickland; Craig Stroupe; Gretchen Thies; Cindy Wheatley-Lovoy; Ron Wiginton; Thia Wolf; and Trisha Yarborough. My next nod of appreciation goes to several years of first-year through senior writing students who have discussed these essays with me and helped me see how to improve my work as writer, teacher, and editor. And of course, my daughter Morgan and son Tait always provide windows into the world of reading and writing by sharing their humor, energy, and insights into texts and text-making.

## Works Cited

Murray, Donald M. (1990) *Shoptalk: Learning to Write with Writers.* Portsmouth, NH: Boynton/Cook Heinemann.

# The Subject Is writing

# Part I

# Writing to Invent and Imagine

I've been learning to write since before I can remember—since first holding a crayon in my hand—yet I've only scratched the surface of what there is to learn and to write about. Some of my best writing has grown out of my journals, has come instantly, like magic. I didn't know what I was going to write, it just came out. Other writing has taken months to research, or years to simmer and season in my memory and my heart, before I could bear to write it down. I write better than I did, say, a year ago, but I still don't write as well as I want to. . . .

—Carolyn Kremers, writing teacher

I say to myself, Can this be done? Well the only way to know is to write it and see. Like all struggling writers, I am still searching for a voice, a place to call home, a place to talk or scream or whisper from. I think I have found a foothold to start with.

—John Beck, writing student

What matters, when you first sit down to write, is that the who you are writing for is yourself and the why is to make that writing a process of discovery. It is the act of writing that makes the search for new meaning possible. You may decide to share this initial thinking with a fellow student or with your teacher, but hold on to the certainty that whether to share or not, at this predraft stage, is your decision.

—Pat D'Arcy, writing teacher

1

The members of our group are surprisingly similar with respect to the way we write. Almost all of us do some form of formal categorizing. Some of us outline, some brainstorm, some write lists, and some of us just write. One thing remains constant among all six of us—we all procrastinate. I used to think I was a horrible individual for waiting until the last minute, but now I realize that everyone procrastinates—maybe we do it to actually "psych" ourselves up. We all preferred to write straight through with breaks only for their nutritional value. Most of us need quiet in order to keep up our train of thought but one of us (surprisingly) preferred lots of loud music. With regard to writer's block we agreed that the only way to beat it is to keep working.

—Writers' group report on writing processes

# 1

# Writing as a Tool for Learning and Discovery

## Thia Wolf

Thia Wolf is Associate Professor of Composition Studies at
California State University, Chico, where she coordinates the
English Composition Program. She teaches courses in writing and
rhetoric to undergraduates and courses in composition theory to
graduate students. The birth of her son in 1995 has inspired her to
investigate learning development in children. She resides in
Richardson Springs, a canyon just outside of Chico, with her family
and three rambunctious dogs.

This essay examines ways of using writing to improve memory, foster
insights, and accelerate learning. Few of us stop to consider that writing can
be more than a functional activity (something we do when we need to apply
for a job or prepare for a trip to the grocery store) and different from mandatory assignments. Writing is a uniquely human tool, a means to stimulate
memory, construct new knowledge, and explore both ourselves and our environment. Even people who don't like to write essays, letters, or research
papers may find that they enjoy using writing to increase their learning potential. I want to introduce you to writing activities that can support you in learning and in living. You'll probably get the most out of this essay if you have
paper and pencil handy. Rather than reading straight through, plan to sit down
with the essay more than once. On each occasion of your reading, try one or
two of the activities suggested here. They are scattered throughout the text.

Let's begin by looking at some ways that writing stimulates and enhances memory. Although researchers still have a long way to go before understanding all about the ways our brains work, they have created useful hypotheses, or theories, about brain function. Obviously, our brains store information over the entire course of our lives; this stored information forms the basic building blocks of our memories.

We'll try a simple writing activity that demonstrates how memory becomes activated through language. Start with a word that seems neutral, even uninteresting, and print it in the middle of a sheet of paper. (In my example, below, I started with the word *bread*.) After you've printed this word, print other words or phrases that it reminds you of. (You'll see that I wrote names of breads, but pretty soon I found myself writing names and places where I'd eaten bread, people I know who like bread, childhood memories about bread, etc.) Keep track of the thoughts that go through your mind by noting as many words and phrases as you can around other words and phrases on the page that trigger a memory or association. You may be surprised at how many memories come back to you and how many associations you have for simple words such as *tree*, *lamp*, or *blanket*.

The map below (Figure 1.1) is a visual representation of the ways my brain became stimulated when I thought of the word "bread." I began by categorizing breads: sourdough, French. And I suddenly remembered something I think of only rarely—the Helm's Bakery truck that used to visit our neighborhood when I was a child. The Helm's truck was like an ice cream truck,

## Figure 1–1

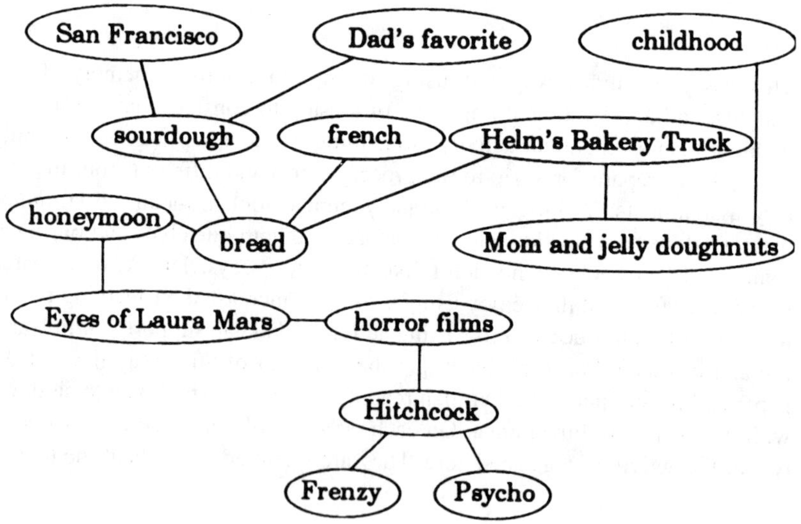

except that it was filled with shelves of breads, doughnuts, and other bakery goods. Although I didn't mention it in my map, remembering the Helm's truck brought back memories of some of the most delicious smells imaginable. When the Helm's man opened the large back doors to his truck and invited us up a step and into his bakery, my mother and I found ourselves enveloped in the thick, sweet smells of freshly baked treats.

Remembering what it felt like to enter the truck with my mother, I also remembered her favorite food: lemon jelly doughnuts. But my thinking didn't stop there. Coming back to my original word trigger, bread, I realized that sourdough bread reminds me both of my father, who loves it, and of San Francisco, a place renowned for its sourdough loaves. Thinking of San Francisco reminded me of my honeymoon, and of a film my husband and I saw while we were there. That film, a horror film, made me think of other horror films I've known.

Create a map yourself and see what it shows you about how your memory works.

# Activity

When I made my map and reviewed it, I realized how important the sense of smell is in my memory process: the smell of the Helm's Bakery Truck and the smell of the sourdough loaves on San Francisco's fisherman's wharf brought back the richest memories for me.

Writing researchers Linda Flower and John Hayes (1977) explain that we store memory in "rich bits," chemically encoded pieces of information that incorporate many experiences and associations. Flower and Hayes liken them to intuition and explain that without the intervention of language these bits never become useful to us. Although I have stored many complex bits of information about my family and my daily experience in my brain, I can only examine, enjoy, and use this information fully when I put it into words. Looking over my map I can also see that relationships occupy a central place in my memory process: most of my memories center on my relationships with my family members. The words in my map serve as memory triggers, allowing me to relive significant moments in my life and to make new connections between my past experience and my present situation. If you examine your cognitive map, what memory triggers seem to matter most to you? Did you remember any details when you did your map that surprised or pleased you? What were they?

Most people who use writing as a way of remembering the past find that many small details they had entirely forgotten resurface during the writing activity. This is not to say that all of these memories are accurate. Experiments on the working of memory reveal that many factors—including stress, distorted self-assessment, and elapsed time—alter the way we remember past events. Also, the way others remember or represent the past can influence our memories of it (Loftus 1988).

To demonstrate how malleable memory really is, write a one-page description of something you remember from your childhood. Make sure that it's a memory that is fairly vivid for you and that someone in your family will probably also remember. After you've written your description down, talk to the family member who shared the experience with you. Ask for his or her description. What discrepancies did you find?

I've often found that my memory of a situation differs radically from others' memories. When I finished high school, I expected to be given my father's old Volkswagen Beetle; I clearly remembered that he had promised it to me when I was a freshman. My graduation day arrived at last, but my father had no memory of any such promise! He eventually traded the car in on a new car for himself. Because I know my father is an honest man, I know he really didn't remember having promised me the car. It's not impossible, in fact, that I made up the promise in my own mind and came to believe in it because I wanted it to be true.

The malleability of memory is one reason why some people like to keep daily journals: a written record of the highlights in one's life can help to keep memory more accurate. In business situations, many individuals like to create a "paper trail," a series of memos and notes that record each worker's responsibilities for a certain project. In these cases, writing becomes a way of preserving memory and creating a history of a business undertaking or a private life.

But writing has many more interesting uses than to preserve or explore memory. In and out of school settings, writing can help individuals synthesize new information with previously learned information and thus create new, complex structures of *understanding*. So let's move from the realm of memory and examine some writing activities that help us to think more clearly and create new ways of knowing what we need to know.

# Activity

One writing activity my students and I both enjoy is the "teacher exercise," an activity passed on to me by a friend who took a workshop on creative diary keeping. The teacher exercise is an example of a dialogue activity, a way of externalizing some of the internal conversations that take place between different voices within yourself. To create a successful dialogue with one of your internal teaching voices, start by listing important teachers in your life. These may be people you have known and admired, people you've never met, characters in stories or film, places you've traveled, even objects. (For example, I learn a lot by watching the ways trees share ground and sky with one another; they're a cooperative group that live together peaceably unless dire necessity forces them to struggle for the same ground. From trees I've learned the importance of being as much as one can be wherever one stands.) I've included a partial list of my favorite teachers below:

My music teacher, Virginia Petersen

My dissertation director, Professor Don Daiker

My colleague, Elizabeth Renfro

My neighbor, Jean Graybeal

Trees

After you make a list that suits you, try writing a dialogue between yourself and one of your teachers about a problem you want to solve. Write as quickly as you can, allowing the dialogue to surprise you. Continue to write for several pages.

Written dialogue exercises like this one frequently allow writers to experience sudden insights about problems as diverse as family fights and difficult chemistry equations. Even if your internal teacher doesn't have an answer for your problem, he/she can often provide a strategy for approaching the problem so that you can think about it more calmly, analytically, and effectively.

Another useful dialogue exercise involves recreating an argument you've had with someone, but approaching the argument from the other person's point of view. Include not only the spoken part of the argument, but also the thoughts of the person you argued against. How does that person respond internally to the things you did and said during the argument? When you consider the argument from his/her viewpoint, can you better understand why he/she responded to you in the way he/she did? Try this dialogue exercise here, including the other person's internal thoughts in parentheses.

Being able to understand your opponent's point of view has long been a recommended technique for learning how to persuade others to see your side of an argument. Psychologist Carl Rogers (1965) has claimed that only through validating the viewpoint of another can we hope to have our own viewpoints validated. Analyzing and validating an opponent's view before opposing it may lead to better negotiations for a third, socially constructed viewpoint between all of the parties involved. And you may surprise yourself by finding that, after studying someone else's view, you agree with his/her opinion more than you'd realized.

I recall a turbulent time in my household when I was still in my teens. During an argument with my mother, I claimed that she always put her own needs and interests ahead of my own. She countered by telling me that most of her activities (cooking, cleaning, driving, shopping) revolved around my needs, and that if I didn't understand this, I had better start trying some of her responsibilities on for size. If I had stopped to think about the world from her point of view, I would have seen that she contributed a generous share of her time and energy to keeping me happy. Because I didn't stop to think about her perspective, I made her angry, had some of my privileges revoked, and took on a new household responsibility, that of family cook. She and I didn't have a conversation about our misunderstandings: we had a fight. And fighting, although it produces a satisfactory amount of adrenaline and a momentary surge of self-righteous indignation, rarely transforms the problems it seeks to address.

Now that you've warmed up your imagination by creating the voices of a teacher and an opponent, consider some of the other ways that imagination can intersect with writing to help you create connections and new insights. Below, I've described a few activities that students of mine have found useful. Read them over, then try one.

# Activity

*Letter from the Future.*    Write yourself a letter from an older version of yourself. What will you be like in twenty-five years? Where will you live? What will you do for a living? What will matter to you most? Write to yourself from this older perspective. What advice should your older self give your present self to make sure you arrive at the future you most want?

*Intersection.*    List five subjects you've studied in school. Choose the two that seem most different from each other and write a paragraph describing all of their similarities and connections, even if you really have to stretch to find these.

*Drawing into Writing.*    Draw three pictures of a recurring problem in your life, whether it's studying mathematics or making satisfying friendships. Date one of these pictures from an earlier time in your life, one from the present, and one from the future. Write a paragraph or two that explores the connections between these pictures. What patterns can you start to detect by exploring the ways these pictures relate to each other? What alternative behaviors or approaches might help you solve the problem you've explored?

These activities work equally well for advancing your understanding of your private life and of your scholastic endeavors. You can just as easily ask a future version of yourself about the many reasons why studying writing or mathematics now might help you later in life as you can ask that self about the benefits of vigorous exercise over the course of many years. One important feature of activities like these is that they give you a chance to become more involved in your learning process. Research on cognition, our internal thought processes, indicates that personal involvement in any learning activity increases the chances that learning will be sophisticated rather than superficial, and memorable rather than easily forgotten (Mandler 1984). With a little thought and creativity, you can see how activities such as these could help you in a variety of classes and situations. In a history course, you might write a journal entry from the point of view of a historical figure; in a chemistry course, you might write a conversation among the elements in an equation. You'll enjoy learning more and learn more effectively if you can construct approaches to learning that engage your attention and challenge your imagination.

One of the most powerful ways to challenge yourself through written language and to learn any lesson well is to develop a facility with metaphors and similes. Some researchers argue that metaphors—comparisons between like things—are the fundamental building blocks of all interpretive endeavors. This is because metaphors tap into our most basic ways of knowing about the world—through our senses and our bodily motions. Everything we understand, every new piece of knowledge we add to what we already know, connects with some physical experience of our environment. This is the critical function of metaphor: to provide us with linguistic links between abstract or unexamined thoughts and our physical understanding of the world in which we live.

That last sentence may be hard to understand without a concrete example of the way metaphors and similes work. Let me provide you with an example from my own life. As a freshman in college, I enrolled in an astronomy course, a class I nearly failed. I have hated astronomy ever since but never stopped to think about why. By constructing a simile, I can begin to examine my reasons for responding so negatively to this academic subject. To construct the simile, I'll use the abstract, unexamined problem ("I hate studying astronomy") and a physical experience to which I can compare it. For my physical experience, I use the technique of association, jotting down the first example that comes to mind of something else I hate: eating a rotten bing cherry. So here's my simile: Studying astronomy is like *eating a rotten bing cherry*.

What sense can I make of this comparison? I'll start with the physical side of the equation. Bing cherries are my favorite food. I look forward to cherry season every year and have been known to consume a whole bag of cherries for lunch or dinner. So when I get a rotten cherry, I'm disappointed and disagreeably surprised. My mouth is all set for one kind of taste sensation, but the cherry feels mealy and tastes moldy on my tongue.

Having sorted through these reactions to the rotten cherry, I can start thinking about ways the eating experience reminds me of the astronomy class I took. I remember now that before I enrolled in the course, I expected to like it. I've always been a science fiction fan, and I assumed an astronomy class would focus mostly on facts about distant planets (with some speculation about extraterrestrial life-forms thrown in for good measure). In fact, the professor talked mostly about physics. He wanted us to learn a variety of mathematical calculations that would help us understand how scientists interpret the information they receive from telescopes. Because I expected one kind of experience in the course and got another (very much like expecting a good cherry but biting into a rotten one), I reacted to astronomy with distaste. Realizing this makes me wonder if I wouldn't be wise to give astronomy another try. After all, I may have caused my own problems in learning because of the expectations I carried with me into the class. Now that I'm older and a bit more open-minded, I might enjoy learning something about telescopes and the use of physics to understand the stars.

Writing theorist Peter Elbow (1981) suggests an interesting metaphor activity, which students in many of my writing classes tell me later is the single most useful discovery tool I taught them. This activity will help you make surprising, creative connections if you do the first half quickly and the second half thoughtfully. First, choose a problem (scholastic or personal) that you haven't yet solved. Quickly, without stopping to think about your response, write down its color, its shape, its size, its smell. Now take several minutes to explain, in writing, why you gave this problem each of these physical properties (for a whole series of metaphor activities, see Elbow 1981). Were you able to discover what some of your metaphors meant?

Often, using metaphors to redefine a problem can give you an entirely new perspective on your situation. Developing skill with metaphors will also enhance your use of descriptive and poetic language in your more formal writing tasks.

Finally, you can also employ writing in classes across the disciplines to help strengthen your learning process. Most students take notes during lectures, even though many classroom lectures only repeat material that can be found in the course textbook. If you notice that the professors in some of your classes go over reading material in their lectures, consider using writing in their classes to do something other than take notes. Here are some suggestions: periodically summarize the key points the lecturer has just covered; decide what puzzles you about what you've heard, and write down questions that you'd like to ask in class or during the teacher's office hours; listen for and jot down discrepancies between what the lecturer says and what you thought you knew about the subject (discrepancies should be cleared up in a conversation with the teacher or by rereading the course's text). All of these writing strategies allow you to interact with your learning, to question the material actively instead of sitting like a porous lump in the lecture hall waiting to be filled with someone else's knowledge. Students who take an assertive, interested approach to learning get more out of the courses they take and enjoy their educational experiences far more than students who learn material by rote for exams.

The writing strategies mentioned above can help you during your assigned reading. Keep blank paper handy to copy out intriguing or confusing portions of the text. Select some of these passages for brief writing: what questions do the passages raise or what new ideas do they give you? A particularly rewarding technique for examining your assigned reading is to make connections between unrelated courses. Ask yourself hard questions, such as How does this rule in physics connect with what I learned about the law of supply and demand in my economics course? or Did the conquest of the New World by the Spanish that I'm studying in my history course contain any of the ethical dilemmas I'm studying in my philosophy class? If you take a few minutes to note these questions and respond to them briefly in writing, you'll begin to see many opportunities for drawing on information from all of your classes in developing an educated worldview. You'll probably come up with some interesting paper topics this way, too.

Above all, remember that writing for learning need not be correct, sophisticated, or polished. Writing for learning should serve you as a tool for analyzing and synthesizing many kinds of information in your life. This is writing for *you,* not a teacher, employer, or classmate. Although you may choose to share some of this writing or to develop ideas from this writing into more formal prose, writing for learning should be stress-free, exploratory, and mind-opening. Use it to enjoy and enhance your mind's activity as you study, reflect, and live.

# Works Cited

Elbow, Peter (1981). *Writing with Power.* New York: Oxford Press.

Flower, Linda, & Hayes, John (1977). "Problem-solving Strategies and the Writing Process." *College English, 39,* 456.

Loftus, Elisabeth (1988). *Mind and Body.* New York: Norton.

Mandler, G. (1984). *Mind and Body.* New York: Norton.

Rogers, Carl (1965). *Client-centered Therapy.* Boston: Houghton Mifflin.

# Sharing Ideas

- In an essay later in this collection, Kate Ronald explains that "with computers and copier machines, we don't worry much anymore about memory." In Thia's essay, however, a writer's memories are very important, and writing is a way to "improve memory, foster insights, and accelerate learning." Are these essayists contradicting each other or are they discussing memory in different ways?

- Thia suggests that you can tap into your memories through writing in general and through particular writing strategies like mapping, setting up dialogues with internal voices, and drawing. What, then, is the importance of memory to writers?

- As you tried Thia's activities while you read, which proved most useful to you and why?

- You may have used memory maps before (the technique is sometimes called clustering) or you may freewrite or list to capture the vivid and important details of your past. Share your personal methods (listening to music, walking, etc.) for triggering memory.

- How have two different memories of the same event (yours and another family member's, for example) affected your life?

- Thia suggests that it can be very important for a writer to be able to understand the viewpoint(s) of others. Share a time in your life when that was true.

- Everyone knows that poets use similes and metaphors, and Thia claims they have a lot to offer to any writer. What do you think of her claim and her example (astronomy and rotten cherries)?

- Metaphors seem to come naturally to some people. Do you know anyone who regularly compares one thing to another? Write a sketch of that person, capturing his or her language, and the way he or she makes comparisons.

- If you don't normally make comparisons easily yourself, take a piece of your writing and try to consciously add some metaphors. What changes? How do you like the new version?

---

# 2

# Changing as a Writer

## Audrey Brown

---

Audrey Brown was a student at the University of Vermont when she
wrote this essay.

---

I don't like to write
I never did.
It always takes me a long time to get done.

—age 9

Eleven years later and I still feel this way. So what am I doing? I don't like my
writing. I'm mad right now. I'm irritable. I just bit my sister's head off because
she came in my room with an essay she wanted me to proofread. I always liked
math. Maybe I should have been a math major. Math is good because it's
straightforward and always either right or wrong. There's no emotional
involvement with math. Writing, any kind of writing, drains me.

When writing, I have always felt that I am struggling with myself. The
only reason I have continued to write is that once in a while I like what comes
out. But I really don't want to write this paper that is supposed to trace the
development of my voice. I've been sitting here for hours. Struggling. My
brain is so jammed with all the possible ways to write this that I'm having
trouble producing anything at all. Well, I have to write something, and analytical writing is a safe way to go, so. . . . I wrote my first descriptive piece when
I was eight.

September 14, 1976
I like flowers. They smell nice. They are pretty.

I didn't take advantage of my youth and inexperience to write something off the wall here like "flowers are ugly" or something fantastic and imaginary like "the flowers are dancing." Although at the time, I'm sure I didn't even realized I had that option. I described flowers the way I saw them and the way I still see them. They *are* pretty and they *are* nice. Basic words for a basic subject.

Much of my writing actually reminds me a little of math. Don't take any chances, because if you take chances, you get the answer wrong. Just like math. Subject + verb + object = a sentence. 2 + 2 + 2 = 6. Sometimes this strategy works well, as in the flower piece. Other times, this mathematical prose makes me sound very emotionless.

When I was nine my family had a dog named Tan. He was a great dog, and we all loved him a lot and were really upset when he disappeared during hunting season one year. But this is how I relayed the event in a school journal:

February 18, 1977
Last year my mother found a dog with no collar. We called some of our friends. The dog didn't belong to any of them. We had it on the radio but we couldn't find the owner. We kept him for a little while. One day in winter he didn't come home. We didn't see him the next day we didn't see him either. We never saw him again.

I never even mention being sad in this, but this lack of expressed emotion is typical of a lot of my writing.

Even when I was excited about something, I didn't express it well on paper. Having school canceled because of bad weather was always a highlight of the school year. That fact is completely obscured by the following bit of writing.

January 1977
Yesterday morning about six-o-clock my father came in to see me before he went to work. He told me school was canceled. He said my mom was going to work but she wasn't. When I got up my friend called and I went to her house for a little while. We went outside for a little while and the snow was past my knees.

Believe it or not, I was very excited about that day, although there is not much evidence of that in my words. There's a sense of distance here between me and the reader. In all of my early writing I was very conscious of writing for some sort of audience. I can't quite identify who that audience was, but I know it never varied much, regardless of whether I was writing an analytical paper or a school journal or even a personal diary entry.

This mystery audience never knew me too well. I felt the need to identify the people I wrote about, to justify my beliefs or emotions, and to tie up any loose ends in my life's events. I think sometimes, mostly in the diary entries, the audience was myself. Not me as I was then, but as I would be in the future. I assumed, when writing, that in the future I wouldn't remember much of my past so I was careful to clearly explain everything. In the above passage, I was sure to say "my mom" and "my friend" instead of just "mom" and "Celina." I am careful not to confuse my audience by using a name without any explanation. This adds a touch of formality, of distance, to my writing.

In my final year of high school, I took a course in expository writing. I had intentionally put off taking this class, which I usually called the "dreaded Expo," until my senior year because I was terrified to take a class that was all about writing.

It turned out that the dreaded Expo wasn't really too bad. I actually liked the class, and I learned that writing is not *always* dreadful. I wrote some really good papers in that class and some really bad ones, too. But my absolute worst piece was the essay I wrote for my University of Vermont application.

One of our assignments for Expo was to write a practice essay for a college application. Since I had already sent in my UVM application, I just handed in a copy of the essay I had written. My teacher, not knowing I had actually sent in this essay, ripped it apart in front of the class, as an example of what *not* to write for a college essay. I was in tears the minute I left the classroom, convinced I would never get into college. Here's why:

> My main reason for wanting to attend this college is to expand my education and therefore develop a satisfying career.
>
> At this time, I have many interests, but no single outstanding interest. I would like to attend this college because of its wide range of areas that interest me both academically and socially. I hope that by attending this college I will be able to use its wide range of curriculum to develop a single strong interest. . . .

The subject of the essay was "why you want to go to this college and why you should be accepted." My teacher wrote four comments on my paper. "This is awfully *vague*," "vague," "such as?", and "repetitive and vague."

I think the reason I wrote such a "vague" essay was that I was uncomfortable writing about myself. There is a sense of discomfort in much of my writing. Even in my diary (I call it "the book" because I hate the word diary) where I write my most personal things, my words often sound stiff and contrived. My writing there is always controlled. Whenever I was mad or excited I would always express it in the size of my letters or with exclamation marks. In my life too, I tend to control my emotions, to hold a lot of my feelings inside: especially negative feelings. I don't express sadness very openly, and if I'm angry, the object of my anger rarely knows it, and I just hold it in until the feeling blows away.

Here is what I wrote in the book at age 11 about the traumatic death of a kitten. Don't laugh. People always laugh when they hear about this, but it's not funny, it's very sad.

August 9, 1979
Last night Wellington got killed. He was in the dryer when mom turned it on.
At least he died fast and we can keep Mish.

When first considering what I would write about in this paper, I thought I might be able to get some good information from the book. I sat down and read the thing from cover to cover, entries from 1978 until 1989, although the entries in the last several years are few and far between. After all that reading, I felt I owed an entry. So this is what I wrote:

November, 1989
I have to write a paper on my personal voice—an analysis of it. So I just read this whole book hoping to get some good material but the whole thing is mostly the ravings of a lunatic.

And it is too. I really thought that the book would be the best place to see my true voice. But I'm having a hard time with that because in most of the book I am a stranger. Now I want to say that what I wrote was not my true voice, but how could it not be? I have mentally divided the book up into three categories: the obligation entries (including the death of the cat entry), the hate entries, and the high school entries. The obligation entries evolved somehow into hate entries like this one:

February 23, 1979
Today was terrible. I went to the Wheelers. I hate Dawn and Dawn hates me. There were these dumb girls there named Heather + Holly. Now my parents won't let us see "Hulk" on TV. My mom gets to see "Roots." Why can't we see "Hulk"? My braces don't hurt any more.

This series of unfortunate entries are probably the most emotional things I ever wrote. Even here though, it still sounds as if I am writing for someone other than myself. I say "*my* mom" rather than just "mom," and I'm careful in my attempt to define "Hulk" and "Roots" as television shows with the use of quotation marks. Pretty academic considering the writing was completely personal.

The high school entries are unmentionable, and if I wasn't such a pack rat, I'd throw them out. I refuse to quote any of these entries, but this is what I wrote about them in May of 1989:

I wonder if it's normal for almost this entire book to revolve around the male sex? . . . Why not write about my friends or my family or school or my apartment or the sunset or my car or exercising or any other thing that is important to me. Writing might just not be for me—seems like pictures are better. . . .

My voice starts to change slightly during my senior year in high school. I become a little more present in my writing and start to relax a little. The following passage was written in a journal for an American Writers class:

> Nov. 5, 1985
> I really admire Thoreau for what he did about his taxes. . . . I respect and agree with Thoreau that he shouldn't pay his taxes when he doesn't agree with what they are for. I also know that if I was in the same situation, I wouldn't be able to do what he did. I would pay my taxes so that I wouldn't have to have the difficulties that not paying the tax would present. I'm not proud of that but I know that's what I would do.

The best paper that I wrote my senior year was called Oceanside. It was the first piece of writing that I actually remember feeling good about. The description was of a house on the Outer Banks of North Carolina that my family stayed in for two weeks one summer.

> The white and gold tiles on the kitchen floor are cool to the feet. The cupboard shelves are full of plates, glasses, mugs, bowls, and cooking utensils. The dishes from breakfast are stacked in the sink while the supper dishes still sit, sparkling clean and untouched in the dishwasher. Sand, collecting in the corners of the room, is hardly noticed and the broom and dustpan are left stationary in the corner. A note to all late sleepers says "Gone to the beach. It's beautiful out!" The radio plays soft music from "Beach 95, F." A few smile-faced magnets gaze cheerfully from the refrigerator door.

It's interesting that I do not physically exist in this paper even though the place I described was very special to me. I said that the tiles were cool to "the" feet, but they were really cool to *my* feet. It's as if this robotic eye is viewing the surroundings and putting the data down on paper. A note has been written but who is the author? Who is the reader? I suppose the reader must be the same person who is listening to the radio and I suppose that person is me, but the magnets in this are more alive than I am.

Just last spring I wrote another memory description of a favorite place: Montmartre, in Paris. This is how I began my paper:

> I smile uncomfortably, shake my head and try to blend into the crowd, but I am stopped by a persistent hand on my elbow. I had made the mistake of looking a little too interested in this particular artist's charcoal portraits. "Come, sit. Let me draw you," he insists in a heavy French accent. I ask how much. Three hundred francs. I do some quick mental arithmetic; 300 francs equals 30 pounds, which equals about 40 to 45 dollars. I shake my head, more emphatically this time, and start to back away. "Okay, 200 francs. Just for you, 200 francs." But I really want to look around first, at the other artists. "No good," he says, "now 200 francs, if you leave, you have to pay 300. I am good. If you don't like it, you don't pay . . . huh? Where are you from?

America! Ah, rich American, come . . . come on," he beckons. I look to my friend for help, but she just smiles and shrugs.

I am tempted. Perhaps because I would like my portrait done, but it's more likely that I'm flattered because he is the first Parisian who had treated me with anything better than annoyed indifference.

This was scary for me to put myself so fully into that paper, but since then I've done it more and more. I'm realizing that it's OK to be expressive and emotional in writing. And in person too. If I could write poems I would. Lots of times when something really strikes me, I want to write a poem or draw something to convey how I feel. But if I ever start doing that, some more rational part of me springs out, and I tear up the paper.

Last weekend I did something weird. On Saturday morning I went with Nancy to Swanton to see a fortune-teller. The fortune-teller is an elderly Abenake Indian woman. She is very poor and living in a run-down house behind a block of warehouses, with nothing but trailers for neighboring houses. We each paid $15 for her to read us through a regular deck of cards. Don't conjure up an image of her as a gypsy-type with a crystal ball in front of her; she's very normal looking, and we sat at her kitchen table with the breakfast leftovers still on it.

Nancy went first and got a pretty accurate reading. Then I went. Now, I don't necessarily believe in everything she said to me, but I don't not believe it either. You see, she's not really a fortune-teller, but more of a present-teller. Either way, it was pretty amazing. This woman told me things about my life that there is no way she could have known because she didn't even know my name when I went in to see her. She started my reading by talking about—of all things—men. She described my relationship with my old boyfriend to a tee and told me that he was BAD for me (which I had already discovered), and I should send him to "you know where" (which I have already done), but reinforcement is always good.

She described my brother as a devil but a good devil (which he is) and saw a lot of darkness around my sister (which there is). She asked me why I stopped playing the flute (which I did) and told me I should start again (something I have considered). She told me that whatever is bothering my mother is not my fault (it's not) and that I shouldn't be worried because everything will be OK.

What made me angry was coming home from Swanton and being very excited about what had happened and telling another roommate some of the things the woman said and having him say, scornfully—well of course she just made an easy guess—or something to that effect. Why can't people believe in things that are a little stranger than normal? Why does everything have to be so rational all the time? Life is interesting because of things that are magical and strange and unusual and really beautiful or really ugly, and it upsets me when people say That's stupid or That's weird and turn up their noses.

I think in this country, and in a lot of other places, people are often raised thinking it is bad to be emotional. If you feel something or write something or say something that veers away from the traditional, then you are making a big commitment to being "radical" like that and setting yourself up for criticism. The reason I struggle with my writing is because what I write is usually not exactly what I feel. Instead, it is what I feel is a proper presentation of what I feel. It's the same thing as smiling when someone asks you how you are and just saying Good, thanks, when you are actually feeling lousy or even when you are feeling really great.

I have done a lot of growing up in the past few years, and my writing has grown with me. I have become a more outgoing and expressive person. I am happier and more comfortable with myself, and my writing shows this. In fact, just the other day, I wrote a poem. And I didn't tear it up.

---

## Sharing Ideas

- Audrey talks about different attitudes she has toward numbers and words. Sometimes I hear individuals talking about themselves as number people or word people. Is that distinction meaningful to or necessary for you? What do you mean when you make it?

- Have you ever found yourself in Audrey's situation, keeping your emotions out of your paper? Why did you do that? Were you worried, as she was, about your audience? Did you use any of the same techniques—passive voice, avoidance of first person, the robotic, reporting eye? Did you use any other techniques?

- Audrey talks about her struggles to achieve a personally satisfying writer's voice; still, I think her essay certainly sounds like someone talking to someone else. Can you describe her voice? How does it strike you? Who do you think she imagined as the audience for her piece? Why?

- In Audrey's essay, what do you think about her visit to the fortune-teller and her thoughts about emotion and writing?

- I noticed that Audrey mentions the importance journal writing had for her as she traveled to other countries and experienced different cultures. Have you had similar experiences? Have you kept a journal? With what results?

- After reading the next essay "Journeys in Journaling," return to Audrey's essay and analyze her journaling.

---

# 3

# Journeys in Journaling

## Chris M. Anson and Richard Beach

---

Chris M. Anson is Morse-Alumni Distinguished Teaching Professor of English at the University of Minnesota, where he teaches all sorts of courses in language, literacy, and writing. He has written several textbooks on writing, as well as scholarly books and articles exploring how people write and can learn to write. He has a special interest in formal writing used across the college curriculum as a way to help students learn. In his spare time he writes, remodels old houses, runs, and enjoys the outdoors with his wife Geanie and his two boys, Ian and Graham.

Richard Beach, a former high school English teacher, is Professor of English Education at the University of Minnesota, where he teaches courses on literature, composition, and media methods. He is coauthor of *Teaching Literature in the Secondary School* and is author of *A Teacher's Introduction to Reader Response Theories*. He doodles in his own journal for at least an hour a day. He has also found that student journals, particularly dialogue journals, improve the quality of talk in his own classes. He enjoys running (even in below-zero Minnesota winters), going to movies, and reading spy thrillers.

---

## Prologue, the Authors Explain Their Journey

When we first thought about writing a chapter on journal writing for this textbook, it was as if we were starting on a journey by choosing the most direct, boring route we could find. We talked about what we could tell you about journal writing, what sort of *information* we could impart about this useful and complicated genre. To us, the landscape is familiar; we've traveled the journal road many times, both by keeping journals ourselves and by conducting research on how people, especially students, learn and write by journaling. We were planning to take you down a kind of textbook superhighway, telling you in a blur of ideas what you should think about journals and how you should use them.

But then we started wondering about the sort of journey we were mapping out for you. We would most certainly cover lots of ground and expose you to the "main ideas" about journal writing, even if at breakneck speed. Would you be interested? Possibly. Would you speculate much about journals? Maybe. Could we get across how varied and complex and interesting journal writing is? Doubtful. We could tell you all that, but you might not want to take our word for it.

Still undecided, we went home to do what we usually do when we're not sure how to begin a piece of writing: we journaled. And we kept journaling for many pages and many weeks, first writing to and for ourselves, in the form of "solo" journals and then, later, slipping into a kind of dialogue as we sent each other what we'd written.

Shortly before a draft of our (still unwritten) chapter was due, something curious happened. As we talked about all our journal writing, we began to realize that our own journey *into* this chapter was likely to be more interesting, with more (in)sights to see at a slower and more enjoyable pace, than the chapter we imagined producing for this book. Then it dawned on us that the best way we could tell you about journal writing would be to share with you what we did.

Our journey, then, begins early on in our journal writing, as we wrote loose, exploratory entries focusing on what we wanted to tell you. To help you to see us at work, we've inserted our initials in brackets to indicate who's writing [CMA] or [RB].

## The Journey

### November 10 [CMA]

Rick [RB] came up with a great idea: We simply journal our way into the essay for Wendy Bishop's book, and it could "show" us ideas that we'd otherwise have to conjure up academically. And even as I do this entry I feel that my usual journaling process is becoming different somehow, and I think it comes from knowing that maybe Rick will see this, not so much that it should be polished and formal but that someone is going to look into my thinking and my own learning as a way to understand this crazy genre. Because it *feels* more text-like. That may be a difference we want to explore in the piece because in most academic settings journals are, in fact, read by someone (a teacher? Other students?), which doesn't necessarily change their informality but makes the sentences more complete, fewer personal abbreviations and short cuts, maybe. Something to do with the syntax. This project should be fun.

*November 11 [RB]*

Academic journals vs. personal journals. In discussing the journal, we're really talking about "academic journals" used in college courses to write about and reflect on the class readings, discussions, observations, related experiences, presentations, lectures, etc. This probably differs from a more private "personal diary" form of journal or a journal often used in therapy or as an observation log in creative writing. We need to make this clear. Also, I think journals have gotten bad press from seeming too "wishy washy" in some educational circles. Journals may be informal, but they *lead* to and *require* hard thinking. That's their point.

I think we should include at least the following information:

• What's an academic journal? How does it differ from the stereotypical diary?

• How do you keep one? This seems basic (who cares what sort of actual notebook you use?). But people do feel that the physical side of journals make a difference.

• Different sort of journals. Monologues vs. dialogues.

• How do we show journals at work? I like the idea of including examples from students' work in different courses. Maybe we could include some of our own?

*November 12 [CMA]*

Rick wondered whether we should include anything about our own personal use of journals. I'm not sure what he means—focus overtly on how we use journals? Who wants to read all our professional musings? But it occurs to me that he might have meant how we ourselves started using journals, our personal histories. Makes journal writing seem close to writing autobiography. So here goes.

I guess I was about 11 or 12 years old when I started journaling. It was back when the (now common) American gerbil had just made its way into a few pet shops around the country as some sort of exotic new rodent (I don't think anyone knew at that point how prolific the little beasts were going to be!). I had a tank full of tropical fish and some of those little chameleons (I think they were just a common form of lizard from Mexico but they did turn from brown to green occasionally) and a guinea pig or two. And one day, clutching my 26 cents for a replacement carbon filter for my aquarium aerator, I went into our local pet shop. I remember how the door jingled when I opened it, and I went past the cages and tanks and barrels of bird food and cracked corn and there, right next to the charcoal filters, was a 25-gallon tank containing two gerbils.

I stood there for what seemed like a good half an hour, transfixed by these two strange little creatures, dashing around in their cedar chips, burrowing and nuzzling in their frenzied way. There was something jerky about their movements that I'd never seen in any other pet-store animal, and that fascinated me. I stood there, mesmerized by the way the gerbils would sit up with their little front paws dangling in front of them and then move a few inches to the left or right in one single, split-second twitch, stop, then twitch again. Stop, twitch. Stop, twitch. I wondered what that would be like, moving in that way. I was fascinated, and I just had to have one.

Then came the shock. As I stood there, the pet store owner had been preparing a little sign, his magic marker squeaking across a piece of white cardboard. Finally he brought it over and taped it on to the wall next to the gerbil tank. "Gerbils (South American rodent): $7.50 apiece."

*Seven fifty!* Two month's allowance, not including the cage!

Somehow, and I think it was probably my all-time greatest feat of parental persuasion, I managed, within the week, to get not just one gerbil but both. And a tank. And food. And a bag of cedar chips. *And* a little glass water bottle with a metal drinking spout. My father, who did amateur carpentry in the cellar in his spare time, then decided to build five gerbil cages for me, so that when my pair started to breed (which Dad, in all his wisdom, predicted they would do with a vengeance), I could start up a kind of cottage industry. Twenty five dollars for two gerbils and a fully set up cage. Who could resist? After all, these were new, exotic animals. (I think that image, of our entire cellar turned into a profit-making breeding station for gerbils, was what finally got to Dad and got me my gerbils.)

One minor problem. After waiting for several months, with our five empty cages neatly lined up on a cellar shelf, we began wondering whether our pair of gerbils were capable of breeding. My father had never really looked too closely at them (he was still, I think, immersed in his dream of becoming the state's largest producer of exotic rodents). Finally, one Saturday, he took the gerbils out of the cage to conduct a close inspection. The verdict was instant and final: they were both males.

The following week, I managed to get another pair of gerbils (both female) by agreeing to wash the windows for a year and take out the garbage when asked and even clean up the sawdust in the cellar whenever Dad retreated there to build something. By that time, they were only $5 each (and falling). Before long, my five cages each sported two or more young gerbils. I twisted by best friend's arm to take one cage off my hands for ten dollars, but in spite of this first sale it didn't take long for the remaining four cages to grow in population, each housing a little kibbutz of five, eight, twelve gerbils, Dad frantically built cages. The price continued to drop. And soon, within the year, I was begging our friends, neighbors, distant acquaintances to take them, cage and all, for free.

Now, I had other pets. And when I needed advice about them, I'd turn to one of my little 50-cent pamphlets on "Caring for Tropical Fish" or "The

Domestic Guinea Pig." But nothing, anywhere, on gerbils. I tried the library. Nothing. I combed the pet shops in three nearby towns. Nothing. Not a single word about domestic gerbils. This was it—my very first foray into Authorship. "Gerbils as Pets" by Christopher Anson.

So in the dim light of the dusty basement, amid the squealing of the gerbils' exercise wheels and the weep-weeping of my two guinea pigs and the bubbling of my aquarium aerators, I started my first, almost Darwinian journal, a little lined notepage of clinical observations about my rapidly proliferating pets.

My gerbil journal lasted for over six months, page after page of the most scholarly notes a 12-year old could conjure up about his pets' behavior. Once a gerbil got out of the cage and was lost in the cluttered basement for three weeks. When I finally did find him behind a box of wood, he'd killed a small field mouse (whose little dried up body lay nearby) and taken up residence in the mouse's winter home, a nest of tiny pieces of newspaper, thread, insulation material, part of an old sock from the laundry area, straw, and bits of cedar chips that had fallen from the gerbil cages. Now wild, the gerbil bit me so hard when I tried to pick him up that my finger bled for half an hour. Worse still, when I reintroduced the prodigal gerbil to his commune, the entire cage instantly became a battlefield, father turning on son, brother on sister, cousin on cousin, in a frenzy of indiscriminate attacks. When the dust and cedar chips settled, my renegade gerbil was dead, two others had lost substantial pieces of ear, and a fourth was missing the end of his tail.

After this incident (and a ritual burial of my first gerbil casualty), I remember sitting for a couple of hours in the dank cellar, writing and writing and writing about what it all meant. I figured an entire chapter in my pamphlet would have to be devoted to this problem of the escaped gerbil. And there was more: what could make such peaceful, adorable creatures so aggressive? Why did the gerbil turn on me—his caretaker and source of life—and then on his own kin? And how could they so ruthlessly kill him in his madness? As I wrote, my entries began slipping from rodent to animal kingdom, domestication, zoos, cages. And then to the idea of hostility and war, and humanity. And then to who I was and what I wanted to be.

And that's it, that's all to tell, I guess. I started journal writing that year, the year of the gerbils. I never did finish my pamphlet, but I found out that wasn't really the point.

I've never stopped journaling since.

*November 17 [RB]*

I want to look at characteristics of journal writing (informal, etc.), to contrast them with formal academic writing. What I noticed about Chris' gerbil story is how it's a blend of "polished" and informal writing. When he sent it over he said he was surprised at how well it turned out for something just done very quickly. So in a way he *aimed* to write informally and then ended up doing something that could pass as a formal narrative. The usual difference between journal writing and academic papers looks like this:

| *Formal Writing* | *Journal Writing* |
| --- | --- |
| Organized | Unorganized |
| Formal language | Informal language |
| Definitive | Exploratory |
| Polished | Unpolished |
| Used to communicate | Used to learn, think, reflect |

Most of the journal writing used to help students *learn* is informal, etc. But it may be possible to see the act of journal writing as a great way to write your way into a formal piece.

### November 18 [CMA]

The most powerful thing about journal writing, for me, can be visualized as a sort of wheel, a snake with its tail in its mouth. At some point, the wheel is labeled "writing." Somewhere on the other side, it's labeled "thinking" or "learning." Writing, in other words, *leads* to thinking and learning. Thinking and learning lead, in turn, to more writing. And on and on, like a mantra. I think this concept works especially well with journal writing because it suggests the exploratory nature of journals and emphasizes their chief value: contemplation.

### November 20 [RB]

One use of the journal is to extend or explore your thinking in order to construct your own knowledge. Rather than simply restate or rehearse ideas shared in a course, you're using the journal to reformulate and reflect on ideas *in your own words*. In that way, you're assimilating these ideas into what you already know and believe. For example, you might begin in a philosophy class by restating or rehearsing what the text, students, or instructor has said about the idea of "free will." To extend or explore your own thinking about free will, you may then consider the following ways of extending and exploring (etc., finish this thought):

1.  A loping freewrite: Peter Elbow suggests that one way to extend your thinking is to pick out a word, phrase, or key term, and do a 5- to 10-minute freewrite about that word, phrase, or key term.

2.  Reflecting on your own thinking. You may also use your entries to reflect— to stand back and interpret or evaluate the larger meaning of your thinking.

3.  Using the journal as prewriting. You may also use your journal entries as prewriting to develop ideas for your papers. As you begin to define and clarify a possible paper topic, you could highlight or circle material and entitle that material in the margin according to its relevance to your overall topic, etc. *Chris—What do you think of this sort of listing/bulleting?*

*November 30 [CMA]*

Rick: You notice that since we started exchanging journal entries we've slipped into a dialogue journal, and it's worth, I think, really making that distinction in the chapter for *The Subject Is Writing*. Because some classes may involve students in just plain journal writing, for and to themselves, while others might get students writing in dialogues like this. And frankly I'd rather just dialogue about our journal writing from now on, because I think we have to start getting more specific about what direction we want to take.

*December 9 [RB]*

Chris: We need to explore more of those functions I started working on the other day. Another one I want to add is something like mapping—in keeping a journal, you may want to use some mapping to explore your thoughts (or something like that). For example, in an economics class, you may be discussing the differences between socialism and capitalism. Using a circle and spoke map, put the key ideas—socialism and capitalism—in central circles. Then draw spokes out from the central circles and make smaller circles that represent the different characteristics of the central ideas. (And so on—each smaller circle can then suggest other circles so you begin to fill the page with concepts. Then draw lines and label them with "d" or "s" to represent differences and similarities.) We could actually show a map or maybe one of our own. You didn't do anything like that for the gerbil thing, did you?

*December 15 [CMA]*

Rick—I like the idea of adding something conceptual/visual to journal writing, because it always seems so "wordy," if you know what I mean—all language, in full and sometimes very elaborated sentences (like these, I guess). It would be wise to show how appropriate it is to carry on even the most highly conceptual doodling, mapping, diagrams, and so on in a journal. I also like the way you stuck in a reference to economics, to show the academic diversity of journals.

You asked if I used mapping with the gerbil piece, and no, I didn't. For some reason I find it less useful for narrative, but the main difference was that I didn't think I was actually writing anything formal. This is, for me, one of the most powerful aspects of journal writing: I *tricked myself* into writing something that with a lot of work might actually become a fairly decent, lighthearted piece, but when I was writing it I was just writing as fast as I could to tell you about when I started journaling, and somehow, maybe because I felt so relaxed and uninhibited, my words started coming out more descriptively. It's weird, but it never struck me as such a powerful way to start writing as it did then, and maybe it's precisely because I wasn't actually setting out to "start writing."

What do you want to do with the notion of dialogue journals? Since we started writing articles together (was it six years ago!?) I've noticed how much our stuff has really turned into dialogue journaling even when we're trying to do pretty formal chunks (notice, for example, how both of us, when we tire of writing a formal chunk, almost always do a kind of dialoguing at the moment we fizzle out, like "Rick, what else should we include here?" or (and you do this a lot) "Chris—fill in." It shows how dialoguing can become collaboration, and I like the idea of explaining that to students.

*December 29 [RB]*

Chris—here are some pieces on dialogue journals. Tell me what you think or just redo them.

*Carrying on a written conversation.* Keeping a dialogue journal differs from a solo journal in that you are sharing your thoughts with another person in a written conversation. You and your partner(s) can collaboratively explore your responses to readings, ideas, similar experiences, or difficulties. While you may do the same thing in an oral conversation, one advantage of using a written conversation is that you have time to reflect on each other's entries. There may be a gap of several days before you react. You can therefore mull over what your partner says in order to formulate a response.

Chris: How theoretical do you think we should get in this? I want to refer to Michael Halliday's finding that oral language portrays things more as unfolding processes, in a complex and dynamic way, while written language tends to describe products, turning those into a structure, so its complexity is static and dense. He notes that "writing creates a world of things; talking creates a world of happening." So that the dialogue journal, by combining the features of both oral and written language, encourages both an ongoing interactive exploration of ideas with the more structured exploration of written language. But that's a little too heavy, don't you think? Do you have any ideas for how to explain that?

*January 5 [CMA]*

Rick: I just looked back through the stuff we've been doing. I wondered whether instead of doing the same old boring *formal* kind of paper we could try to explore journals in a concrete and interesting way by actually *doing* what we're talking about. Do you think this could work? Because I'm worried that if we try too hard, we're going to end up doing a sort of "scholarly piece" disguising as a how-to chapter and maybe end up pandering too much or something.

I have one fear about this, and it's the conflict between the sort of journal writing we've been doing and the fact that if it's published in this form, then it sanctions sloppiness, random organization, etc. Let's face it, nothing is ever published unless it's formal and tidy and stylistically slick. We don't want to give the impression that a writer can be conceptually and linguistically messy and then just stop there. Do you think we'll be sending that message?

*January 10 [RB]*

   Chris: The dialogue journal idea is tied up with the notion of building relationships, a kind of good conversation that leads to learning and thinking. So why not share the process we're going through?

*January 15 [CMA]*

   Rick: Help! I don't know. I've read back through all this and I'm tempted to polish it up, especially my gerbil narrative (I was sort of amazed looking back at it to remember that it took me the lesser part of an hour to write, just blasting through). But if we do that, we defeat the whole purpose of the chapter, which is to show journals in action, to go on a kind of journey of journaling. In other words, if the whole thing starts to look contrived and polished and slick, then it's not journal writing any more. And that's hard, because it takes a certain will power to resist "fixing it up."

   We've put ourselves on the line by going public with something so informal. But what I like about the idea is that we *had* to learn our way into and through this piece to begin with. We might have ended up with a polished article, but it wouldn't have shown *how* we learned our way into and through it.

   And another thing I like about it in this form: We don't have all the answers about this sort of writing. It's too varied (I think we did five or six really different kinds of writing in the process of writing about it). I'd rather that people talk about journal writing and experiment with it than think that we have all the answers about just how and why it works. Again, that's a risk, don't you think? We're researchers, we have all sorts of data and expertise on journal writing. But I'd rather just be honest.

*January 20 [RB]*

   Chris: I liked your phrase about a journey. Why don't we call it "Journeys in Journaling" and leave it at that?

## Coda, the Authors Reflect on Their Travels

This is the first and probably the only time we will ever write about journaling by publishing our own journal writing. The advantage, for us, comes from the potential for our chapter to display some of the benefits of journaling: more and better thinking about a topic; less anxiety and procrastination because of the sense of having "started" a writing task; better planning for formal writing; and a more collaborative writing situation, especially when keeping a dialogue journal.

But, like the dramatic commercial in which someone flies over ten piles of tires in a stock car or bungee-jumps 500 feet above a rocky river, we suggest that you don't try this at home. Turn in formal, polished writing. But by all means begin it by journaling. You'll find, as we do, that keeping a journal, alone or with someone else as a dialogue partner, really does work. Take our words for it.

## Sharing Ideas

- Whenever I read other writer's journals, I tend to grab some of my old travel journals and start reading them again. Describe your own journeys in journaling. Have you kept journals? When, why, for how long, in or out of school, and so on.

- Chris and Rick have shown as much as told about journaling. Play teacher and draw some points from their presentation to share with a class of writing students—your own class.

- Look at Rick's entry from November 11; did this essay manage to include the information he outlines as being essential? Can you provide additional information in these areas, based on your own journaling experiences?

- Chris and Rick's journal entries echo letter writing since they offer a dialog between writers. Some of my most engaging writing interactions these days are taking place on electronic mail where I "journal" with other writing teachers around the country. If you are using this form of journaling, share your experiences.

- At this point, what new ideas do you have about writers' conversations? Some of the essays in this book describe writers talking in class or in journals. Writers also hold many other conversations through electronic journals, letters, or phone and dinner conversations; writers hold conversations with themselves, aloud or internally, or on paper when they use invention exercises to hold a dialogue with a memory, and so on. How do you make sense of all this talking about writing?

- Make yourself a promise about journaling and stick to it for a set period of time.

# 4

# Time, Tools, and Talismans

## Susan Wyche

Susan Wyche is an Associate Professor in Human Communications at California State University Monterey Bay, where she also directs the University Writing Program. She still struggles with writing, still uses writing rituals to be a productive writer, and sometimes dreams of giving it all up to become a surfer.

Famous writers have been known to do a lot of crazy things to help them write: Dame Edith Sitwell sought inspiration by lying in a coffin. George Sand wrote after making love. Friedrich Schiller sniffed rotten apples stashed under the lid of his desk. A hotel room furnished with a dictionary, a Bible, a deck of cards, and a bottle of sherry suits Maya Angelou. Fugitive writer Salman Rushdie carries a silver map of an unpartitioned India and Pakistan. Charles Dickens traveled with ceramic frogs.

Writers also mention less bizarre practices. They describe eating, drinking, pacing, rocking, sailing, driving a car or riding in a bus or train, taking a hot bath or shower, burning incense, listening to music, staring out windows, cleaning house, or wearing lucky clothes. What do these rituals do for writers? The explanations are as varied as the rituals themselves. Tolstoy believed that "the best thoughts most often come in the morning after waking, while still in bed, or during a walk." Sonia Sanchez says that she works at night because "at that time the house is quiet. The children are asleep. I've prepared for my classes . . . graded papers . . . answered letters. . . . [A]t a quarter to twelve all that stops . . . then my writing starts." Although interpretations differ, one need not read extensively in the journals, letters, essays, and interviews of writers to know that they consider rituals an essential component of their work.

Do these behaviors serve a purpose in the composing process? Are some practices more common than others? Do rituals make for better writers? Until recently, the answer was usually "No," but anthropologists and others who study the subject of consciousness now say that private rituals are used by individuals to selectively and temporarily shut out the daily world. Researchers in psychophysiology have observed that rhythmic activities that can be performed "mindlessly" alter brainwaves into a more relaxed, creative state. Walking, pacing, and some kinds of exercise have this effect. So does staring out windows, which some researchers now believe may actively trigger daydreaming rather than being a symptom of it. Although coffins and frogs are probably effective only in the personal psychology of a Sitwell or a Dickens, scientists at Yale have discovered that rotting applies produce a gas that suppresses panic—a reminder that we should be careful not to scoff too soon at writers' rituals.

I became interested in the subject of rituals after suffering through my master's thesis with a bad case of writer's block. When a counselor asked me to describe my work habits, I became aware of the condition under which I had chosen to work: at school in the afternoon (my worst time of day) in an office where I was constantly interrupted or at home (also in the afternoon) while my husband's band practiced in the living room. I answered the phone, made coffee, and tried to shut out mentally what the walls could not. As Tillie Olsen points out, writing under such conditions produces a "craziness of endurance" that silences the writer. After awhile, even when I wasn't interrupted, I'd create my own distractions by calling friends, scrounging food in the kitchen, or escaping the house to run errands.

At the counselor's prompting, I began looking for a protected place to work—at first in the library and later at coffeeshops, where the conversational buzz and clatter of dishes provided consistent background noise. Somehow the interruptions in these places were less disruptive than those at home. I also began to pay attention to those moments when ideas bubbled up effortlessly, like on my walks to and from the university or while soaking in a hot bath late at night. I realized that ideas had always come in offbeat moments, but I had rarely been able to recapture them at "official" writing times. In the next three years, I gradually revamped my work habits and was able to face writing my doctoral dissertation, not with fear-producing blank pages, but pocketfuls of short passages scribbled in the heat of inspiration.

As a teacher of writing who works with unprepared students who are "at risk" in the university, I began to wonder what they did when they wrote. I knew there were times when they, too, became frustrated, blocked, and turned in work that did not represent their actual abilities. In Spring 1990, I conducted a project with two writing classes in the Academic Skills Department at San Diego State University. I wanted to know

What rituals did students practice when they wrote for school?

What explanations would they offer for their practices?

Where did they get their best ideas?

What did they do when they blocked?

Were they aware of habits that sabotaged their composing processes?

Students filled out several pages of a questionnaire on their schedules, their rituals, and the amount of time they allocated for writing school assignments. Afterward, several met with me for follow-up interviews. In the following section, I present edited transcripts of three students who represented the range of responses I received.

# Interviews

The first student, Adriana, provides a profile of work habits typical of other students in her class. She takes five classes, works twenty hours each week, and spends six to ten hours per week on homework:

> I create a schedule for a day but if there's one particular thing I'm supposed to do, and I fall behind, I just throw it out. Sometimes I call my friends on the phone and tell them what I'm writing about in the essay, and they give me ideas.
>
> Everything has to be clean and neat because if I see my clothes hanging everywhere, I can't study; I can't concentrate. So I have to straighten it up—everything—before I start.
>
> I do most of my writing at night. Last night I stayed up till three o'clock. Before, I used to go to the public library, but it got too loud because of all these high school students jumping around. Now I work primarily at home.
>
> Pacing gives me time to relax and jot down what I'm doing. I can't stay in one place, like for five hours and write a paper. I have to stand up, walk around, watch a little bit of TV and then start again. If my favorite program comes on I just have to watch it. Sometimes its hard to do both—writing and TV.
>
> To relax, I breathe deeply, stuff like that. I lay in my bed, looking at the ceiling. Nothing special. I work sitting down or lying down. I stare out a window. That's how I get my thoughts all together. I guess it helps, I find myself doing it a lot. I also have this one cassette with all piano solos by George Winston.
>
> At times I put off working on an assignment until it's too late to do my best work, because I work better under pressure. If I start maybe a month before, I won't really concentrate. If I start three days before, then I'll get on it. If I have a month to do a project, and I sit down the week before, I'm not even thinking about it the other three weeks. Sometimes I work when I'm too exhausted, because I have a deadline to make. I've got to do it or fail the class.

> I get my ideas sometimes right away, but most of the time it takes an
> hour to sit and think about it. I also get ideas from reading essays or from the
> person next to me. I'd ask what they're writing about, and sometimes I get
> some ideas. When I do go blank, I get frustrated—don't even know what I
> do. I think I just sit there and keep staring at my paper.

Adriana has difficulty creating and following through on self-made schedules.
Her problems are further compounded by being unable to concentrate for
extended periods of time; instead, she takes numerous breaks, including
watching television. By her own account she begins drafts cold, using only the
hour prior to drafting to give the paper serious thought.

Given all this, it is surprising to note how many beneficial rituals she practices. She cleans her workspace, paces, and breathes deeply to relax. She stares
out windows to gather her thoughts, and focuses her attention by listening to
instrumental music. However, she mitigates the effect of these practices by
placing herself under the pressure of imminent deadlines. It's no wonder that
she becomes frustrated when she blocks. She has little time left for delays, and
her coping strategy—to sit staring at the blank page—is more likely to create
stress than to relieve it. The conditions she chooses would torpedo even a
stronger writer's chance for success.

The second student, Marcia, also has five classes, averages eighteen hours
each week at a job, and spends sixteen to twenty hours each week (twice as
much as Adriana) on homework.

> Usually I study in the evening. I start at seven or eight, and lately I've been
> finishing about one or two. I talk my paper over with my friends. I ask if it's
> OK to write on this, or I ask them to read it when I'm finished, to see if it's
> OK. I usually work in my room, sometimes on my bed or in the living room
> on the floor. For some reason, I can't do my homework on my desk. When
> I'm in the family room, I just lie down on the couch, and do my homework
> with my legs up on the table. I play the radio, sometimes I'll watch TV. If it's
> an interesting show, I'll continue working during the commercials.
>
> I guess I'm just a procrastinator. I always tend to do my writing assign-
> ments at the last minute. Like when they give it to you, and they say, this is
> due a month later, I'll start on it a week before it's due. Sometimes when I'm
> thinking about a paper, I think, oh, I could write that in my paper, but when
> I come to writing it, I forget. I get distracted when I watch TV, or when
> there's people there and I say, OK, I won't do this now, I'll do it later when
> I'm by myself. Sometimes I'm on the phone or I go out. Then I end up not
> doing it, or starting late. When I was doing one assignment, I wrote it in
> about an hour.
>
> If I block, I put it down for awhile, or I ask somebody to read it, or do
> something else. Then I'll go back to it. When I block, I feel mad, yeah, frus-
> trated. I don't cry. I just think, I hate writing, I hate writing. Why do I have
> to do this? That kind of stuff. Writing is not my subject.

Marcia writes in the evening, after a full day of work and school. Like Adriana, she describes herself as a procrastinator. She has no designated workspace and often seeks distraction in friends or television. Although Adriana describes using an hour to generate and organize her ideas, Maria mentions no such practice. She doesn't write down ideas and often doesn't remember them when she is ready to draft the assignment. There are other clues to serious problems. Although help from peers can be useful, she seems overly reliant on her friends for ideas and approval. She looks to them to tell her whether her choice of subject is a good one, to help her when she blocks, and to tell her whether her draft is adequate. She spends very little time on the work and may not even finish if interrupted. Her frustration with writing is obvious; her rituals—what few she practices—sabotage her efforts.

The third student, Sam, represents a highly ritualistic writer. He is enrolled in four classes, works twenty-five hours, and spends six to ten hours on homework.

> I'm really into driving. When I drive I notice everything. Things like, Oh, that billboard wasn't like that yesterday. I notice if my car feels different. I'm constantly looking and thinking. What's going on? And so, when I have time to prepare for my paper, all the thought goes into that, from there.
>
> In high school, my thoughts used to go down on microrecording. But I haven't used it since college. My batteries went dead. I do a little bit of performing stand-up comedy, so now I carry a little book for when I see something funny or some kind of story I want to keep. I've probably been through three of those books. I lose a lot of creative energy when I don't write things down.
>
> My roommates and I lift weights every day. A lot of thoughts come from that. I don't like to sit. When I'm thinking, I pace. I do a lot of what you could call role playing. I think, if I come from here, then I gotta hit the next paragraph this way. I actually look this way, then turn the other way. I really get into my papers, I guess. I'm Italian, I talk with my hands. It's a way to release energy both physically and mentally.
>
> Ideas come at different times. I've been known to write paragraphs on napkins at work. At home, I don't have a desk. I have my computer which just sits on top of my dresser. I usually sit on my bed. A lot of times I lie down; a lot of times I'll stand up, just depends. I write in the afternoon, I feel a lot better than I do when I write at night. I look out a window and just write. But, when it comes to the mid hours, six o'clock, seven o'clock, there's too many things going on. I'm too jumpy, too hyper to concentrate then.
>
> I'm a very procrastination kind of guy. If I had a paper due in two weeks, there would be a lot of afternoon writing, a lot of jotting down. I'd probably end up pulling it all together late one evening. You never know, that last week, I might come up with something more. But at all times, I'm actively thinking about it.
>
> I never keep working on a problem once I've blocked. I feel this is use-

less. So, I'll stop, and a half hour later, it'll hit me. If I block at night, I'll stop for the rest of the night. If it's in the day, I'll try to get it again at night. I prefer a sleep period in between. Everybody believes in a fresh new day. A new outlook.

Like Adriana and Marcia, Sam considers himself a procrastinator. But unlike either of them, he actively makes use of the interim between assignment, noting down ideas, even writing entire sections if they take shape in his mind. Because he works better in the afternoon than late at night after he's put in a full day, he tries to schedule his work periods early. He seems to be a kinetic thinker—getting ideas in motion—and he takes advantage of that by allowing himself to pace and act out ideas rather than work at a desk. His interest in stand-up comedy has taught him to pay attention to the world around him, and this has become a source of material for his school assignments. In a way, Sam is always preparing to write. The result? He spends less time on his homework than Marcia and rarely experiences, as Adriana does, the frustration of being blocked.

I appreciated the candor of these and other students in responding to my questions but, as a teacher of writing, I was disheartened by many of the things I learned. Over half of the students surveyed spent fewer than ten hours per week on homework for a full schedule of classes, and three-quarters averaged twice as many hours on the job. The picture that emerged of their composing processes, from both statistics and interviews, was even bleaker. Few practiced rituals to help them write, most wrote under conditions hostile to concentration, and more than two-thirds admitted that procrastination regularly affected the quality of their work.

## How Rituals Help

Rituals cannot create meaning where there is none—as anyone knows who has mumbled through prayers thinking of something else. But a knowledge of rituals can make a difference for students who want to make better use of the time they spend on writing. For one thing, rituals help writers pay attention to the conditions under which they choose to work. Some people think, for example, that fifteen minutes spent writing during TV commercial breaks is the equivalent of fifteen minutes of continuous, uninterrupted time. If they knew more about the nature of concentration—such as the destructive effect of interruptions on one's ability to retain and process information—they would recognize the difference. If they knew that language heard externally interferes with tasks requiring the production of inner speech, they would know that instrumental music or white noise (like the hum heard inside a car) might enhance their ability to write but that television or music with lyrics is likely to make work more difficult.

A knowledge of rituals can also encourage more effective use of the time spent on assignments. While many teachers consider two hours of homework a reasonable expectation for each hour in class, the students I talk to spent half that time and projects were typically written in one stressful sitting. Writing teacher Peter Elbow calls this "The Dangerous Method" and warns that it not only increases the pressure but depends for its success on a lack of any mishaps or mental blocks.

The problem with waiting until the last minute to write is that ideas rarely appear on demand. Instead, they come when listening to others, while reading or dreaming, or in the middle of other activities. Certain conditions stimulate their production, such as when a writer is relaxed and the mind is not strongly preoccupied with other matters. These moments may occur at particular periods of the day, for example, during "hypnagogic" states, the stage between waking and dreaming. Automatic, repetitious activity has a similar effect, which may be why writers often mention the benefits of walking, pacing, or exercising of some kind. They learn to make use of those times by noting down ideas or combining naturally productive times with their scheduled writing time.

Having some ideas to start with is an advantage to the writer, but not enough in itself. Ideas seldom occur as full-blown concepts, complete with all of the details, order, and connections that are required for formal writing. More often, they begin as an image, sensation, key word or phrase, or a sketchy sense of shape and structure. Transforming these bits into a full-fledge piece—whether poem, essay, or short story—usually requires one or more periods of concentration. The term concentration means "to bring together, to converge, to meet in one point" and in reference to thinking, it refers to keeping one's attention and activity fixed on a single problem, however complex. For the kind of writing required at the college level, concentration is crucial.

Most of us know that it is hard to concentrate when we are tired, when interrupted or preoccupied, ill or under stress—thus we recognize, experientially, that writing requires the concerted effort of mind *and* body. Some people can concentrate under adverse conditions—they could work unfazed in the middle of a hurricane if they wanted to—but most of us aren't like that. Concentration comes naturally to a few things that we like to do or are vitally interested in—music, perhaps, or sports. The rest of the time, we juggle several things at once, like jotting down a shopping list while we watch TV or organizing the day ahead while we take a shower. Switching from this kind of divided or scattered mental activity to a state of concentration often generates resistance, especially when the task is unpleasant or formidable.

Mihaly Csikszentmihalyi (1975), a psychologist at the University of Chicago, refers to this state of intense concentration as "flow," and from interviews with athletes, artists, and various professionals, theorizes that flow can only be achieved when a person is neither bored nor worried, but in control, possessing skills adequate to meet the challenge at hand. The key to achieving and maintaining flow is to balance one's skills against the challenge. "What counts," he says, "is the person's ability to restructure the environment so that it will allow flow to occur" (53).

Although rituals can take a bewildering number of forms, they help writers restructure their environment in one or more ways: clear the deck of competing preoccupations, protect from interruptions, encourage relaxation, reduces anxiety, and provide a structure (through established limitations of time) for dividing projects into manageable increments. This last use is especially important as writing assignments increase in length and complexity. The transition from the shorter assignment that can be completed in the space of two or three hours to an assignment that requires weeks of reading, research, and multiple drafts can be devastating to those who have conditioned themselves to write in only one, high-pressured session. In such cases, the writer needs strategies to help him or her overcome mental resistance and make good use of scheduled work-time.

## Using Rituals

Because no two writers are alike, no formula for effective rituals exists. Even the same writer may use different rituals for different projects, or for different stages of a project. One writer may need several rituals involving workspace, time, and repetitive activities; another may need only a favorite pen. Every writer must learn to pay attention to his or her own needs, the demands that must be juggled, the mental and biological rhythms of the day, and the spontaneous moments of inspiration. Here are some suggestions for establishing productive rituals:

1.  Consider the times of the day in which you are most and least alert. Most people have two or three cycles each day. Note the times that are your best.

2.  Identify those times and activities in which ideas naturally occur. These may include certain times of day (when waking up, for example), during physical activities, or when engaged in repetitive or automatic behaviors (driving a car or washing dishes). Carry a tape recorder, small notebook, or some means of recording your ideas as they occur.

3.  Draw up a schedule of a typical week. Mark those hours that are already scheduled. Note those times that are left open that correspond with the times identified in items 1 and 2. These are the most effective times to schedule writing. If possible, plan to do your writing during these times instead of "at the last minute." Each semester, once I know when my classes meet, I draw up such a schedule and post it on my refrigerator. Although I can't always use my writing time to work on writing, the schedule serves as a constant reminder of my priorities.

4.  Consider the amount of time which you are normally able to maintain

concentration. Even experienced writers tend to work for no more than three or four hours a day. They may spend additional time reading, making notes, or editing a text, but these activities can tolerate more interruptions and can be performed at less-than-peak times. Remember, too, it sometimes takes time to achieve a full state of concentration—an hour may provide only fifteen to twenty minutes of productive time. Writing frequently for short periods of time may be best. Many writers advocate working a little bit every day because the frequency helps lessen the initial resistance to concentration.

5.  Consider the conditions under which you work best. Do you need absolute silence or background noise? Does music help you to focus or does it distract you? Do you prefer to work alone or with other people around? Do you prefer certain kinds of pens, inks, or paper, or do you need access to a typewriter or computer? Do you work best when sitting, standing, or lying down? Does it help you to pace or rock in a rocking chair or prepare a pot of coffee? Do you prefer natural, incandescent, or fluorescent light? Is the temperature comfortable? Is this a place you can work without being interrupted? Identify these needs and assemble an environment in which you are most comfortable.

6.  Cultivate rituals that help you focus. Many writers use meditational exercises, write personal letters, or read recreationally to relax and prime the inner voice with prose rhythms. Some writers eat and drink so as not to be bothered with physical distractions; others eat or drink while they work because the repetitive activity helps them stay focused. Some writers feel they are more mentally alert if they write when they are slightly hungry. Experiment with different rituals and choose what works best for you.

Once concentration is achieved, writers tend to lose awareness of their rituals, but when concentration lapses or writers become blocked, they may consciously use rituals to avoid frustration and regain concentration as quickly as possible. The rituals vary according to the writer, the situation, the task, and the cause of the interruption or block, but common practices suggest several options:

1.  Take a short break from the work and return later. If pushed for time, a short break may be most efficient. The trick is to stay away long enough to let strong feelings that may sabotage the writing subside, without letting one's focus shift too far away from the project overall. This is time to get something to drink, stretch out, or put the clothes in the dryer—activities that don't require one's full attention.

2.  Shift attention to a different part of the same task and work on that. If you don't need to take a break, work on a section of the project with which you are not blocked. If you know, for example, that you plan to describe a personal experience later in the draft and you know what you want to

say about it (even though you are not yet sure how that experience fits within the overall organization of the piece), go ahead and write it and set it aside for later.

3.   Shift attention to a different task and return later. Other tasks can provide a break from the writing and, simultaneously, maintain the feeling of productivity; some professional writers juggle more than one writing project at a time for this very reason.

4.   Switch to reading—notes or other texts—to stimulate new ideas and to help regain focus. If you are working from notes or research materials, sometimes browsing through them will remind you of things you wanted to say. If that doesn't work, try reading materials that are not related to your task. One student told me that he used articles in *Rolling Stone* to help him get into a "voice" that helped him write. If you are working on a computer and have lost your sense of direction ("What should I say next?"), printing out your work and reading that may also help you regain your flow of thoughts.

5.   Talk to someone about the problem or, if no one is around, write about it. Writers frequently use a friend or family member to talk through their ideas aloud (notice how often family members are thanked in the acknowledgments of books); reading or talking to someone not only offers a respite, but may result in the needed breakthrough.

6.   Take a longer break, one which involves physical activity, a full escape from the task, or a period of sleep. If the block seems impenetrable or if you are so angry and frustrated that a short break won't make any difference, then spend enough time away from the task that you can begin afresh. Get out of your workspace, go for a hike, see a movie, or spend an evening shooting pool. Intense physical workouts can burn off tension created by writing blocks. If you're tired, take a nap. Some people can work well when tired, and pulling an all-nighter is possible for them, but others are far better off sleeping first and working later, even if that means waking up at 3:00 a.m. to write.

# Coda

Writing this article has reminded me that knowing about rituals and making use of them are not always the same thing. Parts of this developed easily; others had to be teased out line by line. Ideas came while walking the dog, stoking the woodstove, taking hot baths, and discussing my work with others. After reading the last draft, my husband asked me how I intended to conclude. By discussing X, Y, and Z, I answered. I knew exactly what I wanted to say.

That was several nights ago, and today, I can't for the life of me remember what I said. If only I had thought to write it down.

## Annotated Bibliography

The writers' rituals described here were gathered from a variety of sources—interviews, published diaries and letters, biographical and autobiographical materials—but anecdotes about rituals appear almost anytime writers discuss their writing processes. For further reading, see the *Paris Review Interviews with Writers* series, Tillie Olsen's *Silence*, or *Working It Out: 23 Women Writers, Artists, Scientists, and Scholars Talk About Their Lives and Work*, edited by Sara Ruddick and Pamela Daniels.

For further reading on writing and altered states of consciousness, see Csikszentmihalyi's *Beyond Boredom and Anxiety*, Richard Restak's *The Brain* (based on the PBS Television Series "The Brain"), and Diane Ackerman's *A Natural History of the Senses*. For an older but excellent introduction to the subject of psychophysiology see *Altered States of Consciousness*, edited by Charles T. Tart.

Although the subject of rituals is not a common one for most teachers of composition, a few have discussed the personal and idiosyncratic needs of writers. See especially several of the self-reflective articles in *Learning by Teaching* by Donald M. Murray, Peter Elbow's *Writing with Power*, and James Moffett's essay, "Writing Inner Speech, and Meditation," in *Coming On Center*.

## Work Cited

Csikszentmihalyi, Mihaly (1975). *Beyond Boredom and Anxiety*. New York: Jossey-Bass.

## Sharing Ideas

- Describe your best writing conditions and your most effective (even your most secret) writing rituals. For instance, as I write these questions, I have my two cats sleeping behind me, a quiet house, a desk with lots of pencils in a room that is just messy enough (my mess, no one else's), and a mug of coffee. Surely I could write without any of these conditions, but I spent some time arranging the atmosphere I wanted for writing to you.

- What do you sympathize with most or view as most like you as a writer: Adriana, Marcia, or Sam?

- What advice would you give each writer for improving his or her writing processes?

- Tell some stories of times when you achieved flow states (as a writer or during other activities, too).

- What would be involved for you in adopting some of Susan's advice for establishing productive rituals?
- Explore the connection between rituals and inspiration.
- Interview professional or amateur writers of your choice; describe and analyze their writing rituals.
- Use this essay to discuss Joe Quatrone's writing habits as he reports them in his self-analysis in Chapter 20.

———————————

# Part II

# Invitations to Write

I want student writers to show themselves to me in what they write, to give themselves to me, as I try to show and to give myself back to them in what I write. I want them to remember their lives, their histories, the particularities of their existence, and to show them to me. I want to know what they think and how they think and why they think that way, and I want to know the particular experiences that count to them.

—Jim Corder, writing teacher

I think that we are very closely linked to our texts. It comes from inside us and is part of us. I feel that my writing is definitely a part of me and that is why I am often very self-conscious about it. I'm not always pleased with my writing and I wish I could be better at it. I don't think I'm that BAD of a writer, I just know I can, or wish I could be better at it. It is the same way with me as a person—there is always something more I can do to help others in order to make me a better person—sometimes I just need a swift kick to get me going.

—Anonymous in-class freewrite

My voice isn't exactly what I want it to be. When my writing is working for me, I'm clear and conversational. . . . Now I'm at the point where my voice is finally becoming less self-conscious, perhaps consciously less self-conscious. The talky stuff seems to work better for me than the attempts I made at being a high-brow artiste. So that's what I'm concentrating on—just talking.

—Brad Usatch, writing student

43

# 5

# From Oral Narratives to Written Essays

## Ormond Loomis

---

Ormond Loomis teaches composition at Florida State University, before which he worked in private business and government. His interests include folklore, technical writing, and the history of rhetoric and writing instruction. To take his mind off writing, he likes to go canoeing, watch movies with his wife, daughter, and son, and swap stories with friends.

---

My story starts on June 18, last Wednesday. I was getting ready to move to FSU to start my first year at college, and my two best friends, Ginny and Amy, were moving me up to school in Ginny's car. My mom wasn't moving me up to school because we had been arguing. . . .

In a way I'm almost thankful for the wreck. . . . I think the accident was a good thing in a way. I know that seems kind of odd, but it really opened my eyes and I have like this whole new light on everything.

        —Lindsay, a first-year writing student

These lines open and close "Just a Week Ago," a paper about a car wreck Lindsay was in. She wrote it for a freshman composition course I taught. The assignment was to develop an essay from a story she had told before. Evaluating her writing at the end of the course, she considered it her "best work for the term." "That paper was all heart and soul," she wrote. "The purpose was implied and understood" (cover memo).

In the assignment, which I call "Tell, Tape, Transcribe, and Transform," students select a story from their own repertoire of familiar oral narratives and retell it aloud in class. The activity encourages them to move from language and narratives they know well to writing in the university. As students share the story with peers in a small-group workshop, they tape-record it and the discussion that follows. Afterward, like Lindsay, each writes a paper from a transcription of the oral text. The process lets them tap their storytelling ability to empower their writing.

The directions I give my students should show how to use the activity and give me a chance to explain why I think this writing sequence can be as important to you as it was to Lindsay.

### Tell, Tape, Transcribe, and Transform

This exercise helps you write an essay from a story you've told before. The story can recount a personal experience, describe a friend or an acquaintance, relate a joke or tale you're fond of—tell any complete narrative. It should be one you've learned informally and told often. Drawing on the narrative for the essay, you work with material—language, narrative elements, and background information—that you know well and can interpret to others.

Put aside whatever anxiety you may have about your ability to recall and retell a story. Everyone tells stories among friends. Remember conversations you've had with friends when you shared narratives, and you'll have plenty of choice for the assignment. When my students relate a story they've told before, they are easy storytellers (even if they feel like incompetent writers). Their narratives range from such subjects as appearing on "Family Feud" to losing $1,000 in Las Vegas, working with a private investigator to playing basketball with Michael Jordan. Yours may range from "the first time I cooked a turkey" or "the time I made everyone laugh by zipping a tablecloth in my fly" to "when Jim and I drove to Mexico one night" and "the trouble that happened when I forgot to bring the salad." They may even include your favorite joke or an account of how your neighbor's cousin met a famous person like the President.

Prepare for your class workshop by selecting a story you enjoy. It can be about anything that has meaning for you: cooking perhaps, computers or the internet, a sport, or some other subject. Remember the settings in which you've told the story before. Think about how the story was usually told; how it was organized; what elements were interesting, entertaining, or necessary to the narrative; what background listeners shared that made the elements of the story significant. Plan to present enough of the story and enough of the background to make sense to people in your workshop. You might want to

write notes to follow, but DON'T WRITE THE TEXT TO READ IN CLASS.
Allow yourself about five minutes for the presentation.

The story you pick draws on your knowledge of culture, people, and verbal arts. When you retell it in your workshop, you need to add background that will help your peers appreciate it as you do. Along with the narrative you should provide information about where it comes from, how the characters in it relate to each other, when it's been told, who usually tells it and who usually listens, what events accompanied previous tellings that might increase its significance. You should also include insights you have about the way people use the story to express themselves and about the influence the narrative has had on you.

As you reflect on the background and significance of the story, you're doing work that essayists and other serious writers do with their material— work that is perhaps the most important part of academic writing: thinking critically to make meaning. Explaining your story in your workshop furthers the development of your narrative into an essay. Speech, the medium you're familiar with for sharing the narrative, allows you to recreate the story as you've known it; your retelling gives you a starting point to discuss the story's meaning. You might think of talking in your workshop as "oral narrative invention."

People who study and teach writing frequently refer to "developing narratives," "using voice," "addressing an audience," but they usually employ these terms metaphorically. They seldom deal with oral texts although the concepts they use derive from speech. In textbooks, using speech is often recommended as a tool to develop papers. Some suggest that talk can help with brainstorming and revision. Many encourage reading aloud as a step in proofreading. These activities are valuable; they work well. The use of speech in the "Tell, Tape, Transcribe, and Transform" exercise is different from other activities, however, because you start with a familiar oral narrative.

When you retell and explain your story in a class workshop, you're the authority. A text based on your memory of the narrative already exists in your mind. It has a shape and contains scenes, dialog, and details that work independently of the writing exercise. It makes, or made, sense to tell outside class. You have a sense—from comments and nonverbal cues your listeners gave when you told the story before—of what was good about it and what wasn't. This knowledge is an asset in retelling and will help you later in writing.

Present your narrative aloud in your workshop, and tape-record it and the discussion that follows. You may want to begin by telling the story exactly as you have in the past, or you may prefer to introduce it by giving some background. The choice is yours. As you present, help your class audience by providing an explanation of where the narrative comes from, when you've told it before, who you usually tell it to, and what it means to you and people you usually share it with. After telling the story, ask for responses from your workshop. What did your peers enjoy about the narrative; what about it confused them; what should you have added to help them understand?

I'm not the only teacher who encourages writing students to work with oral texts. Some have students adapt ethnography—observing people and recording facets of community life—for composition. The way people in different groups and communities use language reflects their history and culture. Other teachers have students write about folktales that initially began as oral narratives. Using ethnography and folklore fosters intercultural awareness. In effect, your story amounts to an ethnographic document, a part of your folklore. The "Tell, Tape, Transcribe, and Transform" assignment challenges you to interpret what your narrative reflects.

> After class, transcribe the narrative—word for word, pause for pause, inflection for inflection. Use any punctuation or arrangement of lines on the page that helps you capture what you said. But at this point don't subtract from or add to the words and sounds you uttered. Reflect on the words or phrases you repeat frequently, punctuation marks and paragraph breaks you use, and the way you write slang or dialect. What do they suggest to you about the meaning you intend audiences to get? Print this transcribed version and save it as is. If you're working with a computer, save the computer file as well.

A verbatim transcription serves as a reference. It preserves what you said in your workshop. If you're tempted to edit as you transcribe, please don't. Easy, obvious editing now takes you away from your narrative experience. Eventually you'll shape the text into your essay. Before you make changes, however, you need to consider the words you spoke—your actual voice.

Your speaking style reflects your culture. Your transcription captures that style. As you revise and edit the verbatim text into an essay, your goal should be to preserve your style with language—your metaphorical "voice"—and at the same time move your prose toward conventions (such as reasonable connections and supporting examples as well as recognizable spelling and punctuation) that literate people use for making sense to readers. Your transcription gives you a text for revision—which should be a source of confidence that your essay is well begun—and, often, editing text prompts you to write new lines that expand and improve on the old.

> Next, review the comments that came out of the workshop: points that interested your listeners; questions your story and the way you told it raised for them; ideas and connections your narrative stimulated. Once you've considered the transcription and the responses, expand your narrative into an essay. It should describe your narrative and explain its meaning. Elaborate on points that interested your listeners; clarify points that confused them. Use quotations from your oral presentation to give life, color, and detail to your writing.

Much of what you said is worth keeping in your essay. I expect you'll find details that conjure powerful mental images; jargon and distinctive grammar that catches the way people authentically talk; events that turn dramatically, revealingly, perhaps instructively. You can use this material. Working from an oral story helps you to discover compelling images and appealing language. Lindsay told, and wrote, with this type of detail about the moments immediately after her accident:

> My head then busted out the side window, my legs were caught between the two front seats, my ear was bleeding, and Ginny was screaming at the top of her lungs because part of her ear was torn off, Amy's mouth was bleeding, and it was raining through the back windshield. There were paramedics running everywhere sticking umbrellas in the windshield so we wouldn't be cold. ("Just a Week Ago," 1–2)

Often if you pay attention to your audience's reactions, your listeners, and later your readers, will respond with increased attention. Try to recognize and include these "moments of appeal." They're part of what makes your oral narrative memorable and repeatable. For your essay you want to build on this material to bring out the meaning your story carries. You'll also probably notice repetitious words and phrases, clichés, and ideas grouped without logical connections in your text. You can drop or modify them depending on how important you feel they are to explaining your story.

Your transcription and the comments from your workshop members serve as a bridge to the meaning you want your audience—listeners or readers—to take from your narrative. The ideas behind your oral text don't all come across in a verbatim transcription; you expressed some meaning with pauses, intonation, and gestures. As you revise, you may be able to put nonverbal parts of your presentation into words, or you may need to suggest them on the page with punctuation, paragraph and extra line breaks, italics, and other typographic conventions.

Akua Duku Anokye is a teacher who has her students write three papers from different types of oral narratives: one from a folktale, one from a "narrative . . . about one of their personal ancestors" (1994, 49), and one from "a personal life narrative" (53). She explains that "oral storytelling works as a prewriting device, cultivates critical thinking and analysis, and fosters self-esteem" (56). When her students revise their transcriptions, she suggests to them that they:

> might move from an oral version of the story to a written one by adding: a title; formulaic sentence; literary diction; features of detachment such as changing a direct quote to an indirect one ("I hate you, man" to "I used to look in the mirror and say that I hated myself"). . . . The rhetorical devices used in the oral version—figures of speech, repetition, parallelism in the grammatical system—will be retained but the paralinguistics must show up in paragraphing and punctuation. . . . When conversation is not face to face ideas must be stated in clear, precise language . . . metaphors and imagery create vivid pictures where facial and body gestures were adequate in orality. (57)

If you are sensitive to listeners when you present your narrative in your workshop, to hold their attention, you probably add or drop some of what you'd planned to say. Notice the points in your transcription where this oral editing happened and extend the impulse to edit as you revise your text. Develop those sections further. Trim apparently interesting sections and expand where listeners seemed to lose interest. Points that your workshop audience asked you to clarify in the discussion after you presented your story need to be addressed in your revisions as well. Weave these clarifications into your essay where they will help readers most.

> Share the transcription and a draft of your essay in your next group workshop. With the help of your workshop members, confirm places in the draft that contain strong details, have emotional impact, and use language distinctively and find places that cause confusion, distract, or seem irrelevant. Get your peers' advice on using valuable material from your oral text and on explaining ideas in the draft of the essay. Finally, based on their suggestions, your understanding of how your text affected them, and your ideas of what you want to achieve, revise the paper again to produce a polished essay.

Transforming your story—first from an oral text to a transcription, then from the transcription to a thoughtful essay—raises issues about your awareness of your audience, reference to authority, structural patterns, formulas and clichés, grammar, spelling, and punctuation. The more you understand these issues and the more you resolve problems that arise from them the better writer you become and the better your writing becomes.

Akua Duku Anokye observes that transcription and revision "lead to a discussion about orality, . . . literacy and what is acceptable, expected, and different from . . . oral tellings" (1994, 56). Walter Ong, Patricia Bizzell, and others who've studied the effects of literacy find that writing enables people to think and express themselves—in speech and writing—differently than people who depend on speech alone. Repetitive words and phrases; concrete images; ideas placed next to each other without logical connections or coordinating elements, at times seeming even random; and episodic and formulaic structures are characteristics of orality. Literate people tend toward an analytic use of words and phrases; generalizations; ideas arranged hierarchically and with logical connections; and a linear, sequential structure.

Because literacy pervades modern society, most people today—including you and me—are primarily literate. Even if you don't consider yourself literary, you blend oral and literate patterns in your thought, speech, and writing. Such blending appears in Lindsay's paper. The details she used in her oral narrative—those describing the scene at the accident as well as other details describing the panic and the stupor among victims in the emergency room and her own incapacity during recuperation—lead to her general profession of gratitude for her mother's efforts: "It makes me realize how much I take advantage of my mom and how I don't appreciate her as much as I should" (5).

Lindsay's paper contains excellent examples of the oral pattern of juxta-posing ideas without clear connections, called parataxis, and the literate pat-tern of subordinating one idea to another logically, called hypotaxis. For instance, she employs parataxis at the end of her paper when she writes from her transcript, "I wasn't ready to leave. I just didn't want to go. I had eighteen days between graduation and college." A few lines later she employs hypotaxis in her remarks about leaving home: "In a way I'm almost thankful for the wreck. One, because it gave me extra days with my family and my friends" (5).

Finding the right amount of connection for your ideas becomes a matter of style—your metaphorical voice again. Too much randomness can be con-fusing; too much logic can be tedious. In a draft from an oral text, it's gener-ally better to revise in a direction that clarifies the apparent connection between ideas. Rearrange sections into a sensible progression. Readers in your workshop can help you with style by identifying places in your draft that need transition or extra explanation. They share a mental impression of your oral text, and they have your written draft to examine.

But wouldn't any personal narrative paper exercise, even one that doesn't involve an oral narrative, have similar results?

There's an undeniable similarity between the themes of conventional per-sonal experience papers and the themes of papers based on oral personal expe-rience stories. In fact, the array of students' personal narrative topics I receive fits recognizable types that have been noted by other composition teachers. My students write essays on what Lad Tobin identifies as "getting into a near-fatal car crash," "getting drunk," the "time me and my friends played a great . . . prank," and the "success [or failure] as a shoplifter" stories (158)—even on the "'wild canoe trips' noted by Linda Peterson" (1991, 175). Such topics may be seen as clichéd. *(Writer beware!)*

A cursory survey of the oral narrative papers I've received during four semesters revealed that, apart from technical concerns, nearly all of them used similar topics, settings, characters, motifs, frames, structure, and themes. The features may be summarized as

- topics: cool and crazy life; accidents and legal violations; encounters with bullies; or the influence of sports

- settings: home; school; local neighborhood; sports arena; or entertainment venue

- characters: the speaker/writer; family members; friends; classmates; neighborhood associates; and celebrities

- motifs: cars; alcohol; sporting events; concerts; stereotypes of other people

- frames: openings with an establishing time, place, and action involving principal characters and closings that express a lesson or moral

- structure: linear—chronological or near chronological—progression

- themes: romantic or sexual relationships; embarrassment; growth through discovery or the work ethic; loyalty; and standing up for one's rights

I see these similarities not as mere cliché but as cultural exploration and understanding in the making. By picking a story you've told before to share aloud with peers in your workshop, you're more likely to select topics, characters, and narrative structure that appeal to people like yourself. In the process you learn some of what you have in common at this place and time with others in your class and at the university. Your essay involves part of what Bizzell would call your "audience's canonical knowledge."*(142)* It has power to engage the other students. When you take the time to explain your narrative—at first to peers in your workshop and eventually, as you revise and develop your paper, to an audience of other university students and teachers—you have an essay that's invested with your personal understanding as well as your experience.

When I read essays from this exercise, I am pleased and disappointed to varying degrees with the writing in each paper. Some show more originality than others, some more technical polish; some reflect both. Nevertheless, each provides a foundation for class discussions of the differences between oral and literate texts, informal and formal writing, popular media and academic prose. Do the words of a rock singer you quote carry as much weight for an anthropology major as they do for a business major? Why are cars, alcohol, and sports more frequently discussed than novels, political theories, or scientific discoveries? If you and others in your workshop start your stories with "It happened on . . . at . . . ," how does that compare with the opening of a short story you enjoyed reading, a newspaper article that stimulates debate on campus, or a lecture that impressed you?

In the pursuit of the answers, you begin writing about issues that matter to you, and you discover ways to express what you mean. And that's what the work of writing is all about.

## Questions to Ask After Reading:

What group of people is the source of most of your stories? Are there subjects that are of particular interest for them? If so, how do those subjects relate to their age; sex; neighborhood, town, and region; education, income, and social class? Do the stories contain terms and phrases that have special, perhaps exclusive, meaning? What and how much should you explain about the group to help your audience understand the story?

How are your favorite stories organized? How and where do they begin and end? Do events proceed chronologically, jump randomly from past to present or present to past? Are there digressions—extended descriptions, tangents about events outside the main narrative, side comments about people or places—and if there are, how do they contribute to the effect?

Who, besides you, are the authority figures in one of your favorite stories: mother; father; sister; brother; other family members; friends; teachers; bullies; athletes; singers and musicians; movie and TV stars; employers; police; "they"? What special knowledge or stature do these people add to your narrative? How do you treat quotations from them?

What's the main point to one of your favorite stories? How does your audience get the message you want from the story? Does the story communicate more than one point? Do subordinate points distract your listeners/readers or lead them to and help them understand the main point?

Do you regard the story the same way now as you did when you first heard or told it? Why has, or hasn't, your attitude changed?

## Works Cited

Anokye, Akua Duku (1994). "Oral Connections to Literacy: The Narrative." *Journal of Basic Writing 13*. (2), 46–60.

Bizzell, Patricia (1988). "Arguing About Literacy." *College English 50*. (2), 141–153.

Lindsay (30 July 1997). "Cover Memo." Memo to the author.

———— (26 June 1997). "Just a Week Ago." Unpublished essay.

Ong, Walter J. (1982). *Orality and Literacy: The Technologizing of the Word*. London: Methuen.

Peterson, Linda H. (May 1991). "Gender and the Autobiographical Essay: Research Perspectives, Pedagogical Practices." *College Composition and Communication 42*: 170–183.

Tobin, Lad (February 1996). "Car Wrecks, Baseball Caps, and Man-to-Man Defense: The Personal Narratives of Adolescent Males." *College English 58*. (2), 158–175.

## Sharing Ideas

- Many of the essayists in this collection use stories to illustrate their points. Make a list of these stories and consider which ones were most effective in helping the author get your attention and make a point he or she was trying to make. Do you think these authors told their stories before writing them down? Or do you think they developed them just to illustrate the essays here? What textual clues or experiences with storytelling did you draw on for deciding this?

- Looking at Ormond Loomis' analysis of student writing topics in his class, decide which you'd most like to read. Which have you written on in the past? Which seem like "school topics"—writings done with the assignment, class, or teacher in mind—and which seem to you to be topics that probably matter a great deal to the author? Are these always separate issues or can a writer care about a school topic? How do you know?

- Ormond claims some of the topics generated from personal experience can be seen as clichéd. Take two clichéd topics and talk in your group about how those topics could still be written about in interesting and provocative ways (it may help to read Toby Fulwiler's essay, Chapter 8, to get ideas for this).

- Spend some time with your local newspaper and favorite magazines or nonfiction writers you've enjoyed. Where and how do you find stories of personal experience illuminating a text? Collect several of these instances and share them with members of your writing group. Did these writers introduce and use stories in the same way class writers did? Do the examples you collected offer you some revision ideas?

- What do you know about the art of interviewing? In this exercise, you're interviewing yourself in the sense that you're mining your own memory for stories to share. But you also have the traditional interviewer's task of rendering taped information to a legible written transcript—how can you best do this?

- After you complete this paper, continue on, conduct primary research for another paper by interviewing others. What advice can you share for doing this? What are the challenges of face to face? Telephone interviews? E-mail interviews? How can you use these in an essay and cite them in your Works Cited?

# 6

# How to Get the Writing Done

## Donald M. Murray

---

Donald M. Murray is a writer who publishes novels, poetry, a news-
paper column, and textbooks on writing and teaching writing. He is
Professor Emeritus of English at the University of New Hampshire.
As a journalist, Murray won a number of awards including the
Pulitzer Prize for editorial writing on *The Boston Herald* in 1954.
Currently, he writes a weekly column, *Over Sixty*, for *The Boston
Globe*. His most recent books include new editions of *Write to
Learn* and *Read to Write*, as well as *The Craft of Revision,
Expecting the Unexpected*, and *Shoptalk: Learning to Write with
Writers* were published by Boynton/Cook.

---

Famous writers and writers who hope they will become famous, published
writers and unpublished writers, master writers and miserable writers, good
students and poor students have one problem in common: How can we get the
writing done?

I am going to take you into the back room of the writing shop that readers never see and show you how one professional produces his daily quota of
words.

There is no one way to get the writing done. Many of my strategies are
contradictory, what works on one project will not work on the next. I have to
keep trying new ways—or retrying old ways—to produce effective writing.
The strategies keep changing as I steal a technique from a fellow writer or
from another craft, remember one I have forgotten, or discard another that
works for someone else but never seems to work for me. Here are the strategies hung above my workbench this morning:

*1. Write Now.* Write before you know what you have to say or how to say it. Ignorance is a great starting place. Write as fast as you can—and then increase the speed! Don't worry about penmanship or typing, punctuation or correctness, making sense or being silly. Velocity is as important in writing as in bicycle riding—speed gets you ahead of the censor and causes the accidents of meaning and language essential to good writing.

Later you can read what you have written and the draft, rough as it is, will often reveal what you have to say and how you can say it.

*2. Rewrite.* Take a rough draft and get into the writing by rewriting. The old draft will stimulate a new one. I used to revise by hand, cutting (I love to cut—this chapter is growing shorter at the moment), adding, moving around. Now I work on a computer, and I write right over what I have written, layering new meanings on top of old ones the way you build up an oil painting.

Rewriting is not failure but an essential part of the process of writing, each draft leads us to our meaning and allows us to tune our voices to that meaning.

*3. Delay.* But sometimes writing early doesn't work. In that case stand back. E. B. White says, "Delay is natural to a writer. He is like a surfer—he bides his time, waits for the perfect wave on which to ride in. Delay is instinctive with him. He waits for the surge (of emotion? of strength? of courage?) that will carry him along." And Virginia Woolf wrote: "As for my next book, I am going to hold myself from writing it till I have it impending in me: grown heavy in my mind like a ripe pear; pendant, gravid, asking to be cut or it will fall."

I find it helpful sometimes to take a walk, drive somewhere and do errands, watch the Celtics on TV, take a nap, or assign my subconscious to consider a writing problem as I go to sleep at night. The writing goes on, and when I return to the writing desk I discover I know what to say and how to say it.

*4. Rehearse.* We rehearse plays and concerts, rehearse what we will say when applying for a job or a loan from a parent, and rehearse our approach to a member of the opposite sex, and writers rehearse writing. Talk to yourself, try beginnings and key paragraphs in your head before you get to the page, hear what you may say before you see it. I am at my desk a couple of hours a morning but I write in my head during the twenty-two or so hours I am away from the writing desk. To help me in this process I keep small cards in my shirt pocket so I can catch a phrase or thought if one flies through my head. I also keep a daybook, a writing log or journal, in which I can talk to myself in writing, playing with what I may write when I return to my writing desk.

*5. Consult.* Develop a writing community with which you can talk about what you may write, what you are writing—and rewriting. I have developed my own community by sharing my writing first. Then some of them share theirs. We consult on what we may write, what we are writing, what works, and what needs work. I not only receive help from the writers in my community; I hear the answers to my writing problems in what I say to them.

I have one rule for admission to my writing community: I only invite people to join who make me want to write when I finish talking to them.

6. *Plan.*     Some writing is unplanned. You freewrite and a text seems to arise spontaneously from the page. Wonderful. Accept the gift, but don't count on it happening regularly like the six o'clock news. Most writing is planned. But rarely do writers plan in rigid detail, outlining with complete sentences—"The Harvard Outline"—or an intricate A, a, B, b; Ii, Iii; 1.1, 1.1.1 sequence. The planning techniques I find most helpful are

> *Line.*     I know I have a piece of writing when I have a line, a fragment of language, sometimes a word, most likely a phrase, rarely a sentence, which contains the essential conflict or tension within the subject. I knew I could write this piece when I heard the phrase "master writers and students have the same problem: how . . ." The article would be released by the tension within those words.

> *Title.*     I find the title helps me get started if it contains the energy to push the writer—and the reader—forward. Write a title such as "How to Get the Writing Done" and the draft follows directly.

> *Lead.*     As a journalist, I have to get the lead right, the first few sentences or paragraphs, before I go on. I play with those lines in my head, in my daybook, on my computer screen, drafting half a dozen or three dozen leads quickly until the essential tension within the piece is established, the voice is clear, and the reader is drawn in, as I hope I did in developing the line into the lead, or first paragraph, of this article.

> *Cross Heads.*     In writing most nonfiction, I write the headings and subheadings first, as I did in this article. They may change as I go along but as I draft the heads I can see the sequence and pattern the article will take.

7. *Attitude.*     Every writer goes to the writing desk with a set of assumptions that may make the writing difficult or easy. For years I wanted to impress teachers, editors, and associates I didn't even like. I also wanted to write perfect copy the first time out. But I learned to follow William Stafford's advice:

> I believe that the so-called "writing block" is a product of some kind of disproportion between your standards and your performance. . . . [O]ne should lower his standards until there is no felt threshold to go over in writing. It's easy to write. You just shouldn't have standards that inhibit you from writing.

> I can imagine a person beginning to feel he's not able to write up to that standard he imagines the world has set for him. But to me that's surrealistic. The

only standard I can rationally have is the standard I'm meeting right now. . . .
You should be more willing to forgive yourself. It doesn't make any difference if you are good or bad today. The assessment of the product is something that happens after you've done it.

Now I go to the desk determined to write as well as I can write each morning but no better. If I lower my standards, I receive a draft. Then I can rewrite.

*8. Habit.*     Right there, in the center over my workbench are four words in
big black letters *NULLA DIES SINE LINEA.* The Latin command—"never a
day without a line" is attributed to both Horace and Pliny. Never mind who
said it, it is the motto of most writers, ancient and modern, men and women.
Jogging and writing require habit. And it is more productive to write every day
for a short time than one day for a long time.

Brief writing periods can be amazingly effective. One prolific—and excellent—writer, Anthony Burgess, pointed out that by writing only one page per
day, you can have a 365-page book drafted in a year. I find that I can get an
amazing amount of writing done in bursts of half-an-hour a day, twenty minutes, fifteen; three pages a day, one page, half a page; 500 words, 300, 200, 100.

*9. Deadlines.*     There's little that clarifies the mind and increases the concentration better than a deadline, a point upon which you pass and you are
dead. As the deadline approaches, the adrenaline flows and copy comes; it is
too late for excessive thought: don't think, write.

But *their* deadline should not necessarily be your deadline. My deadline
for my Tuesday column is Monday—a week ahead. And I stick to it.

Work backward in time and establish your own deadlines, saying, "On the
twelfth the research will be done, on the fourteenth I'll have the lead and a list
of the main points to be covered, on the nineteenth I'll have a first draft, on the
twenty-second the final draft."

*10. When Interrupted as You Wr. . . .*     Stop in the middle of a sentence so
that you can finish the sentence and be involved in the writing immediately
after the interruption or the next day when you return to your writing desk. If
you have an idea of the sequence of things to be written scribble them down
at the same time.

*11. Change Your Working Style.*     What works on one project may not on
another. I advocate fast writing, but sometimes I have to slow down and work
with pen on paper. I am an early morning writer, but once in a while a project
will seem to require days of ruminations as I do errands, and I end up writing
in late afternoon. I usually outline nonfiction texts and plunge into fiction, but
sometimes I have to plunge into nonfiction and stop to plan fiction.

Know your working patterns, but when a project isn't going well—or
even going—experiment with other styles to see if they fit this new project.
New projects may require new work patterns.

*12. Count Words, Pages, or Hours.*     While writing never ask yourself or answer the question: "How good was my writing today?" You have no idea. You can't tell in the middle of a project. Forgive yourself. Follow the counsel of Jonwillum van der Wettering that has kept me productive:

> To write you have to set up a routine, to promise yourself that you will write. Just state in a loud voice that you will write so many pages a day, or write for so many hours a day. Keep the number of pages or hours within reason, and don't be upset if a day slips by. Start again; pick up the routine. Don't look for results. Just write, easily, quietly.

*13. Work Within the Draft.*     When the writing doesn't come easily, do not look outside the draft to textbooks, including mine; to the principles and traditions of writing; to the expectations of teacher, editor, or reader; but first look within the text. Read the paragraph you have just drafted. It will tell you what to deal with next; it will call for more description, an opinion, some evidence, whatever is needed to develop what you have to say, paragraph by paragraph.

*14. Answer the Reader's Questions.*     Effective writing is a conversation with a reader. Anticipate the reader's questions—and answer them.

*15. Make What Works Better.*     I used to write the way most schools teach writing, by pointing out the errors in a draft and then trying to correct them. I always felt guilty, unsure, hesitant, and, more and more, a stranger to the draft. It was less and less mine.

Then I photocopied each page of my first draft on a large sheet of paper and made notes on what I was doing when the revising went well. I was increasing and strengthening those qualities and elements in the writing that went well. If the draft was well organized, I worked on making it even better; if the voice was clear, then I made it clearer; and if the documentation seemed the strength of my argument, I made it even stronger.

My writing went easier when I learned this lesson, the drafts were more my own, and most of the problems of the early draft disappeared. If they didn't, then I corrected them—in the context of an effective working draft that had established its own method and its own standards.

*16. Make Use of Failure.*     I continue to learn to write from what works well and from the instructive failures that are a necessary part of any writing act. I do not like to fail, but I no longer see my writing failures as judgments against me personally as if I were flunking the human race. They are the normal, instructive failures of an experimental art in which you commit yourself to discover what works and what needs work.

*17. Write in Chunks.*     John Steinbeck once wrote:

> When I face the desolate impossibility of writing 500 pages a sick sense of failure falls on me and I know I can never do it. Then gradually I write one page and then another. One day's work is all I can permit myself to contemplate.

All of us feel despair and hopelessness when we contemplate a long writing project. I was comforted by Steinbeck's quotation and by the answer of a woman who spent many days and nights climbing a huge rock face in California. When asked how she stuck it out, she answered: "You eat an elephant one bite at a time." Break long writing tasks into daily bites.

*18. Write with Force; Unleash the Draft.*     Let it rip. As Annie Dillard states:

> One of the few things I know about writing is this: spend it all, shoot it, play it, lose it, all, right away, every time. Do not hoard what seems good for a later place in the book, or for another book; give it, give it all, give it now. The impulse to save something good for a better place later is to signal to spend it now. Something more will arise for later, something better. These things fill from behind, from beneath, like well water.

You can cut later, but you cannot cut from an undeveloped, under written text. Write from abundance to get the draft done, let the energy rise out of the writing; cut, shape, polish later.

*19. Write.*     Write when you think you don't have anything to say. Write when you are tired. Write between classes. Write during TV commercials. Write when what you see on the page makes you want to vomit. Write when the writing isn't going well—and when it is. Write fast. Write slowly. Use a pencil, use a pen; type on typewriter and on a computer. Dictate to a tape recorder. Write when you are sick. Write. Write. Write. Write, and something will begin to happen, a word, a line, a sentence, and when you least expect it, the writing will come.

Writing is the way to get the writing done.

---

## Sharing Ideas

- Don provides you with several provocative quotes by poets and novelists. Use one as a starting point for a freewrite of your own, considering or expanding on the author's advice.

- Decide which five of the nineteen categories of advice you find here are the most important to you as a writer. Are those five the same as the ones chosen by other class writers? Consider how your learning and personality preferences may influence your choices.

- Think about ways to break out of school-imposed deadlines. Decide when it might be useful to set your own writing deadlines. For instance, in any class there are always some writers who get work done ahead of schedule. It's certainly not cool, but it is productive. What would you have to do to be one step ahead of your normal production schedule and what, if anything, would you gain?

- What do you think about the suggestion that writers should write every day? Chris Anson and Richard Beach's discussion of journaling shows you one way to get the words down. What would happen if you set your own word count, as Don suggests, and what would that word count be— 100, 200, 300, 500 words?
- Spend a week changing your working style and report on the results.
- Don's section 14 on readers is quite brief. Spend some time deciding who your readers are, and how they do (and should) affect your writing.
- It's certainly hard to accept, but we all fail as writers sometimes. Tell stories of times when you learned from writing that didn't quite work.
- What writing conditions are necessary if you want to follow the advice to unleash a draft and let it rip?
- Think more deeply about Don's advice that writing anything at any time is *always* better than not writing.

# 7

# Access: Writing in the Midst of Many Cultures

## Hans Ostrom

Hans Ostrom is Professor of English and codirector of African American Studies at the University of Puget Sound. He has also taught at the University of California, Davis, and at Johannes Gutenberg University in Mainz, Germany. In 1994 he was a Fulbright Senior Lecturer at Uppsala University, Sweden. His books include *Three to Get Ready* (novel), *Langston Hughes: A Study of the Short Fiction,* and *Lives and Moments: An Introduction to Short Fiction.* With Wendy Bishop, he edited *Genres of Writing.* He likes to garden and listen to the radio.

I listen to the radio every day, and every day I hear at least one advertisement for this or that company "offering" (selling) "Internet access." Great word, *access,* as verb or noun. *Internet,* as a word, I can take or leave. *Access* seems to be a crucial word these days. Consider:

access to quality education

access to health care

"access denied"

breakdowns in security that allow terrorists
    access (to embassies, for instance)

computer crashes that prevent access to the hard drive

"freeway access"

"easy access!"

"let me access your account"

"don't go there" (i.e., access inadvisable)

Jerzy Kosinski wrote a novel, later turned into a film, called *Being There,* but it seems our lives have become all about Getting There. In the magical place of There, *there* is something we need or something we need to protect from others or protect others from. All the action, though, is in the access: a key; a door; an on-ramp; the right software; a map; a code; a password; an account; a card. Ours is not the Age of Information, Chivalry, Reason, Innocence, Space, or X. Ours is the Age of Access.

Naturally, once we "get" (access) There, we learn that There is a place from which we shall require access to other theres. The Internet especially seems to be an infinite string of accesses. The Oxford American Dictionary (1980), page six, warns me not to confuse *access* with *excess*. Okay, I promise. However, I am bound to observe that our culture's concern with access seems excessive, to the point of being obsessive.

Offered access to this book, I hereby announce my interest in how we access the many cultures around us—how we do so especially in college, particularly through writing and reading, specifically in first-year writing courses. Let me now move the mouse of this essay and click twice on the *Anecdote* icon and share some microstories with you. (Names of students are fictitious.)

*Place: Departmental Reception for Graduating English Majors,* on the morning before graduation. A father comes up to me. He is a native of Charleston, South Carolina. He is wealthy, polished, polite. His daughter, Grace, transferred to the University of Puget Sound when she was a sophomore. He thanks me for the wonderful experience she has had, but his face is grim as he continues: "Her beliefs were really challenged here." "Oh," I say. He moves on to talk with others. Although "Oh" was probably an appropriate response, given the context, other responses came to mind: "We'll try not to let that happen again." "You're entitled to a full refund." "Which beliefs?" Or, "It must have been an accident" (for Puget Sound is a small liberal-arts college; the student body is 85 percent white; the curriculum is most traditional). Or, "Her beliefs were challenged and—what?—what was the result?"

*Place: First-year Composition Class.* We've been reading Primo Levi's book, *Survival in Auschwitz.* This day our conversation drifts to the subject of anti-Semitism in the contemporary United States. A student mentions that she heard someone on a talk show claim that "Jews control the media." Most students greet her report as she intended it: as an example of an unsupported claim in service of stereotyping and anti-Semitic lore. But one student, Stan, says, "Well, they pretty much do control the media." The discussion heats up. My contribution is to encourage the students to interrogate, not Stan, but the claim.

What is meant by "control" and "media"? The use of the word "they"—what does that suggest? Who owns NBC, CBS, ABC, CNN, BET, MTV, TCI, your favorite radio station, the company that produced your favorite CD, your hometown newspaper, the campus paper (an interesting question, this), the local avant-garde weekly? On the ownership question, we come up with answers like General Electric, Ted Turner, Rupert Murdoch, Time/Warner, I don't know, the McClatchy Family, doesn't Time/Warner own Ted Turner?, Knight-Ridder papers, and so on. The claim evaporates before our eyes. But we move on to ask why some people (in general, not Stan) seem to need to believe that "Jews control the media." We discuss, and try to define, scapegoating. We discuss *theyspeak,* as in "they control the media." Eventually we get back to the unforgettable book by the Italian chemist, to our journal writing about stereotypes, to the hard work of developing topics based on *Survival in Auschwitz.*

*Place: Another First-year Writing Class.*    We've been reading Lorene Cary's book, *Black Ice,* much of which details her experience as an African American woman attending a virtually all white, upper-crust boarding school in New England. One of the men in class blurts out, "I'm from Idaho—black people just *look* at me and get mad!" Another student—Kathy, the only African American student in the room—says, with friendly exasperation, "Jay. I'm black. We've been in class together all term." Jay responds, "I know—I'm not talking about you!"

I'm interested in—grateful for—how guilelessly Stan and Jay recapitulate notions of "we" and "they," how they act out—no one could script it so well—issues raised in the reading and discussion, how they demonstrate a collision between beliefs they brought to college and studies they do here. I'm interested in students who keep their views to themselves, playing it safe, or holding back, or being confused, or just not caring. I'm interested in the way Kathy spoke, as a colleague, directly to Jay—in how strange (or familiar) it was for her to realize, as the class did, that for Jay the "black people" in his mind were, even after a month or more of class, disconnected from her. Ironic that, in the book, the famous lawyer Archibald Cox visits Cary's school, and while chatting with the students, turns to Cary and, about Richard Nixon, says, "He hates us, you know." Cary is thrown off balance as she realizes that Cox is talking about upper-class New Englanders and including her, a black middle-class woman not from Cox's turf.

I'm frustrated sometimes by how little difference the reading and writing seem to make, astonished at other times by how much they make, never sure how to tell one way or the other.

*Place: (One More) First-year Writing Class.*    We've viewed the film, *Come See the Paradise,* which concerns the internment of Japanese American citizens in "relocation camps" during World War II. We talk about how Hollywood seems to need to put a white person in the middle of stories regardless of the subject matter. In this case, it's a character played by Dennis Quaid. The character does help highlight issues of cultural differences and brings in interesting labor issues. But still. We talk about how, just fifty-some years ago, several Puget Sound undergraduates were removed from the college and sent with their families to a camp in nearby Puyallup (pronounced *Pew-al-up*), then on to an Idaho prison camp. Their families' business, farms, and homes were taken from them and in most cases never returned.

A student, Lori—extremely capable, thoughtful, and well read; a graduate of an ostensibly "good" West Coast high school—says, with a mixture of sadness and disbelief, to the other students, "Had you all heard about this [internment of Japanese Americans]? I'd never heard of this before we saw the movie." If it was news to other students, too, they aren't saying.

The drafts and essays that materialize impress me by how they distinguish between the movie and history, how they focus on a variety of issues—absence of due process and other illegalities, absurdities, what is "American"?, tragedies, bitter ironies. After the reading, talking, and writing are all done, I find I focus on Lori's comment, "I'd never heard of this before. . . ." I am forced to remember that multiculturalism depends on information, on plain old news—some of it very old indeed.

## Click Twice on *Interview* Icon.

*Q:*  What do you mean by *multiculturalism?*

*A:*  May I plead the Fifth Amendment? I mean an active awareness of many cultures, and of cultures within or beside cultures. I mean a willingness to acknowledge cultural differences and similarities, a willingness to acknowledge what we don't know or what we think we know as opposed to what we know we know. I mean read, read, read, learn, learn, learn, write, write, write.

*Q:*  What is *culture?*

*A:*  A cluster of learned behavioral traits.

*Q:*  Huh?

*A:*  Example: *Swedish culture.* That would include geography (its influence on such things as farming and shelter), language, art, music, history, a people's sense of history, laws, attitudes toward sex/marriage/education/children/theft/murder/guns/hockey, toward Norgwegians/monarchy/copper/crystal/potatoes, and so on. Swedes have a Swedish answer to the following questions: If someone invites you to come to dinner at 7:00 P.M., when do you arrive? (Exactly at 7:00, not even five minutes before or after.) Once you arrive, what is among the very first things you do? (Take off your shoes.) Maybe arrival times and shoe removal are trivial bits of the trait-culture; maybe they symbolize more significant traits.

*Q:* Is there such a thing as cultural purity?

*A:* No. Everything in one culture came from another culture—no exceptions (he said, issuing a challenge to find examples to the contrary).

*Q:* So all cultures are the same?

*A:* No. Absence of purity does not mean absence of difference or sameness of history.

*Q:* Why all this talk of differences? That causes trouble and just keeps dividing us.

*A:* Not necessarily. To observe differences—to discover, explore, even enjoy them—is not by nature a trouble-making affair. What we do with the information is our choice. We can choose to make trouble—or not. And *trouble* needs defining—another story.

*Q:* *Multiculturalism* seems so trendy, so politically correct. Such a buzzword.

*A:* I have been on the lookout for more than ten years, but I have yet to hear or read a definition of *politically correct* that makes any sense to me, so I can't help you there. If the *M*-word buzzes, ignore the buzzing. Consider the ideas. One idea is to study histories, customs, perspectives, beliefs. Trendy? Perhaps. But a trend is a pattern, and patterns aren't inherently good or bad. If multiculturalism suggests awareness of different histories and such, then it is not trendy in the sense of a fad. Anyone who ever tried to learn about and from other people was essentially multicultural. Anyone who ever caught the travel bug was multicultural. Anyone who was ever aware of "the many" who always, without exception, lie behind the illusion of "the one" (nation, people, kingdom, culture, state, city) was multicultural.

*Q:* So, the big *M*—it's a good thing?

*A:* Not necessarily. It's a little *m*. A perspective, a practice. It can be used for bad ends. One might become aware of a cultural difference and decide to exploit it unethically. One might equate the discomfort of being left-handed with the difficulties and pain associated with racism. This is to trivialize.

*Q:* What does multiculturalism have to do with first-year writing?

*A:* Let us now visit the Argument Web site.

*A List.*      Racism. Anti-Semitism. Religious conflict. Terrorism. Police "profiling." Affirmative action. "English only." Immigration policies. People from different backgrounds trying to make their way in ever more populous cities. The relative ease with which we travel and communicate globally. The abundance of translated literature and subtitled cinema and television/radio in numerous languages. The terrifying ease with which ethnic conflict becomes genocide. "The race card." Segregated communities/neighborhoods. White supremacists. Haves and have-nots. Adoption of children as a global affair. This is the world in which we live.*

If one purpose of first-year writing is to reinforce your readiness to thrive in college,* and if one purpose of college is to educate you as a *citizen,* and if a citizen should be multiculturally aware,* then multiculturalism is not, to say the least, out of place in first-year writing—*if* you buy those four premises, each marked by an asterisk (*).

*More.*      First-year writing is the contemporary version of rhetoric.* Rhetoric is, in part, the art and craft of public discourse: persuading; discussing; debating; asserting as a citizen (member of communities).* Communities = an internet of cultures.* Therefore (*if* you buy the definitions/equations [*]), multiculturalism plays a big role in our writing, bears directly on what, why, for whom, about whom, and to whom we write.

*Also.*      To enter college is, literally, to enter a new culture, a new cluster of learned behavioral traits (some of which I shudder to think about). It is to encounter persons from different cultures. It is, as the father at the reception noted, to enter an arena in which your beliefs, attitudes, morals, hopes, dreads, prejudices, weaknesses, strengths, fears, ambitions, "family values," and so on, are tested. By tested I don't mean, necessarily, challenged or attacked. I mean *tried.* I mean seen in a new light. Placed in comparison and contrast.

*Connection.*      "Essaying" is *trying* (sometimes very trying indeed). It is testing ideas—your own, someone else's: written; heard; read. It is expressing, linking, supporting, questioning ideas. First-year writing, then, is a fine test site where essaying and the multifaceted culture of college can meet and begin a beautiful friendship.

*And Finally.*      Let us return to access, not to be confused with excess. Writing may be the ultimate access-software package for your cerebral hard drive. With it, you access images, memories, arguments, ideas—your own, others'. To write about a book is to access it, more powerfully than just to read it. To write *out* an idea is to see it anew. To write about yourself is to meet and greet yourself anew. Therefore, if we assume that surviving and thriving as a citizen in and of many cultures requires this capacity to access, then writing is one of a citizen's most important tools.

## Click Twice on *Advice* Icon

Be the primary tester of your own beliefs and attitudes. Rely on writing to do this. Recall the father at the reception: He perceived his daughter to be a holder of beliefs and college to be a force threatening to take them away. It is common to see multicultural questions pictured in such a way—as attack and defense, even as warfare. He implied that his daughter had weathered a storm or survived an onslaught.

But if we see being a citizen in and of many cultures in terms of adaptation, evolution, and discovery, then it is quite natural, productive, and smart for us to test our own beliefs and attitudes. We become more culturally nimble. We prepare ourselves for those rare genuine moments when our beliefs really are challenged. We become less defensive, in the negative sense of that term: jumpy. We see that changing beliefs is neither necessarily good nor necessarily bad, that it's a process over which we have some control. And truly, even when our beliefs and attitudes remain the same, they change. For example, a person can hold fast for a lifetime to a religious belief but also change within that belief. If you are a Muslim, Buddhist, Jew, Hindu, Christian, polytheist, agnostic, or atheist, are you the same Muslim, Buddhist (and so on) you were last year?

## Find *Practice What You Preach* File

Okay, there I am at the reception. I know a little bit about the father from some things Grace has said. To this I add first impressions, then his comment about challenged beliefs and one about how sorry he is that the Citadel (a university) now has to accept women cadets. I begin to label him: conservative Southern man; wealthy; probably Republican; conservative Christian; views of race and gender probably different from my own.

As I write this essay, though, I have to admit how much I don't know about him. Truly I don't know what his views of race and gender are. I don't know to which of Grace's beliefs he was referring. Republican? Perhaps. But he could have voted for a Democrat or no one. What exactly do I mean by *conservative* and *conservative Christian?* Such imprecise terms. Also, there's what I know. I know from Grace that her father moved from Charleston some years ago to the Pacific Northwest for business reasons. Extended family members refuse to visit the Northwest. Sometimes Grace and her family feel shunned, therefore. So the father has experienced his own variety of cultural conflict.

Also, I know that visitors from France, let's say, if they were spectators at the reception, might note how similar the father and I are. We speak American English. Our sense of space and posture is probably American in some tell-tale way. We are garrulous. We're big.

I know I'm a father, too. At the reception, I think the father is overdramatizing the extent to which his daughter's beliefs were really challenged. Will I be so sanguine a decade later when my son comes home from college and talks about his classes?

Lastly, I know that by writing this essay, I've accessed the reception scene and scenes under the anecdote icon differently and more thoroughly than before. I've changed my sense of those scenes. I've recalled particulars and subtleties. I've had to think about the audience for whom I'm presenting the scenes. Matters have become complicated, in a good way.

## Go Back to *Interview* Mode

*Q:*  Yeah, yeah, but I just want to learn to write well enough to do okay in college and get a good job. Multiculturalism, multischmulturalism.

*A:*  Practicality. I like it. Very American, culturally speaking. But even from your practical viewpoint, *Q,* writing about multicultural topics for different audiences and in different modes is excellent writerly training—or training okay enough to help you get an okay job, okay?

And there is what I call deep practicality. When you Get There—access your degree and your job—*there* will be a dizzyingly multicultural place, regardless of what and where the job is. Bet on it. As worker and citizen, you will travel strands of a multicultural internet that makes the Internet look like mere child's play—Legoland.

## Click Twice on *Conclusion* Icon

The many cultures, and cultures within cultures; and beliefs, and beliefs about beliefs; and stereotypes and fears, and fears and facts and misinformation and conflicts and coalitions: these are the heart of our social, political matter. Writing as access is the heart of our educational matter. This is my conclusion, and I'm sticking to it, as now I move the mouse's arrow to the *Writing Tasks* icon.

1.  Write a self-interview in which you 1 interrogates you 2 about certain beliefs—religious, political, or cultural. Make sure you 1 is as smart, logical, and articulate as you 2. Assume you 1 is not predisposed to agree with you 2.

2a.  About what ethnic, religious, or political group that you do not consider your own do you find yourself making pretty hefty assumptions? List the assumptions in column A. List the support (evidence) for the assumptions in column B. In column C, admit to and list what you don't know for sure about the group. This will be a long list. Make column C the topic of an essay, the working title of which will be "What I Don't Know About [the group]." Devote part of the essay to probing how useful and accurate the Group label itself is.

2b.  Write a researched essay, again based on column C (above); the working title will be, "What I Have Found Out About [the Group]."

3.  Write a journal entry or an essay that recounts your having been excluded from a group (any group.) Or write a journal entry (or essay) that

recounts your having been accepted by a group that was initially unwelcoming.

4. Let's assume there is such a thing as "American (United States) culture." Working with other students, develop a big list of specific items you associate with this culture. Don't edit; just brainstorm. The items can be large or small, central or eccentric, major or minor. Then go back and discuss some of the items. What qualifies a given item as "American"? Even if an item withstands scrutiny and seems still to qualify as American, discuss its source in other cultures. Write in your journal about this item. Also, write in your journal about one element of American culture that does not appeal to you.

5. There is such a thing as culture shock, something we often experience when we travel to other lands or even within our own land. We encounter differences in those infamous "learned behavioral traits," and the differences seem so abundant that we get frustrated, fatigued, stunned, homesick, even angry. Write about a personal experience of culture shock. Perhaps some thoughts about how, in time, the experience may have changed you or altered your beliefs in a good way.

6. Choose a favorite food of yours. Then search out facts about it, tracing it as far back in history and through as many cultures as you can. Let's say you choose fast-food french fries. You would research not just the culinary and cultural history of thin-sliced, deep-fried potatoes but also the history of potato-eating, of how "french" got in there, of deep-frying, of the origins of "fast food."

7. Read a book about slavery in the United States or about one significant aspect of it. Write an essay that summarizes and analyzes the book.

8a. Write a review of one (or more) of the following movies or television series: *The Black Robe; The Chosen; The Color Purple; Come See the Paradise; Do the Right Thing; Eyes on the Prize; Foreign Student; Gentleman's Agreement; Geronimo* (the most recent film); *Get on the Bus; The Great White Hope; The Holocaust; The Immigrants; Jungle Fever; Little Big Man; Malcolm X; The Milagro Bean Field Wars; Mississippi Burning; Mississippi Mandela; El Norte; The Picture Bride; Pinky; Reservation Blues; Roots; School Ties; The Scotsboro Trial; Shoah; Six Degrees of Separation; Smoke Signals; Stand and Deliver; To Kill a Mockingbird; Tuskeegee Airmen; The Wedding Banquet; Zebrahead.*

8b. What other kinds of writing about a film or several films might you do, and how might these be more useful than a review? Write one of such pieces.

9. Read Nikki Giovanni's book, *Racism 101,* and write an essay about the extent to which it applies to your college campus.

10. Based on personal observation, write an essay about exclusion. Many clubs, fraternities, sororities, cliques, and organizations are based as much on whom they exclude as on the alleged common interests they serve. (But perhaps your essay will take issue with this premise.) Chances are you have belonged to, been excluded from, resigned from, or observed closely such a group. Why do people practice exclusion (assuming they do so)? What are the stated and unstated criteria of exclusion? How do people justify, deny, and/or manipulate exclusion? When and on what grounds is exclusion appropriate? How would you describe the "culture" (learned behavioral traits) of exclusion?

## Works Cited

Cary, Lorene (1991). *Black Ice.* New York: Knopf.

*Come See the Paradise* (1991). Motion picture. Twentieth-Century Fox, 1990. CBS/Fox Video. Director: Alan Parker. Writer: Alan Parker. Principle roles: Dennis Quaid; Tamlyn Tomita; Sab Shimono; Shizuko Hoshi.

Giovanni, Nikki (1994). *Racism 101.* New York: Morrow.

Kosinski, Jerzy (1972, 1985). *Being There.* Rpt. New York: Bantam Books.

Levi, Primo (1956). *The Reawakening: A Liberated Prisoner's Long March Home Through East Europe.* Trans. Stuart Woolf. Boston: Little Brown.

———— (1971). *Survival at Auschwitz: The Nazi Assault on Humanity.* Trans. Stuart Woolf. New York: Collier.

## Sharing Ideas

- When you read Hans' ten writing suggestions, which did you warm to most, and why? Which would you assign to a writing class if you were teaching, and why?

- Tell a story about you and culture. Move this story from an oral sharing to a written position statement to share with your writing group (perhaps by following the process suggested in Ormond Loomis' essay).

- How do you think Hans Ostrom's style suits his argument? Were you intrigued or irritated, amused or worried by it? Is it closer to yours or farther away from your own writing preferences than other essayists in the book? Some of his discussion is about very important topics—would you approach these topics in a similar way? Why or why not?

- Think about your city—what are the big topics—the issues that garner letters to the editor? Take one up and wrestle with it. In fact, you might choose a letter to the editor and write back—exploring how you feel about a local and cultural issue. Then, ask someone in your writing group to respond to your response, and so on, around the group. Swap your "case-book of responses" with another group and read their dialogue on local issues.

- What readings would you include in a multicultural reader? (You may be taking a class that uses one right now—analyze what is included and why you think the collection is arranged and organized the way it is.)

- Read the essays on (writing) style in Part V. What does style have to do with access? With success? How do you read those essays in light of Hans' discussion? Is there any issue common to the three essays that you'd like to talk about? If so, click the *Discussion* icon and go ahead.

- Tell a story about political (in)correctness—now extend that to the culture of school. What is the correct and incorrect way to be/act as a student? (You can specify the location, situations, of course.) Hint: Click to Part IV of this collection where teachers give you their insights into the politics and practices of classrooms.

———————————

# 8

# A Lesson in Revision

## Toby Fulwiler

---

Toby Fulwiler has directed the writing program at the University of Vermont since 1983. Before that he taught at Michigan Tech and the University of Wisconsin where, in 1973, he also received his Ph.D. in American Literature. He currently teaches classes in first-year composition as well as upper division courses with titles such as "Personal Voice" and "Writing *The New Yorker*." He is the author of *College Writing*, editor of *The Journal Book*, and a rider of a BMW motorcycle.

---

The real secret to good writing, for most writers, is rewriting. It's true that a few gifted writers compose, understand, and edit all in one draft—but neither I nor my students seem to do our best writing that way. Even when writers are pleased with their first drafts, those drafts don't usually tell the whole story that could be told—the one revealed only in second- and third-draft writing. In other words, it's the act of writing itself that explains the whole story to the writer. There are no shortcuts to full understanding, even for good writers.

There are no shortcuts, either, to careful writing. Just as first drafts seldom tell the whole story or make the best case, so too are first words and sentences seldom as polished, careful, and precise as they could be. What makes words and sentences more polished, careful, and precise is returning to them over and over again, each time with a little more distance, a little more clarity, and a little more rigor, and editing them until they create just the effect the writer hopes to achieve.

As result of teaching writing and writing professionally over the past two decades, I have come to believe that knowing when, where, and how to revise is the greatest difference between my own good and bad writing as well as between the practices of experienced and inexperienced writers. This essay will try to explain in some detail that difference.

The following story describes the effect of systematic revision on twenty-five first-year college students in a writing class at the University of Vermont. All were required by their various majors to take this course; none who entered claimed to enjoy writing. My job was to change this attitude and, in the bargain, help them become better writers.

# Draft I

The first assignment, a common one for first-year writing classes, is to write about a recent personal experience of some importance to the writer—a good place to start a composition course because it starts with what writers already know best, their own experience. While I asked that these first drafts be typed, I specified no particular form or length. Students brought their papers to class, read them out loud in groups of four or five, and commented on each other about "what interested them" and "where more information would help." After class, I took copies home with me to read. Let me show you some of the first paragraphs of these first papers.

—This probably is the most heroic event of my childhood. Everyone has their moments, but I believe that this episode is indeed commendable.

—In everyday life there are so many things that frustrate us, annoy us or make us upset that when we find something that makes us truly happy we should take advantage of it at every opportunity. For me, that thing is chocolate. The experience that I had which helped me to form this philosophy was one that will remain forever in my mind as a beautiful memory.

—Life—it definitely has its ups and downs. Most people don't need to think about what to do with themselves for amusement during life's livelier moments, but have you ever considered the things people do when life seems to be getting quite dull? Well, every so often I realize just what stupid, mindless things I've caught myself doing to fill time.

—Last summer my mother and I flew to Ireland. I've traveled there four times before. I thought it would be the normal three week tedious venture of traveling the countries visiting relatives and seeing the sights. This action-packed vacation turned out to be more than I could handle. From recalling old memories, to falling in love, I helped discover a new side of myself.

Most of the twenty-six papers were variations of these four, where the writers told us of forthcoming heroism, frustration, ups and downs, and action. Nothing is really wrong with any of these beginnings, except that they are slow, foreshadowing excitement to come and summarizing the writer's point before the paper demonstrates it. Would you rather have action promised or delivered? Would you like to be told the meaning of a store before hearing it? While I can't answer for you, I want the story to start fast, and I want to figure out its meaning for myself.

Further on in some of the same papers, however, I found both fast and interesting writing. Here is a passage from Avey's paper, exploring the story of a boarding-school friendship:"

> —Let me draw a picture for you. My first day of boarding school, the first person I see was a girl with black, starchy hair and face was as white as a clown. She wore huge black combat boots (which I never knew existed until I went to the Cambridge School) and a dangling cross earring protruding from her nose.

Avery draws a picture with words, allowing us to see the girl she's talking about "with black starchy hair," and "combat boots," and "a dangling cross earring protruding from her nose." When I read this, I can make my own judgment—that this girl is bold, fashionable, weird, whatever. And the writer shows me the character, asking me to evaluate it myself; I am drawn further into the story and want to see whether my judgment will be confirmed or not. (More on Avey's story later.)

In a different paper, John writes about spending eleven months in Equador and includes the following dialogue:

> "You mean in America people live together before marriage?" she asked me in a childish voice.
>
> "Well, yes, I guess so. Once in a while, it's a pretty common thing," I said back in a casual voice. I had to think a lot before responding because I hadn't learned much of the Spanish language yet. She looked at me stunned as I looked at her and giggled.

I especially enjoy hearing John and his Ecuadorian friend talk with each other—a conversation I imagine taking place in halting Spanish. Hearing people speak, overhearing them actually, puts me in the story and lets me make of the conversation what I will. In this case, because the writer doesn't summarize for me, I infer the difference between a liberal North American culture and a more conservative one in South America.

Look at one more sample from these first papers, this one written by Amanda, a student from Scotland attending college in the United States.

> For most of this summer I again worked on the farm where I removed rotten, diseased potato shaws from a field all day. But I was in the sun all the time with a good bunch of people so it was quite good fun. . . . Later on I signed up with an employment agency and got a waitressing job in Aberdeen, a city thirty-five miles north of our farm. It was only for one week, but I didn't mind—it was the first job I got myself and I felt totally independent.

Amanda cannot quite make up her mind what her story is about: the paper's title is "Waitressing," and we see here some of the details ("Aberdeen, a city thirty-five miles north of our farm") and importance of this first "job I got myself." In addition, however, she also describes in brief but wonderful detail the potato field "where I removed rotten, diseased potato shaws . . . in the sun . . . with a good bunch of people." In other words, she includes descriptive rather than summary detail about two possible directions her paper might take: she could focus on either her week as a waitress or her life picking potatoes on her father's farm.

It turns out that a lot of students were in the same situation as Amanda, trying to write one story that had embedded within it the seed of several others, each of which, if told fully, would itself be substantial and complete. Remember Amanda, we will keep tabs on her throughout this essay.

For their second drafts, I suggested that each writer create (recreate) as much action, dialogue, and detail as possible, while keeping summary comments and judgments to a minimum. In concluded by telling the class: "If you want to switch topics, please do. Your topic needs to be interesting enough to endure several more weeks of attention and experimentation!"

# Draft II

I asked the students to meet again in their same small groups to share the second drafts. This time each writer brought enough copies to share with his or her groupmates, read a draft aloud while the others followed along, received comments on it, then left a copy for me to take home and read. Please look at these paragraphs from different parts of Amanda's second draft:

### Waitressing

"Hey Muriel, how much are the chili-burgers and chips?"

"Two pounds ten pence" came the reply.

"Okay. . . . . . . . . . oh heck, Muriel, I've done it AGAIN! I'm never going to get it right. Blimming tills!"

This was a common conversation between me and the cook with whom I worked in a small snack bar during the summer holidays this year. It was the first time I had worked outside a farm. Normally during my holidays—Easter, Summer or October I would work on neighboring farms or on our own in the North East of Scotland, which is a large agricultural area.

I have also worked on potato fields, where I either picked them in a squad of about fifty to sixty people. We would bend over collecting the "tatties" til there were none left on our "bit" only to have a tractor drive past and dig up some more. This job was always in October, so the weather was never very good. It either rained or was windy, often both. Some days it would be so cold that we would lie in between the drills of undug potatoes to protect ourselves from the wind.

Amanda still can't decide what to focus on; however, she now includes good lively dialogue about waitressing (first paragraph) and specific details of farming (second paragraph). Look especially at the details of the potato field, where Amanda describes herself as [lying] in between the drills of undug potatoes to protect ourselves from the wind." Her concrete, specific language puts us with her in that freezing October potato field, all the while allowing us to be safely warm vicarious observers—which good writing does—and we want more. Lying between those potato rows to keep warm is the kind of detail that it's hard to fake or imagine—only the writer who's been there would think to include it, and so we believe her completely.

I also want you to see the second draft of a paper by a nursing major named Dawn who had spent the previous summer as a nurse's aide in a nursing home. Here are two paragraphs from her story, the first early in the paper, the second later on:

> Well, I walked into the first room, expecting to see women, but no there were two men lying in their beds. My face turned red with embarrassment, I didn't expect that I would have to take care of men. So Charlene gave me a washcloth and towel and told me to wash them up and dress them. As I washed them I thought to myself, I can handle this, I mean these people don't know what is going on and I am just here to help them survive.
>
> It was this year when I got my last surprise. It was on a Saturday when a dear patient of mine died. His name was Frank, he was my first death. I sat there and watched him go on his journey to heaven. The time was 12:45 p.m. when I heard his wife yell to me. I ran as fast as I could. I kept thinking, "Oh my god, what do I do?" When I got to his bed, Frank's eyes were rolled back and he was breathing with difficulty. I yelled to the nurse and stood by Frank, making him as comfortable as I could. The nurse ran to call the doctor and the rest of his family. As all this was going on, I just stood their applying cold compresses to his face and wondering what happened. Earlier that morning he was smiling and laughing, and now here he was dying. All of a sudden Frank stopped breathing. I felt for a pulse but couldn't get one.

Dawn now includes the reader with her on the hospital floor as she begins work. Her surprise at finding "men" in the room ("My faced turned red with embarrassment") is another of those telling details; few writers who haven't worked in a nursing home would invent that anxious insight, which, like Amanda lying in the potato field, is entirely convincing. I now want to see even more details of the washing of the men. How did she get over her anxiety? How does she actually dress and shave them?

You might also notice in her second paragraph both some tense action ("I felt for a pulse and couldn't get one") and some fanciful summary ("I sat there and watched him go on his journey to heaven"—How does she know?). Note the differences between what a writer can authentically know (the data supplied by her senses) versus that she cannot (what goes on in someone else's mind). In recounting personal experiences, writers create the strongest belief when they record what they experience and know firsthand, rather than their guesses, speculations, and judgments.

By now, in draft two, at least a dozen other papers also include rich and specific details that make the writing exciting to read. Many are shared in the small groups, and I read as many of these passages as I can to the whole class, knowing they will encourage still other students to reconsider their own next drafts. They do. I found the following entry about these second drafts in John's journal (Figure 8–1).

Then, a few days later, in another journal entry, John assesses his own second draft before beginning a third. The story he set out to tell covered one whole season when he coached an eighth-grade basketball team. John, a business major, now understands that to recreate a truly believable narrative, he must write with careful detail—a kind of writing he has never done before (Figure 8–2).

John's problem has changed from the novice writer's dilemma of filling enough pages to fulfill the assignment to the working writer's dilemma of selecting from among "SO MUCH MATERIAL." He now sees that he has stories within stories and must decide which one to tell and in how much detail.

# Draft III

Many writers are now beginning to see that the more they write, the more their stories grow, develop, and evolve into tales they didn't at first intend to tell. However, most still need coaching about how to actually make this evolution happen and their stories continue to grow. In the spirit of play and experimentation, I placed two new limitations on draft three: (1) that the time covered in the narrative be limited to a single day or less and (2) that the setting be limited to one specific place. With this draft everybody's writing really took off. Students had more material than could be shared in one period. Look at what Dawn's paper has become, an internal monologue inside her head written in present tense with new specific details:

### My Job as a Nursing Aide

Up the steps I go, through the big white door again. The fowl odor of urine strikes my nose. Sounds quiet. . . . for now anyway. Of course it is quiet, it's 6:30 a.m. in the morning. Got to get on this elevator that creeks when it moves. Time to punch in already! Seems like I just got out of here. Another eight hours for a small paycheck. I hope my feet stay under me.

It is my last day, YEAH, tomorrow is a day off. Oh no! I've got to listen to this report, it takes too long and what do I care about who gets what medications anyway.

"Dawn, you have assignment five!" yells Terry while laughing at me.

"Gee thanks, why do I get stuck with the mens end? Oh I get it, just because I'm younger than all of you, so I have more time on my hands!"

Well, stuck with the men again. I kind of figured I would, but it would

## Figure 8-1

9/12 Today in english Toby took
parts of some peoples papers to teach
us how to write better. I think I
am starting to feel my writing coming
together ~~Is very hard to tell a
story and not show~~. you begin to
totally reshape the actual incident when
you want to get down to the littilest
detail to give the reader the feeling
you have. I really think the idea of
having all the diff't drafts really
helps. You totally can get to the root
of your topic. It makes you feel
like a surgeon. Tonights assignment is
to focus on a very short time span.
I think this one is going to be
the toughest.

## Figure 8-2

I'm going to try to use more
dialogue in my paper. That is
what I really think I was
missing.
    The second draft is very
dull. As I read it, it has
no life. I should have used
more detail.
    I'll try more dialogue,
lot's more, in draft #3
    I'l have it take place
at one of my practices. Goiving
a vivid description of what those
practices were like when
the kids showed up.
    I have SO much MATERIAL.
But I have a hard time deciding
what seems more interesting.

have been nice to get a different assignment. Report is finally over, now I have to hurry and get my bucket filled. . . . let's see powder, soap, gloves, bags for the laundry, shaving cream, after shave cologne, razors and medicines for my patients treatments. Yup, I've got everything. First I should do my rounds to make sure everyone is still breathing. Then I will start to get up at least two people.

"Dawn, breakfast trays are here!"

"Already, I only got up two people and nine more to go!"

Amanda, meanwhile, has dropped the waitress story and elected to go with the potatoes. Look at the first full page of her third draft:

### Potatoes

Potatoes, mud, potatoes, mud, potatoes, that was all I saw in front of me. They moved from my right side to my left, at hip level. A conveyor belt never stopping. On and on and on.

I bounced and stumbled around as the potato harvester moved over the rough heath, digging the newly grown potatoes out of the ground, transporting them up a conveyor belt and pushing them out in front of me and three other ladies. Two on either side of the belt.

The potatoes passed fast, a constant stream. My hands worked deftly, pulling out clods of dirt, rotten potatoes, old shaws and anything else I found that wasn't a potato. They were sore, rubbed raw with the constant pressure of holding dirt. They were numb, partly from the work, and partly from the cold. It was October, the ground was nearly frozen, the mud was hard and solid. Cold. Dirt had gotten into my yellow and yet brown rubber gloves, had wedged under my nails, increasing my discomfort.

On and on the tractor pulled the harvester that I was standing in, looming high above the dark rich earth, high above the potatoes.

My back ached right at the bottom of my spine. A searing, nagging pain. I stooped over the belt unlike the other ladies who were short and able to lean their hip's and waist's on the side of the belt, resting their bodies as they worked. "Oh to be short."

A bump and a shuggle, all movements hurt as the harvester moved. My feet throbbed, tired from lack of support in welly boots and standing all day. My eyes blurred as they moved over the potatoes in front of me, guiding my hands to the dirt and noting the difference of a rotten or dirty potato.

My brain is dead, dormant. Boredom, tediousness and pain. I was tired, tired of thinking, looking at and picking at potatoes. My mind wandered to the old days, before I went to boarding school seven years ago. Where potato picking was with your friends, and families would turn up at the field early on the cold October mornings to labor all day and make some extra cash.

I was there, lines up, waiting for the tractors to start. A bunch of men passed, red baskets fell in front of me ready to be filled. The sky was still duskey, it was seven in the morning, the sun was beginning to rise. A hush is on the field. The squad are silent remembering the feel of their warm beds and the personalness of their dreams.

A whirr and clatter, an engine starts. A sigh escapes my body, I watch the pattern of the hot air condense in the cold. A buzz is felt on the field. The day has begun. It is work, but the fifty of us are experiencing it together, as a team.

Nobody in class had yet written like this, making the rhythms of sentences match the rhythms of the experience ("Potatoes, mud, potatoes, mud"). When Amanda read this draft out loud to the class, the students sat in awed silence. Here was their classmate, eighteen-year-old Amanda, to whom her Scottish teachers had said she could not write, demonstrating new and exciting techniques, writing an interior monologue complete with sentence fragments, flashbacks, made-up words, colloquial language, and compelling details. In the comments that follow I could hear the admiration for a classmate's work well done and an unspoken resolve to try still more experiments with next drafts: "I could really feel your work!" "Good job, Amanda!" "Nice going!" "Good writing!"

## Draft IV

What next? Actually, more of the same. Revision, when taken seriously, is a process that generates ever more and deeper thought, telling the writer that "Yes, you're on the right track. It's getting better," or "No, I think I've exhausted what I have to say on this subject. Better start something else." I wanted to give my writers one more shot at discovering still more about the story they were trying to tell, so for draft four I suggested writing from still another perspective: "Change either your TENSE (from the past to present), POINT OF VIEW (from first to third), or FORM (from essay to drama, letters, or diary)— or all three."

Some students, especially those who were pleased with the shape of their writing, resisted "new" drafts, but only because their old ones were developing in pleasing directions. In a journal entry I find later, Dawn takes me to task (Figure 8–3).

At this point in the course, these student writers had been trying out new and different approaches to telling their personal stories. Now, with virtually everyone accepting the idea that good writing was the result of intensive exploration, frequent and frank feedback, risk taking, and seeing good models, I felt it was time to slow down and see what the whole might look like.

So, during the fifth week of the term, I scheduled conferences where we talked one-on-one about each writer's several drafts: What did the writer like best or least? What story was emerging? Where would the next draft lead? We conducted each conference with plans for a fifth more focused and comprehensive draft, which would give shape to each experience.

## Figure 8–3

*Write a new paper he says! I was doing great with the one I was working on. I really had a strong feeling about it!*

*I guess this draft, I will do two different deaths but in a diary form. That sounds interesting but it will be tough. It only has to be 1-2 pgs good!*

With these last drafts, virtually every one of the twenty-six students had arrived at a pleasing story of self. Dawn's story in the nursing home finally took the form of "a day in the life," where she invited readers to accompany her throughout her whole eight-hour shift. Had I space here, I would share with you Jon's recreated journal of eleven months in Ecuador as an exchange student—which is how he solved the problem of writing in detail yet still covering a long span of time. Or I would show you Avey's portrait of a deteriorating relationship with her boarding school best friend over a four-year period, which she finally told as a series of telephone conversations each a few months later—and more distant—than the previous one. Or John's decision to capture his basketball coaching season by focusing on a three-minute talk with the rival coach sitting in the bleachers before one game began. As you can see, some writers, such as Dawn, found their stories early on and stayed close to it, while others, such as Amanda, kept moving their pieces outward, adding ever newer dimensions to what they started with, finding out ever more about their own stories.

Let me conclude this study of one writing class with excerpts from Amanda's last draft, for which she invented a narrative in three scenes, to tell the story of her work in the potato field. In Part One, Amanda described her most recent season (1988) working on the farm before coming to college, working in her father's newly purchased mechanical harvester so now only four people are needed to complete the entire season's harvest. As she explained in our conference: "The last year when I worked there, it was only four of us and the relentless machine." This was the experience she recounted in the "Potatoes, mud, potatoes, mud" draft.

In Part Two—separated by white space and a new date (1983)—Amanda flashed back to when she was younger and one of sixty local people who hand-picked the potatoes—the origin of the passage about lying "down among drills of undug potatoes."

For Part Three Amanda wrote only a single paragraph, set off from the other sections by white space and dated in parallel fashion to the other parts (1989). Here is the whole of her third and last section:

> 1989. October 17th
>
> This year the potato harvester is still working, the same women on board, with the same bored expressions on their faces. Soon this job will probably not need anyone to work or help the machinery. Labor is an expense farmers cannot afford. There are no tattie holidays anymore, no extra pocket money for the small children of the district. Change, technology, development is what they say it is, I say that it is a loss of a valuable experience in hard work, and a loss of good times.

Do you remember that I said at the start of this chapter that it is important for writers to hold off telling readers exactly what to think about their stories? That readers need to be invited in and allowed to make meaning for themselves? Well, Amanda has done that right up until the end, showing us the two different versions of potato picking on her father's farm. In the beginning she didn't know which story to tell, waitressing or potatoes. In draft three she found the story behind her other stories, and that's what that last paragraph is about—but it only emerged in the sixth week of writing. By then, of course, I didn't need it, having understood her point by the way she ordered her detail, dialogues, and monologues. But I think Amanda needed that last paragraph, for herself. I would not have wanted it earlier, but it closes her paper well.

By now I think you understand the story I wanted to tell about revision. But just in case, let me do as Amanda did and suggest some ideas that might help you when you return to your own drafts—so long as you understand these to be suggestions and not commandments. Although writing gets better by rewriting, there are no guarantees. I know of no formula for revising that works every time or for everyone—or every time for anyone. Revision is a chancy process: Therein lies both the excitement and the frustration.

## Ideas for Revision

The story I just told you involves personal experience writing. However, the premises about the generative power of writing and even many of the specific revision strategies apply, with some modifications, to reports, reviews, research papers, and arguments as well. In argumentative papers, for instance, try writing one draft from the opposite point of view, one as if you were a politician, and maybe one as a newspaper editorial. To that end, the following ideas are sound for virtually any substantial writing task you are called upon to undertake.

*Attend to Matters of Conception First.*     Focus on what you want and need to say, try to get that out, and worry later about how it looks. Keep rereading and keep asking yourself: What is my story? What else should be included? What's no longer necessary? Worry about sentence-level matters, including correct spelling and punctuation, and precise word choice, only after these larger purposes are satisfied. (It's not an efficient use of your time to carefully edit a paragraph that you later delete because it's part of a story you no longer want to tell.)

*Allow Time.*    If a paper is due next week, start it this week, no matter if you have all your data and ideas or not, no matter if the big chem test is on the horizon. Beginning to write, even for ten concerted minutes, will start the incubation process in your own mind, and you'll actually be working on the paper in your subconscious. Plan, at the outset, to do more than one draft—as many more as you need to find and tell your story.

*Start Over.*    Even when you return to a draft that you think just needs a conclusion, reread the whole thing all over, from start to finish, with an eye toward still other possible changes. Every time you read your own paper you create yet another dialogue with it, from which could emerge still a better idea. The conclusion may be all the old paper needed—when last you read it. But that was then and this is now, so don't stand pat; keep looking for what else could happen to the story you are telling.

*Compose on a Word Processor.*    Computers make all the difference when it comes to making changes easy. Save early drafts by relabeling files so that you always have a paper trail to return to or old copy to restore in case you change your mind. If you don't have access to a computer, try to make at least one typed draft before the final one: typed words give you greater distance from your own ideas and invite more possibilities of change. (When Amanda entered my class, she had never typed a paper before and had to learn keyboarding while she learned to revise.) One more hint: For early drafts, start a new file each time and see what else your paper can become. The new file guarantees that you generate new language and, therefore, new thought. You can always merge files later on and synthesize your several insights.

*Seek Response.*    As soon as you have enough copy in reasonable shape, read it or show it to someone you trust and get their reaction. Another pair of eyes can always see what you cannot. Most good writers ask others to read and react to their work *before* the final copy is due. And, of course, you needn't feel obligated to take all the suggestions you're given.

*Imagine a Real Audience.*    Keep your teacher or several skeptical classmates in mind as you write and especially as you reread. Of course whatever story, essay, or report you write is clear to you; it's your story, essay, or report. Ask What information do *they* need to know that I already take for granted? Then put it in because they'll understand you better.

*Play with Titles, Introductions, and Conclusions.* These are emphatic, highly visible points in any paper. Provocative titles catch readers' attention. Good introductions keep readers going. Strong conclusions leave strong memories in readers' minds. But these same elements work on the writer as well as the reader, as a good title, introduction, or conclusion can suggest changes for what follows (or precedes). Sometimes these elements come first—as controlling ideas—sometimes later, but in any case they can capture (or recapture) the essence of your paper, telling you what to keep and what to cut.

*Imagine Other Points of View.* Whether the paper is based on experience, data, or opinion, try to see it from another point of view: your job as seen by your boss or a customer; the pro side of the gun control debate even though you are arguing con; how other reviewers have interpreted a movie, play, poem, etc. Seeing and acknowledging other points of view is especially helpful for anticipating questions and objections to your own and therefore allows your writing to present a more complete case.

*Let Form Follow Content.* Be aware that writing can be and do anything you can make it do, that there are no real rules that all writers *must* follow. There are, however, conventions of genre (writing a twenty-inch book review for the local paper) and discipline (the voice, form, and style of a laboratory report). To violate conventions is to risk not being taken as seriously as you might wish. But, more often than not, so long as your content is substantial and your style clear, the actual form of your writing is more open than you may imagine. Is your paper best written as a report? As an essay? As an exchange of letters? As drama? The point is this: Changing form is not cosmetic; it causes you to see your subject differently.

## My Students Respond

When time came to hand in the midterm portfolios, week seven, we (the class and I) agreed to call these personal experience papers done. Meanwhile, they had started on their second writing assignment, a collaborative research essay on a local issue or institution—which would also be a many-draft process, this time with both the research and the writing shared among group members. At this point, I asked my students to comment anonymously on the process of writing and rewriting this first assignment (see Figures 8–4, 8–5, and 8–6).

At the beginning of the term, I believed that people learned to write by some combination of provocation and nourishment. I set out, dutifully, to provoke these twenty-six students into as many experimental drafts as they would tolerate, reminding them often that the more they tried, the more they would grow. I allowed no one to stand pat and only write what he or she was already good at. Then when someone took a risk and tried something new, I, along with the others in the class, would say "Wow! Good job." In fact, it was amazing how

**Figure 8–4**

---

I have a lot different attitude towards
writing now, than I did during the first class.
At the beginning of the year I was scared
to write. I've written more papers in these
first few weeks, than I did all of last year
in English. As we have gone on this year,
I feel the writing has gotten easier. It isn't
taking me so long to start a paper and once
I am started there is no stopping me. This
early writing has also drastically improved my
typing abilities as well.
    I am hoping that this class will break
me out of this writing shell and help me
    enjoy writing on my own. I don't want
to just write when it is required.

**Figure 8–5**

---

writing has changed for me. I'm
beginning to realize how much
you can do with a single
idea. I like the idea of
writing 5 pages about a
single hour, day or afternoon
on the first day of class
I wasn't really sure what to
think it seemed like such
an odd way to start class.
Yet, maybe one of the best
ways considering the
type of class this is I
still find writing very difficult
I never seem able to
get the way I feel down
on paper My goals are to
be able to do this by the
end of the semester. I
want there to be some of
me in the paper also.

**Figure 8–6**

Writing: I'm more involved in it. But not as attached. I used to really cling to my writing, and didn't want it to change. Now, I can see the usefulness of it. I just really like my 3-d draft. But for the final draft I am thinking of struggling with it. I feel like I have to let go of my third draft, but that's not what it's all about. I can still really enjoy my third draft and create another exciting paper.

Writing is more than just pen to paper or hands to key board. It is also reading, rereading and getting some criticism on it. I have improved my papers so much after getting feedback from my Kelley, Dawn, Gavin, Kelley, Lane, Amy and Toby, and Amanda.

much improvement the word *Wow* seemed to engender. Of course, not everything worked, but everything counted, and the class understood that good writing meant, in the words of one, being "involved," but not being "attached." In the end, however, I learned something else: When students write well, they teach writing teachers to teach well. Thanks, class, for a wonderful lesson.

## Sharing Ideas

- Describe the ways this essay influenced your thinking about revision.
- If the essayists in this book have convinced you that writing is thinking, take that idea one step farther and explore the ways writers *think* through revision.

- Have you ever felt the same way about your opening paragraphs as Toby felt about the opening paragraphs of the student papers he shared? You might want to look through your old work and see if you have any consistent strategies for starting out a paper.

- Toby pushed his students to undertake a demanding and organized drafting sequence. What would happen to your writing under similar drafting conditions?

- What does it take to make you want to revise your writing?

- What environmental, physical, and/or mental conditions get in the way of revision for you? Make a list of ways to overcome those blocks.

- Go over Toby's ideas for revision and connect them to your own writing.

- You'll notice at the end of his essay Toby quotes from students' journals. You might want to think about these in light of Chris Anson and Richard Beach's essay on journaling in the writing class.

- If you've ever had teachers learn (write) with you in the writing class, tell stories about that experience. You'll notice that Toby, like other teachers in this book, thanks students for the journey they take together.

---

# Part III

# To the Writer—
# Writing Classrooms and
# Writing Processes

Part of your life story as a writer will include stories of your previous writing classrooms. You too have an important history of writing, one you will want to explore even as you continue to write today's papers and share them with your peers and teacher. You might share your thoughts in a literacy autobiography, in journal entries, during classroom discussions, or in conferences with your teacher. When reading essays about writing and talking about your own writing past, I hope you'll notice how all of us start writing courses already informed by significant writing experiences. All of us, too, have the ability to grow, more fully, into our writing.

—Wendy Bishop, writing teacher

My past writing classes had not developed too much of me. I've either analyzed texts without really including personal views, or I've written stories that sounded pretty but had no depth. . . . Writing, revising, editing, workshopping, revising again—these all motivated me to rework my texts (or at least think about different ways to revise as I showered, walked to class, brushed my teeth, and ate lunch).

—Haley Belt, writing student

Using a computer will change the way you write. I would like to be able to say that using word processing will transform your writing into prize-winning prose, or at least grade-*A* material. But I cannot. I can tell you that your writing will be different because my students tell me that the computer changed how they write. It didn't make them better writers; it made them different writers. Maybe that's not so bad. Changing old habits may allow us to examine the way we write, thereby prompting us to learn new strategies as we become different writers.

—James Strickland, writing teacher

Textbooks and teachers are sincerely trying to help students become better writers. But you are the person in control of deciding what works best for you. Some people don't want to accept that responsibility because it takes some effort and experimentation to find out how they write most effectively. They'd rather have someone tell them exactly what to do—it's a "no brain" activity since they then merely have to do what they are told. Other people shy away from the close consideration involved in making choices because they are so unsure of their skills. They'd rather trust "the experts." But you are the expert on the subject of yourself.

—Muriel Harris, writing teacher

# 9

# That Isn't What We Did in High School Big Changes in the Teaching of Writing

## Donald A. McAndrew

---

Donald A. McAndrew spends his work days teaching writing to undergraduates and the teaching of writing to college and secondary teachers. When not teaching, he works in his garden, listens to classical music and jazz, fishes from his boat or kayak, beats his three kids at tennis, and enjoys his wife's gourmet cooking. Currently he is writing about the teacher as leader in writing classrooms and about teaching writing as a spiritual act.

---

When I sat down to start playing with this essay, I decided to write it directly to the students I have now—Diane, Shelley, and Lori; Eric and Darin; Julie, Leigh, and Ed; Dwight and Will and Chuck—to see them sitting there, me flopped in a student desk, sipping hot black coffee, gabbing about writing and the teaching of writing. I guess it's fair to say that this piece is dedicated to those students—they are the one who asked the questions that got me thinking about how our class was different from their high school English classes. In fact, as you'll see below, I quote directly from written answers and comments they gave to questions I asked about our class. So, this essay will be both to them and from them, a testament to their risking tough questions and to their insights in helping us all find answers.

On the first day of our writing class, I pass out a course overview sheet, which shows what we will do in terms of work and grades. It doesn't take long for my students to realize that this course is going to be really different from what they expect. They expect a rerun of Grade 12 English, just a little tougher; after all, this is college. Well, very quickly they realized they are wrong—this course isn't going to be much like high school English, or at least most high school English courses. Here they will choose their own topics to write about. They will draft and revise in class. They will work with other students who will read their drafts and try to help improve them, and they will meet one-to-one with me to talk about their developing drafts. They will read what they decide they need to read to help with their pieces of writing and with their growth as a writer. They will turn in only their best papers for grades, and they will have a say in that grade. Here there won't be tests, lectures, raising hands, desk in rows, and a teacher up front. But there will be portfolios, peer response, talk, movement, groups, conferences, and everybody, including the teacher, writing things that are important to them, sharing those pieces for feedback and revision. This is different from most high schools, oh, yeah.

In what follows, I show you some of the differences you might see in a writing class that is taught like ours, taught as current theory and research on teaching writing would tell teachers to teach. I do this by letting you hear the voices of my students reporting on life in our class. After that, I also explain why our class is taught as it is—theory and research that is the basis for the new writing class that many of you will experience. So, let me start by showing you some of the things my students saw as different from English classes in high school.

## Differences from Previous English Classes

### *Atmosphere of the Class*

Students frequently told me that the biggest difference they saw between their high school classes and our class was that the atmosphere was more "relaxed and comfortable" and "wasn't as tense" As a couple of students said, "it's not a sit-down-and-shut-up class" or a "sit, listen, and take notes class." Many also reported that there was "a ton more interaction between the students" than there had been in their high school classes.

### *Class Activities*

Students characterized the activities in their high school English classes as centered on analyzing literature, test taking, and grammar. Most often they mentioned literature, saying that they "read plays, learned about the different ages in history, and read certain works from these ages." After reading, the teacher "stood in front of the class telling us the acceptable interpretations." Next most often they mentioned studying "pieces of English like vocabulary, grammar, and punctuation" and "taking objective tests on trivial facts that I memorized and repeated on the test." Finally, they mentioned doing some writing, but explained that "the teacher was more concerned with grammar, fragments, commas, etc., rather than really what was in the paper."

In our class, whatever reading was done, whether literature or anything else, was decided on by each individual writer because of a need they felt based on a piece of writing they were working on. In our class, we never study the pieces of English, only the wholes, like pieces of student writing or pieces written by professionals or previous students. And in our class, I'm concerned mostly with what is in the paper, its ideas and content, not fragments and commas.

## Writing Assignments

In high school, students told me that "the teacher controlled the topic" and that "you had to write about what the teacher wanted which was usually about a book we had to read" or "something you didn't know much about." Even the topics concerning the book were "very regimented." In our class, students told me they felt that they "could write about what you feel like writing about and this is good because it forces you to really know what you are talking about." One student explained it this way: "I have to write about topics of known interest to me because, if I'm not interested in the topic, my paper usually isn't my best work." Other students reported that writing about topics that they chose helped them to "expand on your own individual ideas" and "to be able to explore my own writing more."

Students also reported that their high school teachers controlled the form of their pieces of writing by requiring papers "always in the same style and always five paragraphs." In our class, the form of the writing and its length are decided by the writer. Also, students repeated that in our class they just flat out did more writing, lots more. In high school they "didn't do much writing at all" except for "maybe a few stories and poem and essays about literature." In our class, they "get a *lot* of practice writing and revising every day."

## Response and Revision

My students reported that in high school they "wrote and revised by myself and turned it in to the teacher for her feedback." They also reported that "it was rare that students read and responded to each other's papers; only the teacher did that." They found this system of response to be inadequate, complaining that "there was no second chance to revise or rewrite a paper; so you couldn't learn from your mistakes." In our class, as you've probably already guessed, we did things differently. While writers were working on pieces, they could ask me or peers for a response. They found the one-to-one conferences with me valuable; they gave them "help when it was needed" during the process of writing the piece, helping the writers see "ways to better their work" and "what we could do to improve them." Students found response from peers equally valuable, stating that it was "beneficial to have your peers read and criticize your paper" because writers are "simply too involved to realize an error or another route to take" and because "being able to read other students' writings is a good way to see and compare the way they write with the way you write."

### Outcomes and Improvements

Students reported that they felt "more comfortable to express themselves" and that comfort "helped you become more of an individual" and that "by writing freely on topics of our own choice, we are learning about ourselves." Students also thought that the frequent interaction between peers "taught me a lot about other people" and gave them "respect for the opinions of others and showed me how to handle them in a mature and respectable way." Others reported that the peer interaction taught them "to be a little more outgoing," "helped us make friends," and "gave me a sense of belonging."

In addition to these personal effects, students also reported that our course had effects on their growth as writers. They reported that writing "was not so intimidating"; so they "became more interested in it" and "put more effort into it." They realized that "it's what goes in the paper, thoughts and feelings, that are most important" and that they can "set aside worries about grammar and spelling and get my ideas on paper instead." They realized "the importance of receiving feedback and revising more than once or twice."

## Theory and Research Behind
## Our Writing Class

One of the most important things for you to realize about our class is that it is well grounded in the latest understandings about how teachers *can best teach students to be better writers*. I like to think of our class as our construction of a state-of-the-art writing class. Your college writing class will not be exactly like our class, but you will see many parallels because your class and our class are grounded in the same body of theory and research, state-of-the-art theory and research, if you will. In what follows, I give you an overview of that theory and research so you'll see that we have powerful reasons for the things we do in our class. Then I close by tying that theory and research back to specific features of our class, showing you the theory and research behind a couple of activities that are at the heart of teaching and learning writing.

## Social Constructionists

When I think of the theorists and researchers who support our writing class, I think of three groups, each with a fancy name and all overlapping each other a bit. The first group of theorists and researchers are called "social constructionists." These people are probably at the center of current understandings about how writing works and about how people learn to use it. As their name suggests, they are concerned about two issues—society and construction.

With "social" they hope to emphasize the fact that language is a phenomenon of societies, created by them and serving them. Language exists at a social level as speakers/listeners and writers/readers communicate. All language use occurs in a social world, among language users. Even when we sit alone writing at our desk, we are constantly thinking of the people we are writing to, the people whose previous writing we have read, and the people we have talked to. We are always in society.

By "constructionist" this group hopes to stress that language, and society itself for that matter, are constructed by humans. This constructionist belief also extends to what society does with its constructed language—it constructs communication, meaning, knowledge. We make our own personal understanding in language, either speech or writing, and share it with others as they listen or read. From this sharing of our individual understandings, we construct still more complex knowledge, both as individuals and as groups. Social constructionists believe we are simultaneously both individual and social, individuals-in-society, and that we build our knowledge and beliefs as a result of our lives and language as individuals-in-society. Knowledge is something we build, we create; knowledge is a social construction. That means that there is no knowledge "out there"; it is only "in here"—in the mind of social beings constructing it through language, not in textbooks, not in libraries. When you learn, you are not taking something from "out there" and stuffing it "in here." Rather you are building, creating, constructing it as an individual-in-society.

## Participationists

The second group of theorists and researchers behind the new writing class is the one I call "participationists." This group stresses that to know something, to have knowledge, means to participate in its making, constructing through language, reading, writing, and talking to others who are also participating in making knowledge. Participation is the key—being active, doing it, joining in history, accounting, nursing, sociology as a language user. For example, a discipline like biology is not in the biology textbook, something objective and outside people; rather biology is what participating biologists say it is as they use language in a community of other biologists to construct their discipline of biology. The biology textbook is just one person's construction of her understanding of the field of biology in written language. Others will read it, talk about it, and write about it. She will read, talk, and write about what they say. And it is this participation in the language interaction of these individuals-in-society that creates biology as a field of study.

Think about schools and classrooms. Participationists say that teachers can't give you knowledge; you have to make it by participating in language activities. Just as biologists have to make biology by reading, writing, and talk-ing, by participating in the discipline of biology, so too you must participate in the language of your classes. Your General Psychology class is just that—yours; you construct it by reading, discussing, writing, in a group of others who are also making their General Psychology. It is the "-ing" on "making" that is important—the process and activity of making. Knowledge is an action—in this case a participation in the language of a certain subject. During language participation in psych class, all members, students and teacher, create General Psychology—it is a social construction made through participation in language.

## Socio-psycholinguists

The third group of theorists and researchers who support our writing class are the "socio-psycholinguists." Where the social constructionists look at our world generally—society, knowledge, language—and participationists look at knowledge and language, socio-psycholinguists look specifically at language, trying to form the big picture of how language works. Many have studied read-ing/writing, and it is these people who give us a lot of support for what we do in our class. Socio-psycholinguists have demonstrated that reading and writ-ing are processes by which we make meaning—writers construct their own meaning and readers construct their own meaning, both actively building the meaning we commonly think of as "in the print" when, in reality, meaning is in writers and readers, in people not ink on the page. Writers and readers bring their prior knowledge of the world and language to bear on the new language event as they make their meaning based on this prior knowledge.

Socio-psycholinguists also remind us that reading and writing are a social action, always involving others. Here they echo the social constructionists and participationists I described above. They also emphasize the significance of context, the environment in which language use occurs, showing us that all language is inextricably tied to its context. The word STOP is a lot different on a road sign than it is in a magazine advertisement; the context in which the word occurs really gives much of its meaning. They demonstrate that real writ-ing and reading only exist in real contexts, the natural and complex events of whole language at work among a group of languagers.

And finally, socio-psycholinguists emphasize how important risk taking and ownership are in improving reading and writing. They argue that learners must feel comfortable enough to risk making a mistake because this is the only way to learn; without risk there is little important learning. They also argue how important ownership is in improving writing and reading. Writers and readers must feel as if they own the meanings they make; they should not feel that they are forced to make a meaning someone else wants. The class focus should always be their piece of writing, written their way, and their response to reading, constructed as their prior knowledge tells them.

## A Final Look at Our Class

Above I showed you two things about our class: first, a portrait of our class based on how my students reported it was different from the classes they had in high school and, second, some of the theory and research that supports our class. Now let me try to draw these two together by explaining how the theory and research specifically supports two activities at the heart of our class.

In our class peers frequently respond to each other's drafts. Why is this a good thing to do based on our state-of-the-art theory and research? Peer response creates a minisocial constructionist world. Writing is social because you share it with other students and you may even have them in mind while you write. You, in turn, read their writing. All of this is done with much talk about your construction of ideas as peers have constructed it while reading your piece. Everyone is participating in making meaning while they write and while they read the writing of others. You and your peer responder make your meanings based on your previous experience of life and language. The class becomes a group of writers and responders, all writing and responding to the meanings constructed. The teacher also joins in the process of writing and responding, focusing on meaning as the highest priority and creating a comfortable atmosphere where risk taking is easy. I hope you hear the echoes of the theory and research I described above: "minisocial constructionist world," "participating in the construction of meaning as the highest priority," and "comfortable atmosphere for risk taking."

Let me show you another example. In our class, students write mostly about self-selected topics. How is this grounded in state-of-the-art theory and research? Since prior knowledge of the world and language is the starting place for all language and learning, as socio-psycholinguists explain, then choosing your own topics, forms, and lengths seems like the perfect place to begin improving your writing. Your prior knowledge is at the center. This creates a context for class writing that is more like real, authentic writing—you write about what you know and value. From the outset of each piece you have almost total ownership of ideas, form, and the processes of your writing. Since the atmosphere is relaxed and comfortable making risk taking easy, and since you are writing about topics and in forms that you know about and are interested in, participation in the life of the class happens naturally. You become an active participant in the construction of your improvement as a writer, something that participationists tell us is essential to knowledge, to knowing how to write well. Again, listen to the echoes of theory and research: "prior knowledge of language and the world," "participation in natural context," and "ownership of ideas, forms, and processes."

I hope that the two examples of peer groups and self-selected topics show you that our class is firmly grounded in state-of-the-art theory and research. Remember this, especially when your writing class is doing things that seem different from many of the things you did in high school. When your writing class shows some of the features I've talked about, be glad because you're getting your money's worth for your tuition. Be glad also because you have a great chance to improve your writing ability, and that's what a first-year college writing course is all about.

## Sharing Ideas

- What did you read and write about in high school? Do you agree with Don's students that your classes focused more on the form than the content of your writing?

- Did you ever have two writing teachers who took very different approaches? Tell the stories of those two classes.

- Do you agree with Don that reading in a writing class should be done *for* the writer's own purposes and that a writer should pick his or her own topics? Why or why not? What does that mean for you as a writer? How do you go about finding your own readings and topics?

- Before your current writing class, did you ever share your work with peers? How did that work? List some ways you could have made the sharing more successful.

- When you're sitting by yourself writing, what are the influences you feel? Do you agree with the social constructionists that you aren't writing alone? To what degree are you remembering other writers and teachers or things you've read and friends you've talked to about your writing?

- Try writing two descriptive scenes. In one, you're composing alone (what does the place look like, what are you doing, what in particular are you eating, listening to, feeling, thinking, etc.). In one, you're composing—or talking about composing—with others (who is there, what is each person saying and doing? How do you feel, what do you see, notice, or need?). Rereading each descriptive scene, how are you a different (more or less successful) writer in each scene?

- If you've never before thought of yourself as a participationist, what does that mean for how you act in the classroom, particularly the writing classroom? If you're shy, what might you do? If you're confused, what might you do? If you're not shy at all, how as a class member can you help those who are shy or confused?

- Now that you've thought about this new type of classroom, think of your strengths as a writer and as a class member. Explain what you contribute.

# 10

# Does Coming to College Mean Becoming Someone New?

## Kevin Davis

---

Kevin Davis, father of two, is an avid baseball fan (St. Louis), bicycle rider, and pasta maker. He writes an occasional poem. In his spare time, he teaches writing and directs the writing center at East Central University in Ada, Oklahoma, where he received an award for teaching excellence in 1991 and again in 1996.

---

As an undergraduate English major, I felt like an outsider. I originally chose to major in English because of my love for reading and writing, but the reading and writing college expected of me was not the reading and writing I was prepared to do. Sure, I could read the assigned literature, and I could make my own good sense of it. Yet that was not enough for my English professors. They wanted me to make their sense of the literature, to understand the texts as they understood them. Not only that, they expected me to write about this alien sense-making in turgid, impersonal, passive-voiced prose. When I became an English major, I didn't just learn certain understandings of what I read; I also had to learn a particular way of reading and writing. Right from the start, it was clear that if I was to become a member of the English-majors community, I had to do more than read and think and write; I had to turn into someone new.

Perhaps that is why I was never a very successful English major and why, eventually, I left the academic world and joined the business community. I was living on the boundary between academic and home communities, between maintaining my identity and accepting another. I found I didn't like the someone new I was being asked to become.

Eventually, I returned to the academic world and discovered I fit into the community of outsiders known as rhetoricians (people who study the way other people effectively communicate). I'm not sure if I fit into this community because I wanted to join it more than I had wanted to join the English studies community, because it was willing to accept me as I already was, or because I had matured enough to be willing to become someone new. I do know, however, that this second attempt at entrance into the academic community has been as successful as my earlier attempt was a flop.

As a rhetorician and because of my past experience, I have become interested in issues of community membership. Everyone is a member of several discourse communities (the term rhetoricians use to describe groups of people who share patterns and strategies of communication). We're all members of a home discourse community, based on our family's regional, social, and economic lifestyles. And many of us are members of other discourse communities because we are familiar with particular language communities through experience such as jobs and hobbies. But entering the academic discourse communities present on college campuses can produce problems and anxieties for students who are attempting the transition.

In the rest of this essay, I want to use my own experiences and research to answer several questions. What happens as students try to become members of new academic discourse communities? What special writing and thinking abilities are required? What personal investments must be made?

When I was eighteen, my writing was an extremely personal activity. I didn't just throw words on pages, I invested myself into the work. Everything I wrote was full of personal insights, personal style, and voice. A good writer, I was regularly praised and awarded for my high school writing efforts. I was totally unprepared for the shocking comments that my college professors would place on my writing.

Part of the problem came from a natural maturing process: The valued and original insights of a high school senior were suddenly the trite and common repetitions of a college student. And part of the problem came from style. The original, personal, whimsical voice of a young writer was not enough to assure my spot in the academic community.

I have now discovered that rhetoricians have an insightful way of looking at the split I experienced (North 1986). "Formalists," people who think that the most important aspect of a particular discourse community is the forms the community's writers use, would suggest that I didn't know the appropriate forms for academic writing. I didn't know what academic writing sounded like, and I didn't know how to present my ideas in the lingo that would bring the ideas recognition and acceptance. On the other hand, "epistemics," people who think that the most important aspect of a particular discourse community is the way the community thinks and solves problems, would suggest that I was not thinking like members of the academic world are supposed to think. I didn't process my thoughts in appropriate academic ways, according to the epistemics, and I wasn't positively involved with my studies.

Several composition scholars have completed research studies that try to understand more fully what happens with students trying to enter academic discourse communities. Recently, for example, Stephen North (1986) investigated the ways three students changed during one philosophy course. He relied solely on his readings of the papers the students wrote in order to describe three contexts in which the students changed: the *rhetorical* (the students' sense of their audience and their purpose for writing), the *intellectual or epistemic* (how the students struggled to understand the ideas they were studying), and the *disciplinary or formalistic* (how the students used language to show membership in the discourse community). By looking at papers similar to those that I wrote as an undergraduate, North was able to ascertain these three changes in writing for students entering new discourse communities.

Another research project, completed by Lucille McCarthy (1987), studied one student as he learned to negotiate his way through new discourse communities in several different freshman and sophomore courses. McCarthy made several conclusions from her work. First, she found that her subject used the same writing process to figure out how to complete a variety of writing tasks; this would imply that a student who can write in one situation, like I could, can extrapolate a process for writing into other situations. Second, she found that the purpose for the writing task and the student's involvement with the task were important to the writer's success; this implies that students write better if they are actively involved in the topic they are writing about, which is certainly true in my own experience. Finally, McCarthy concluded that writing tasks that are familiar in one situation were considered different when the student encountered them in a different situation; this implies that epistemic knowledge of a discourse community is important for a writer to succeed.

These adaptations writers make to new discourse communities are not limited, of course, to undergraduate college students. Everyone enters new communities throughout life. Carol Berkenkotter, Thomas Hucklin, and John Ackerman (1988) verified this when they examined the experiences of a teacher who returned to graduate school after several years of teaching. In their study, they ended up agreeing with both the formalists and the epistemics: They concluded that student writers have to assimilate both the forms and the thoughts of an academic discourse community to function within it. Their subject had to change the nature of his writing, from personal exploration to impersonal declaration, but he also had to change his community allegiance; he had to learn to think like a member of the community.

By looking at these studies and at my experience, then I can begin to make some conclusions about how students have to adapt their writing and thinking to succeed in college's unfamiliar academic discourse community. First, we have to recognize and accept the forms of the community, we have to make our writing look and sound like that of the field. Second, we have to learn to think in the ways that are valued by the field we are entering; we have to be personal or impersonal, focused on ideas or numbers, as the field demands. Third, we have to have a reliable comfortable writing process that we can take with us from task to task, community to community; once established, the process will probably serve us in a variety of settings. Finally, we have to become personally and intellectually involved with the community, wanting to be a part of it; without personal involvement, the formalistic and epistemic changes are merely window dressing.

As I look back on my own experience, I can clearly identify that last change as the most problematic for me. As an undergraduate English major, I never completed the personal commitment important for my success in the field. Eventually, I learned to mimic the writing and thinking activities that the field valued, but I remained unwilling to submit to the authority of those form and thought patterns. To personally endorse the English studies discourse community I would have had to abandon much of what I believed about life. Later, when I returned to graduate school to study rhetoric, however, I easily endorsed the field, finding it much more palatable to my native ways of being.

As I began my own research into discourse community membership, I was particularly interested in the personal involvement issues. Did other people reject communities, as I had done, because they were hesitant to make the personal commitments necessary for success? Could individuals only join communities that endorsed their native ways of thinking? Or did other people accept the communities and, in the process, give up something of their native ways of being in the world?

To investigate the personal changes students make as they enter new discourse communities, I interviewed, several times over six months, two undergraduates who were taking their first courses toward a degree and eventual licenses in social work.

Stella (the names are changed) was in her early twenties and in college for the second time, having delayed her education for a marriage. As Stella engaged the social work community, she became more accepting of differences in others, developing a new sense of open-mindedness. As she put it, "I try to see people as they are and not make judgments. . . . Through my social work classes, I've learned that everybody should be treated that way." But sometimes this open, nonjudgmental attitude caused problems for Stella who suddenly found that her husband was prejudiced in several ways. "My husband is racially prejudiced, and I'm real open and have no problem with that"; "My husband's family thinks welfare people are lazy. I really stand up for people they don't understand." Through her entrance into the new community, her attitudes toward others changed, and she adopted a socially accepting worldview even when the new worldview was in direct conflict with her family. In the process, she became more committed to the community of social workers.

The other participant in the study, Charlotte, had graduated from high school in 1957. After raising a family and working as both a cosmetologist and a practical nurse, Charlotte was finally returning to college to get the degree she had long cherished. Charlotte, too, was willing to make the personal commitment that membership in the social work community required. As she put it, "The course is really making a difference in my thoughts. I had not recognized that I was biased in my way of thinking." Further, Charlotte suggested that self awareness and open-mindedness were mandatory for a social worker; "If you don't understand yourself, you can't help anyone else. Not in the way that will help people take control of a situation." Her studies in social work, she said, changed her overall view of people and communities and culture. And, like Stella, Charlotte tried to become a change agent for those around her: "Just this weekend my husband made a comment, and I said 'Now just a minute, that's not the way it is at all.'"

In attempting to enter the social work discourse community, both Stella and Charlotte underwent a great deal of self-realization. Both acknowledged their native social worldview, critiqued it, began to develop new social worldviews, and even tried to become change agents for their spouses' worldviews. Through this progression, both women began to develop what their instructor described as the "social work frame of reference," a socially accepting worldview that is necessary for an individual to help members of diverse social groups try to improve their position in life. In the process, they became increasingly estranged from their home communities.

Research—my own and others'—exploring discourse communities verified what my personal experiences taught me. Learning to write within an academic discourse community is not a simple procedure.

First, we have to learn to put down words and ideas in community acceptable ways. We have to internalize and apply the form limitations of the discourse community; our writing has to look like writing in the community is supposed to look. In my own experience, this formalistic community entrance was easy to master, quick to develop; I learned to sound like an English major early in my education.

But there is more. We also have to learn to explore ideas by exploring the intellectual manners that are important to a particular field. We have to accept and use the epistemic process of the discourse community. This can be more difficult than the forms, but new ways of thinking usually develop easily through repeated contact. In my own experience, the epistemic knowledge developed a bit more slowly than the formalistic, but it, too, grew rapidly; I was soon thinking and sounding like an English major.

Finally—and I think most importantly—personal commitment to a particular community is involved in entering that new discourse community. Students can develop the sound of a community and apply the thought process of the community without adopting the worldviews of the community, without truly accepting membership in that community. In my own case, I was unwilling to become the person the literary studies community required me to be and to develop the worldview the community expected. As a result, I pursued careers in two different communities, business and rhetoric. Literary studies expected me to become somebody new, somebody I was unwilling to become. I was willing to become a business manager and, later, a rhetorician.

In my research, however, I found that Stella and Charlotte were willing to make the total transition, to write in social worker ways, to solve problems using social worker methods, and finally to adopt a social worker world view, no matter how alien it was to their native communities. In the process of coming to college, Stella and Charlotte found themselves becoming someone new.

## Works Cited

Berkenkotter, Carol, Thomas, Hucklin; and John Ackerman (1988). "Conventions, Conversations, and the Writer: Case Study of a Student in a Rhetoric Ph.D. Program," *Research in the Teaching of English, 22,* 9–44.

McCarthy, Lucille (1987). "A Stranger in Strange Lands: A College Student Writing Across the Curriculum," *Research in the Teaching of English, 21,* 233–265.

——— (1985). *The Making of Knowledge in Composition: Portrait of an Emerging Field.* Upper Montclair, NJ: Boynton/Cook.

North, Stephen (1986). "Writing in a Philosophy Class: Three Case Studies," *Research in the Teaching of English, 20,* 225–262.

## Sharing Ideas

- Draw a diagram of your discourse communities.

- I'm very sympathetic to all three stores Kevin shares—his own and those of Stella and Charlotte. You've probably known people (they may be you) who have changed their minds several times about majors and future professions. How do these stories illuminate such changes and choices?

- For you, what is at risk when you think about succeeding in your chosen field and major? Who agrees or disagrees with your goals and why? Consider your family, your significant other, your teacher, your friends? How do their opinions affect you?

- What is involved in personally investing in your education?

- How important has writing been to your success in school?

- Kevin claims adaptation to college requires that learners recognize the forms of writing used in their new communities, to think in ways that are valued in those communities, and to become personally and intellectually involved in their communities. How are these three elements playing out in your own college life? The lives of your close friends?

# 11

# By the Light of the
# Terminal Screen
## Discovering Digital Discourse

### Pat Hendricks

---

Pat Hendricks studies Rhetoric and Composition at Florida State
University, where she is currently a graduate teaching assistant. She
has what once was called a checkered past—she spent ten years in
the Air Force and five years working for the State of Florida
Department of Transportation. She is often amazed and sometimes
alarmed that she has become so interested in digital discourse as
computers are suspiciously sciencelike.

---

So, there you are staring at a big box with a bunch of electric cables running
out of it and a blank screen is staring back at you. Congratulations, you have
stumbled into the digital revolution. Scholars in a variety of disciplines are
studying what it means to work on and in digital computer environments and
asking questions like:

- Does our writing really change when we work with a computer?

- Can a real community form and be maintained in a computer's electronic
  environment?

- What happens to our physical identity when we go on-line and will we
  merge with the machine?

Other, more immediate questions you might have may be, What happens to an e-mail message when I send it? Who is "watching" what I do when I am on the Internet?

This essay is not going to give you answers to these questions. They are questions you may want to read about as you become more immersed in digital discourse. What I do want to share with you here are a few things you may find yourself taking part in as a student in a computer classroom and/or as you explore on your own.

Now, depending on your particular school, you may find yourself with access to some of the hottest equipment and leading-edge software available. Count yourself very, very lucky indeed. You may find that your class is conducted almost entirely on-line with you taking part in electronic discussions instead of face-to-face (F2F) classroom meetings. You may be required to construct a Web page. You may be responding to your classmates' papers electronically or you might find that you are asked to collaborate on writing assignments with people beyond your local college or university. Your teacher might ask you to publish a class anthology written, designed, edited, illustrated, and printed within the classroom. You might also find yourself conducting extensive research through various computer programs. On the other hand, you may find yourself in a low-tech computer assisted classroom (CAC), one that is limited in hardware, software, and access. Don't despair if you find yourself without the latest bells and whistles—there's still plenty of neat stuff to do.

Most of my students come into the first-year writing course with only a little computer knowledge, mostly word processing and maybe e-mailing. What they haven't done too much of is playing. And playing on the computer is an absolute must. Playing and writing. Playing and writing and thinking about what's going on.*

```
I am computer illiterate and all this technology
intimidates me. But actually once you've played
around on this huge hunk of metal you become a
little more relaxed and a little more confident.
```
*Heather*

## Word Processing

Probably the most used function of the personal computer (pc) is word processing. Two of the most well-known word-processing software programs that you might find yourself working in are Microsoft's Word and Corel's WordPerfect; however, any program that will let you type text into the com-

---

*All quotes are from students at Florida State University; used with permission.

puter and either print out a copy of the text or post it in a digital environment
might be said to be a word-processing program.

> For a messy writer like me, a computer becomes very
> efficient I hate to scratch out something I've
> already written, or worse, having to start all over.
> On a computer though, it is all easy and fast.
>
> *Brad*

Perhaps one of the greatest things about computer word processing has to
do with its ease. If you can type at all, word processing on the computer makes
it easy and quick to get words on paper, to change words, to correct and edit
your work, and to dramatically revise just about any aspect of your text. You
probably already know about deleting, copying, moving, and pasting text. And
you have, hopefully, already found the spell checker on your program. What
you may not have done too much of is play with how your text looks.

If you want to dramatically change the look of your essay, you can accomplish this by playing with all sorts of options. The easiest, by far, is to highlight
the text you want to emphasize and click the **bold**, *italic,* or underline buttons
on the power or button bar or find the options within the font menu. You can
also play a little with font typefaces. Some fonts are *extremely* difficult **to**
read *in small sizes* and some fonts are just *difficult* to read all together. A few programs will allow you to wrap text around a graphic or even manipulate the text
into a shape. You can also add special characters like ✓ ☞ ➤ to draw your
reader's attention to a line or paragraph. And of course there's always the possibility of using color for emphasis. You'll want to consider what you're saying,
why you're saying it, and who you're saying it to. Be choosy. Ask yourself if
you are choosing something because it helps you express something or just
because it's cool. Also, be aware that some teachers really hate this and will
want you to stick with standard fonts in standard sizes.

You can also play around with margins; line spacing; how you want paragraphs to look; whether all the text will run from left to right, be centered, or
be flush right; page numbering; and if you get really involved, you can start
fine-tuning how much space you want between letters or words. You might set
up columns, which can be a real interesting format to work with. All these features can be found in the menus of your word-processing program, usually
under either Format or Layout. Also, don't be shy about going to the Help
menu if you get confused; the Help explanations are not too hard to follow.

> The computer helps to save time and headaches.
>
> *Paige*

# Hypertext

One of the really fascinating things you can do if you stick with an electronic copy of your text, either via a disk or on the World-WideWeb (WWW or Web), is to work with hypertext. Briefly, hypertexts are normally boldfaced or underlined (maybe colored, too) words or phrases that, when clicked on, bring up something else on the computer screen. (If you can't quite picture this, think of the VH-1 pop-up videos.) What you might not know is that you, too, can write with hypertext. Why might you want to do this?

Let's say you are writing a paper and you have a ton of information on your topic; in fact, you have so much information you just can't find a way to get it all in your paper. You could put a whole bunch of footnotes in your essay and use lots of attachments. Or you can go with hypertext links which, when activated (clicked on), will bring up all that information right on the screen so your reader doesn't have to scroll back and forth. When the reader is done with the your explanatory information, he can just move back to the main text.

Sometimes hypertext brings up very brief bits of text, sometimes it brings up very long texts like essays or articles. If your system and software program allow it, you can also have hypertext links that bring up some sort of graphic like a drawing or a photograph. This feature can be particularly helpful if you are discussing an object or location that not everyone is familiar with. Let's say my paper is about common garden flowers. My electronic essay could offer the reader hypertext links that would bring up pictures of zinnias, marigolds, and daisies. When the reader clicked on the word *zinnias,* a picture of a zinnia would appear on his computer screen. Then he could go back to the main text with a clear idea of what a zinnia looks like.

Many word-processing programs today will allow you to add hypertext links to sounds and even animated sequences. Much of what you can do will be determined by your system, your software, how big your final electronic file can be, and what type of software your reader has available to read your file. Many, though not all, of these limitations are eliminated when you work in the WWW environment.

```
I think that computers have revolutionized the way
we communicate with each other - it is not good or
bad, just different.
```

*Monica*

The Web has a fairly standard way to construct hypertext links called hypertext markup language or HTML. There are plenty of good books out there that can explain HTML and help you learn how to use it if you are interested. When you move into the Web environment, not only can you do all the things I mentioned above but you can also offer your reader hypertext links to other Web sites.

Let's say I am writing about the Greek philosopher, Plato. If I do this for a Web environment, I can offer my reader hypertext links to sites that have information about Plato's life, sites that offer full texts of all of Plato's works, and sites where other people have posted articles, essays, and papers about Plato. I can also offer hypertext links to sites that have all sorts of information about historical Greece, about other people who lived during Plato's time, and maybe sites of Plato fan clubs. What's truly great about this feature is that I really only have to have done the research to find these sites and review them for their applicability to my paper; I don't have to paraphrase or summarize or correctly quote all the information that the reader will find there.

On the Web, you really don't have to worry about the size of your file (you aren't going to save it to a disk) and unless you offer a hypertext link to an exotically constructed site, most of your readers will be able to activate and access the hypertexted sites. The main thing to remember about hypertext in either environment is that it opens up all sorts of possibilities for you to play with. If you get interested, learn the basics and go for it.

## Final Text

You may have an opportunity to publish your work in some way. Students often publish class anthologies, 'zines, newsletters, or some other printed document that they can then distribute. Students, of course, write all the material but they also design, lay out, illustrate, edit, and arrange for the printing. As with most computer issues, what you can do is often limited by the equipment, software, and expertise available to you. Some writing classes here at Florida State have published their works and distributed them at campus sites like the student union and off-campus sites such as popular student coffee shops. More recently, classes are designing class Web sites and publishing their work there.

And you thought you would just type a paper, run spell check, and hand it in. Ha!

## Asynchronous Communication

What does asynchronous mean and why should you care? Asynchronous is defined in the dictionary as not occurring at the same time. In this case, since we are talking about asynchronous communication, we would say that it is communication that does not occur at the same time. Confused? Think of the humble letter, often referred to by computer users as snailmail.

Let's say your mother or father writes you a letter and asks how things are going in your classes. Because this is an asynchronous communication, you have some time to figure out what you are going to say and some time before Mom or Dad actually gets your return letter. Or you could decide to ignore a letter altogether and claim you never got it. What's important to remember about asynchronous communication is that it allows you to respond in your own time, which is good if you need to think about a response or if you have a very busy schedule. On the down side, asynchronous communication won't normally get you an instant response to anything you say and other people can always claim to have lost your message. Some of the more common asynchronous forms of digital communication are e-mail, listserv, and bulletin boards.

```
You've Got Mail.
```

*mysterious computer voice*

Of all the capabilities a computer connected to the Internet has perhaps the single most popular one is the ability to send and receive e-mail messages. If you do not have an e-mail account through your school or a commercial provider, get one. I mean it. E-mailing has become so popular and so prevalent that to be without an e-mail address is almost like being with a telephone number. Why are e-mail messages so popular?

- They are normally very short notes.
- Spelling, capitalization, and punctuation standards are fairly loose.
- They can be sent or responded to at any time, day or night.
- Lots of people who are unwilling to write letters will correspond by e-mail.
- You can send e-mail to people you would normally not call on the phone.
- E-mailing is fairly cheap.

You may find yourself writing a collaborative paper or perhaps conducting peer workshops via e-mail.

A variant of e-mail is called a listserv. The difference between straight e-mail and a listserv is that when you send a message to the listserv, everyone who has subscribed to that listserv gets your message. Most often you have no idea who has subscribed to the listserv and so don't know who, specifically, is reading your messages. Likewise, you will be receiving all the messages that everyone else sends to the listserv. Most messages on listservs are not at all personal; messages address issues, not people. Not to say that personal exchanges or comments are forbidden but rather that "personal" takes on a slightly different meaning in this forum.

Typically a listserv attracts people who are interested in a particular subject. For example, I subscribe to the Alliance for Computers and Writing Listserv. Everyone who has subscribed to this listserv is interested in discussing issues about—you guessed it—computers and writing. What happens on an active listserv is that people start sending messages about something they have been thinking about or maybe something they were discussing. People then continue the discussion of that particular issue or send a message about something else. When people continue a discussion on one particular issue, this becomes what is referred to as a "thread." These discussion threads can go on for days or weeks or they can dry up very quickly because no one wants to talk about the issue. Often threads mutate into new threads and the discussion takes off in new directions.

If you find yourself participating on a listserv for a class, the best advice I can give is to be part of the discussion. While it is totally acceptable to lurk (read messages but never send one) when you first subscribe to an established listserv, lurking is probably not going to work for you on a class listserv. Teachers set up class listservs for various reasons. You may be asked to have a listserv discussion about something you are reading for class or your teacher may pose questions she wants you to consider prior to a class meeting. Teachers may or may not participate actively on the listserv, they may or may not lurk. But for the most part I think teachers go through the trouble of setting up a class listserv so you can become actively engaged in discussions and they expect you to participate, even if only at a minimal level.

The last type of asynchronous communication I want to mention is bulletin boards. Generally speaking, bulletin boards are digital places where you leave some sort of document so people can go and read the document at their leisure. Often times students post a document at a bulletin board and other students are required to go read the document and leave comments. Sometimes these students are from the same class but sometimes students from one university will go and read documents left by students from another university and leave comments. Teachers also leave documents on a bulletin board and require that everyone read them before a certain class meeting. If you do work with bulletin boards you'll find that they, like other types of reading and writing activities, require some thought about the text's intended audience and the context in which the text is written. As with other asynchronous communication forms, bulletin boards wait for you to fit them into your schedule.

```
It's kind of fun to guess what the person behind the
keyboard is really like because you can't watch
their expression while they "talk."
```
*Monica*

## Synchronous Communication

Synchronicity, simultaneous, real time. All these terms attempt to describe a type of digital communication that closely resembles a face-to-face conversation or a telephone call. Like both the conversation and phone call, once you start, you're in it. You don't really get a chance to compose a draft response and go through lots of editing, nor are you allowed much time before you are expected to respond. Almost all computer synchronous communications function in a sort of chat room type environment where messages are sent and received almost instantly. There are all sorts of chat room environments out there so I'll just discuss a few here.

One very common chat room environment you may find yourself participating in is limited to use with directly interconnected or networked computers. There are several software programs that enable this type of classroom communication but the one I am most familiar with is Daedalus' InterChange. I don't want to get technical here, but I think a brief example may give you an idea. Let's say that you have just finished reading this chapter in *The Subject Is Writing* and your teacher wants to discuss some of the ideas I've presented. She may ask you to log on to InterChange and discuss a question or example. Basically this is like moving into small groups for discussion or workshopping your paper. So you get onto the computer and into the conference.

Let's say the question is: Why do you like or dislike using a computer for writing your papers? You have strong ideas about how great it is to use the computer so you type in your message: *I love writing on a computer because I'm a rotten speller and it will check my work.* Once you have typed this in, you hit the send button and away it goes to everyone who is logged on. It shows up on everyone's screen looking something like this:

```
Pat Hendricks

I love writing on a computer because I'm a rotten
speller and it will check my work.
```

Each time someone writes and sends a message, a block of text appears. First you get the sender's name and then the message. Sometimes the blocks of text come very, very fast and the screen scrolls up before you have a chance to read everything. If you have a bunch of very fast typists who have a lot to say, it can get very challenging to try to read everything, keep up with all the new messages coming across the screen, plus add your own voice to the conversation.

You might also be asked to conduct writing workshops over a synchronous communication program and this will no doubt provide you with new challenges. When you are participating in workshops via InterChange or another program, you may find you need to spend a bit more time clarifying what you mean since you cannot read anyone's facial expression or body language for hints about how they are reacting to what you say. One thing that my students have said they like about digital workshops is that they feel less constrained to give no-kidding constructive criticism. Maybe like them, you feel a bit uncomfortable questioning or advising a classmate you don't know very well. Somehow the synchronous chat room environment seems to alleviate this reluctance—which is mostly good but sometimes horrible. I'll address some of the more negative aspects that you will want to avoid when working in this environment a bit later.

```
MOOs and MUDs are like wearing cyber-masks.
```
*Chris*


```
It's fun to get out of your normal self and jump
into the life of another. You can do almost whatev-
er you want.
```
*Leslie*

Another chat room environment I want to mention is found in MUDs and MOOs. Before you think I have gone nuts here and think I am going to talk about dairy farms after a rainstorm, let me tell you that a MUD is a multiuser domain environment and a MOO is a MUD that is also object oriented. Right. What does that mean? Basically, these are chat rooms where people have also imagined a physical environment in which they will operate during their time there.

Many people have said they like MUDs and MOOs because these environments provide a sense of community. Regulars spend lots of time "talking" to one another. Another thing people like is an opportunity to take on a different identity. Many MUDs/MOOs are themed and when you participate in a MUD/MOO, you might make up a character you want to be that will fit in with the overall concept of the MUD/MOO. There are many MUDs and MOOs available ranging from Dungeons&Dragons-like motifs to a university or small, city setting. You can be whomever or whatever you choose to be in these digital worlds. You can virtually do outrageous things, be daring, be something you usually are not. It's something you may want to try.

You may be asking why I mention MUDs and MOOs in a book about writing. Well, MUDs and MOOs are writing. First of all, they are all currently text based; you don't actually see anything on your screen except words. Secondly, like all writers, MUD and MOO participants need to have some idea of the audience with whom they are trying to communicate. MUD and MOO communities may be made up of fictitious characters but those characters may have established certain ground rules, may have a long history together, and may have a specialized vocabulary. Finally, you may well be taking on a persona when you enter a MUD or MOO and this is most often what we do when we write.

Chat room environments, either in the classroom or in the zillions of private/commercial sites, are great places to extend yourself. If you are a little shy, this is a great medium for speaking up. Unfortunately, some folks seem to believe they have the right to be rude, crass, and just downright mean because no one is looking directly in their eyes when they make comments. Also, some folks, when they take on a fictitious name and identity, will lie, cheat, steal, and attempt to get you involved in things you may not want to get into. There still aren't many rules out there in cyberspace but there are some basic niceties that most folks go by, a kind of Netiquette, that you'll want to become familiar with before you log on to any form of digital communication.

## Computer Research

A very few comments about research via the computer: You could say there are three types of research you might do with a computer. The one you hear a lot about is research via the Web. There is a lot of information out there and it's not really that difficult to get to. In fact, the biggest problem with research on the Web is that there's so much stuff that you can start to feel a little lost or overwhelmed. The main way you find information is by using a search engine (there are lots of them like AltaVista, Excite, Yahoo). These search engines allow you to type in keywords and then the program searches the Web for anything that matches those words. Until you get proficient at choosing key words, you are likely to get back a lot of junk. Most search engines provide good directions to guide you through key-word options that will help narrow the search. Read these directions and you'll save yourself some time and effort.

A warning about Web research: Be selective about the source of information. Remember that anyone—anyone—can construct a site and put information on the Web. No one is really verifying that anything anyone puts out there is correct or true. Always ask yourself whether the information you get from a Web site is reliable and why you think it is reliable.

A second type of research you might do with a computer involves library computer systems. Without getting into the specifics, let me just say that the library computer systems are probably the next best thing to heaven for anyone needing to do research. No longer do you have to thumb through a card catalogue to find a few books you can use for a research paper. Heck, you may not even have to go to the library to find some articles or essays. Most library systems allow you to conduct the same type of key-word search that I mentioned earlier, as well as the traditional author, subject, or title searches. Additionally, most large university libraries have access to multiple catalogues which means you can find documents that your local library may not have but can get for you. Check out your local library; there are usually classes or workshops scheduled to teach you how to use the library's computer system and to use it to maximum capability.

The last type of research I want to mention is research conducted via electronic asynchronous or synchronous communication. Let's say you want to find out what first-year students at your university think about student government. Well, you can stand around the student union handing out surveys or you can ask a teacher who has a listserv if you can pose the same questions to her class via the class listserv. Maybe you want to interview someone but you just can't quite agree on a time. Why not conduct the interview by e-mail? That certainly would solve the schedule problem and would allow your interviewee an opportunity to think about his response before answering. You might also want to enter a specific chat room and ask the participants if they would be willing to answer some of your questions, either in the chat room itself or via individual e-mail. Another possibility is to construct a Web site where you ask visitors questions or perhaps offer them a survey or poll they can then e-mail to you. And the one thing about these electronic interviews or surveys that makes them so great is you don't have to stay in the local area to get them; in fact, you can go worldwide for your research without leaving your room. You could interview first-year college students in England and Japan and Germany and Canada and, well, wherever you can find someone who will "talk" with you. The possibilities are amazing.

## Teachers in Computer-assisted Classrooms

You may find that your teacher takes on a slightly different role in a computer-assisted classroom. You may be asked to operate at a much more autonomous level than you ever have before. Because no one can really run through all the possibilities of a word-processing program with you; you will have to play around with the program you have. If you do get an opportunity to engage in asynchronous or synchronous digital communication, it will be up to you to take up the challenge and actively participate. Nor can anyone explore the Web for you; you will have to do this yourself. Finally, you may find that you are the technowizard in your class and actually have much more experience than your teacher. Share.

Flip the switch, be a part of it. Write, play, and, most of all, enjoy.

---

## Sharing Ideas

- How would you describe your experience with computers so far? Do you feel totally competent, up on the latest programs, or do you feel a little bit like Heather, a little intimidated by all this? Have you tried playing around with word-processing options like fonts and formats? Are you a regular e-mailer and if so, who do you find yourself communicating with the most? (And in what way does that e-mailing represent your "journey in journaling"?)
- Can you think of some papers you have written in the past that might have been really neat if you could have done a hypertext version? How do you

think the reading of a paper would change if it were done in hypertext instead of traditional footnoting and appendices? Can you think of texts other than reference/research that might be really interesting if done in a hypertext version?

- Is hypertext really so new? Do you know any parallels to experiments in written or other arts that work like hypertext? Collage, performance art, improvisational work? And how successful is paper-bound experimental text making for you and for others (you might look at Hans Ostrom's essay in this collection for an example of the same).

- How do you react to the possibility that students from other schools might read your essays and make comments on them? How might you negotiate feedback in that type of environment?

- Have you ever been in a situation that seems similar to a MUD or MOO— maybe a costume party or in a strange town where no one knows you? Have you been able to get "into" character? How might you establish a different identity on-line? How would you want to be different? Have you ever written anything as if you were a different person?

# 12

# How Writers and Readers Construct Texts

## Jeanette Harris

Jeannette Harris directs the William L. Adams Writing Center at Texas Christian University. Years of teaching writing courses, directing writing programs, and writing composition textbooks have convinced her that students write better and are more comfortable with themselves as writers if they understand the process they go through as they write.

In the past three decades writing has been taught in most composition courses, both in high school and college, as a process that consists of three parts: prewriting, writing, and rewriting. This model has, in general, worked very well, providing writing instructors with a simple, convenient structure for their courses and students with a simple, convenient guide for writing.

Once it emerged, the concept of writing as a process began to erode slowly but surely, the notion that writing, especially good writing, results only from inspiration. To view writing as a process, something like changing a tire or putting on make-up, is to demystify it—to make it known and doable rather than mysterious and mystical. Providing students with a simple model of the writing process helped them understand what was going on when they wrote and gave them confidence that they could write, if not inspired, at least competent prose. Certainly, no one, or almost no one, wanted to go back to the idea that only those who are inspired can write.

But in time the simple three-part process began to seem too simple, and some people (mainly writing researchers) began to question this prewriting-writing-rewriting model. Oh, no one questioned the idea that a process was involved—just what kind of process. Does everyone go through the same three stages in exactly the same way? Is the process perhaps recursive (the result of backward as well as forward motion) rather than relentlessly and progressively linear (moving always forward)? Can the process consist of fewer or more than three stages? And do readers go through a similar process?

Attempts to answer these questions led to various theories of text construction. The idea of constructing a text may seem a little strange to you. A building perhaps, or a highway or bridge, but why speak of constructing texts? The term *construct* suggests that when we write we build or put together something that formerly did not exist in the same form. To construct is to act in a workmanlike or workwomanlike way. To construct is to be productive as well as creative. *Text* is a broad term that can be used to refer to any written document, whether it is carved in stone, inscribed on paper, or reflected on a computer monitor. It conveniently encompasses all forms of writing—book, essay, letter, note, story, memo, poem, and so on. All written documents can be referred to as texts.

What happens when writers construct texts? Clearly, a process is involved, but what is that process and how does it differ from the old three-stage model of prewriting-writing-rewriting? To be honest, no one really knows, but we can make some educated guesses. My own guess goes like this.

A text originates as an idea—usually in the form of an internal dialogue that a writer has with himself or herself. Although in some instances this dialogue may be so fleeting that the writer is hardly conscious of its existence, I believe all texts, however brief and inconsequential, initially assume this unwritten interior form, which I call a mental text. Even the most informal note or list originates as a mental text—a thought that both anticipates and shapes the completed text. The idea to jot down a note or to make a list in itself constitutes a mental text. However unformed and fragmentary this mental image of the text is, it is a very real and significant form of the text.

We might represent this process of text construction as follows:

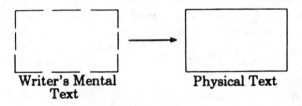

**Writer's Mental Text**          **Physical Text**

But the process is not as simple as the model suggests. Writers do not simply construct a mental text and then transfer that mental phenomenon onto a piece of paper or a computer screen. The construction of a written, physical text involves not just a single movement from mental to physical text but, depending on the complexity and length of the text, a series of recursive movements. It is, in fact, this recursive motion between the mental and physical texts that characterizes the process of constructing a text. The writer constructs a mental image of the text and then attempts to construct a physical text that reflects it.

Unfortunately, this model of text construction is not nearly as tidy and simple as the familiar three-stage process we have been using. Rather it is messy and indefinite. But I believe it is more accurate than the linear three-stage model. As anyone who has written at all knows writing is not simple and tidy. It involves going backward as well as going forward as a writer attempts to reflect in writing what exists in his or her mind. Thus, although there are only two steps to this model of text construction, a writer repeats these two steps, shuttling back and forth from the mental to the physical text and back again, until a deadline or lack of energy or interest terminates the process.

But the process is even more complicated than this explanation suggests because the writer's mental text keeps changing. Once a writer generates something tangible, a physical text of some sort (even though it may be fragmentary), the mental text is modified, often in significant ways. For example, suppose you are asked to identify a problem at your university and write an essay about it. Your initial idea is that you will simply describe the problems with the food served in the campus cafeteria. You write a rough draft of your essay describing how bad the food is and complaining that the cafeteria never serves anything you like. When you finish this draft, you feel pretty good about it. Then a few days later, you read over this first draft and notice that your essay seems rather shallow and subjective. After all, why would a reader want to know about your food preferences? What is the point? So, you try again. This time you decide to argue that the cafeteria should serve a greater variety of food because the students who eat there come from varied backgrounds. You change your introduction so that the focus is not exclusively on you and what you like.

But once more, when you reread what you have written, you are not satisfied with the results. Arguing for a greater variety of food to accommodate the varied tastes of the students who eat there is an improvement over your first subjective version but still seems trivial and perhaps impractical. How can any cafeteria consistently provide food that everyone will like? So you begin to think about criteria other than taste. You now become convinced that the cafeteria's main concern should be good nutrition. In looking back over your first draft, when you were complaining about the food, you realize that most of the dishes you mention are high in fat, salt, and sugar. Thus you decide to rewrite once more, this time emphasizing the need for more healthy food. You revise your essay drastically, arguing this time that students need to learn while they are in college to eat a nutritious, healthy diet. In this version, you go back to your original introduction, writing about what you like, but use this as a point of departure to point out that what you like is not good for you. You then launch your argument that a school cafeteria has a responsibility to introduce students to sensible, healthy eating habits.

Just as the mental text shapes the physical text, so the physical text shapes the mental text. Although the example I've given may be somewhat extreme, subtle modification occurs almost every time you revise something you have written. As you write, your ideas about what you want to write undergo both simple and dramatic changes. If we were to try to represent this modification process in a diagram, it might look something like this:

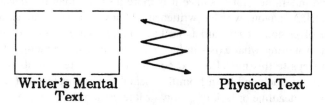

Writer's Mental Text          Physical Text

However, the text construction process does not end here because readers as well as writers construct texts. Although readers do not construct a physical text as do writers, they do construct a mental text, which is their version of the physical text. Thus, a mental text exists not only in the mind of a writer but also, in a different but analogous way, in the mind of the reader.

Because the reader's experiences and information always differ somewhat from that of the writer, the reader's mental text always differs from that of the writer. For example, a person who lives in a large city in which innocent people are often shot would have very different assumptions about guns than those held by a writer who lives in a rural area and likes to hunt. However, the physical text that the writer constructs significantly shapes the reader's mental text. The reader who fears being shot may not accept all of the arguments of a writer who likes to hunt, but may at least begin to appreciate the complexity of the issue.

Thus, to complete the process of text construction, we have to shift from writer to reader, for a text is completed in the mind of the reader. While the writer begins with a physical text and constructs a physical text, a reader begins with a physical text and constructs a mental text. But, like the writer, the reader moves back and forth between the two forms of the text, one modifying the other, until his or her mental text is constructed. Thus, in both writing and reading, a text is constructed by a process that involves a recursive movement between a mental and a physical text. A diagram of the complete process of text construction might look like this:

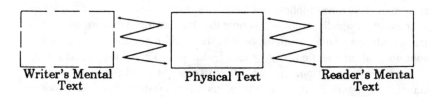

Writer's Mental Text          Physical Text          Reader's Mental Text

At this point you may well be wondering how all of this theory about reading and writing affects you. First, these theories about text construction will, I hope, make you more realistic about writing so that you will not expect to march through the process of constructing a text in a neat, sequential fashion. Although you may still want to follow the familiar guidelines of prewriting first, then writing, and finally rewriting, you should not expect a writing (or reading) project to be orderly. Your mental image of what you are writing will probably change as you write, and each time it changes, the physical text will also change as you attempt to accommodate both and reconcile one to the other. Thus, you may "revise" your mental text before you even begin to write, and may "prewrite"—make new discoveries about your subject and text—well into the project.

Second, understanding how writers and readers construct texts should provide you with a more accurate view of the relationship between readers and writers. As a writer, you are not writing in a vacuum but are rather constructing a text for a reader who will (re)construct that text in his or her own mind. Thus, as a writer, you do not control the reader's version of the text you write. But good writers, understanding the slipperiness of texts, keep the reader's possible responses in mind, trying to guide the reader's understanding. In writing some types of texts, especially fiction and poetry, you may want different readers to have different responses—to find in your words their own meanings. But here too you need to be aware of your readers and their purposes in reading as well as your purposes in writing.

Third, the concept that both writers and readers construct a mental image of the text should help you realize how important to both reading and writing are the mental, interior parts of the process. Thus, the time you spend thinking about what you are going to write is not time wasted. Don't rush into actually putting words on paper or into the computer. Of course, this does not mean that you can put off constructing a physical text forever, but it does mean that what is going on in your mind before you write and as you write is an essential part of the process. Even more important, it means that you should allow enough time between drafts to accommodate this process of modification, to let what is in your head shape your physical text and to let that physical text, in turn, reshape what is in your head.

Finally, knowledge about how readers and writers work should give you increased control over both processes. What you understand you can usually control better. If you have a clear understanding of what is going on as people read and write, you will gradually learn to control your own versions of these processes. Writing is not a gift of the muse nor a mysterious process you cannot understand. Nor is it a simple one, two, three process. Writing involves mental as well as physical activity, involves readers as well as writers, and involves going backward—to the internal mental text—as well as going forward—to the external physical text. By understanding the process by which writers and readers construct texts, you will become a better writer and reader.

## Sharing Ideas

- To construct your own text, you may, as Thia Wolf suggested in her essay, tap your memory. But Jeanette Harris explains that we don't rely only on inspiration for composing. She suggests, instead, that composing is a complex activity and that writers begin with a mental text. Try to articulate some of the inner workings of your own mental text-building processes.

- Some writers compose mainly in their heads and then write a fast and furious single draft. Is that you? Other writers do much more shuttling between mental text and physical text. Is that you?

- Explain how Jeanette's essay gives you insights into reading/writing and writing/reading processes.

- How does your sense of audience expectations modify your drafting?

- Does Jeanette's essay illuminate your own history as a writer/reader?

- Many of us have become used to talking about writing process. It may be more unusual to consider how the act of reading is also a process. You have probably had an experience of bringing your own understanding (past reading, past life experiences, past school experience, your travels, your love life, and so on) to a reading of a text. For instance, when a story is set in New York City, how important is it that you have a knowledge of large urban cityscapes? In understanding a written text, what is the reader's responsibility? What is the writer's responsibility?

- Describe a time when constructing a satisfying mental image of a text proved difficult for you. Does Jeanette's essay help you understand how you might have resolved those difficulties?

# Part IV

# Behind the Scenes
# How Writers and Teachers
# Work (Together)

... speakers and writers are bound to make some errors. In fact,
they could not learn anything new about the language unless they
did make some errors. The errors are likely to be in some way logical or consistent because the learner is searching for patterns. . .
error is an important sign of active learning, for the error shows
how speakers and writers are making predictions and trying out
solutions, and of taking risks with the language they are using. . . .
                                              –Eleanor Kutz, writing teacher

There is a line I see developing in the way the class went. We were
asked to read and comment on the paper itself, and asked to remark
on the devices used, etc. The line was that middle ground between
what is "good writing," and what is acceptable in a social context.
     The question arose, "So, what about content?"
     There were papers that I found very offensive in the beginning,
and I railed on those poor people. There were things I agreed with,
and I gushed my approval. There were people in class that asked me
to look at their work, and I thought, it was terrible, what was I to
say? If you deny them the truth, you are setting them up for a
worse criticism by someone who doesn't care. If you tell them what
you think, will they get discouraged and quit working on something

that had potential and was just not handled properly? And does saying that "This is just my opinion," make it any better for them?
After all, they sought out your comment, and they respect your
judgment.

—Jay Goldbach, writing student

I need deadlines. This class provided me with more than adequate
number of them (I have a gift for understatement). I write my best
from about 10 until 2 in the morning (I edit the following afternoon). I think this is a result of habit, but it is nonetheless true.
Without deadlines, I have trouble forcing myself to work at those
hours. I am concerned that after this class I will do less work since I
am deprived of those deadlines.

—Jason Fink, writing student

# 13

# The Cupped Hand and the Open Palm

## Hephzibah Roskelly

Hephzibah Roskelly teaches a variety of writing courses at University of North Carolina–Greensboro, from freshman composition to graduate theory. She writes about composition and reading theory and has recently published a book with Eleanor Kutz on the theory and practice of teaching English, *An Unquiet Pedagogy*. She received her Ph.D. from the University of Louisville in 1985 and remains an avid basketball fan.

When I was in first grade, I was a bluebird. Funny that I remember that after so many years. Or maybe not so funny. I suspect you remember your label too. I remember being proud of being in the group I was in. Somehow everybody in Mrs. Cox's class knew it was pretty awful to be a yellowbird, common to be a redbird, and therefore best to be a bluebird. One student of mine remembers her experience in first grade this way: "My first-grade teacher waited for us to make a mistake in our group and then she'd pounce. She always stood behind our desks. That's because I wasn't in the fast reading group. I was in the bears." She laughs. "To this day I think bears are stupid." For Susan, like for many of us, the first-grade reading group is our first real experience with group work, and for many of us, like for Susan, it's not remembered fondly. Especially if you happened to be a yellowbird or a bear.

By third or fourth grade, though, your early memory may have dimmed a little as group work began to get less attention. You and your fellow students were "tracked" by this point, grouped into classes according to the results of standardized achievement tests, so the need for "ability level" groups like the blue/red/yellowbirds within the classroom became less pressing. And by the time you entered middle school or seventh grade, probably there wasn't much group work at all. In its place was "seat work," which meant some sort of writing. If you were like most students, you wrote alone. Nobody ever saw your writing except your teacher and, very rarely, other students, if they happened to look at the bulletin board where the teacher occasionally posted the "A" papers. If you were writing answers to questions or coming up with ideas in class, you were often reminded to "cover your work" so that your friend in the desk across from you wouldn't be tempted to copy. So you used a sheet of paper to cover your writing, or you hid your marks behind a wall you made with your hand, cupping it to keep what you wrote private. Covering your work became so natural that you might have even cupped your hand anytime you wrote *anything* in school—the beginning of a short story, a letter to the editor of your school paper or to your girlfriend—the kind of writing where "copying" would never occur. But you continued to cup your hand because by this time you had gotten the message. Writing is solitary, individual, something others can take away from you if you don't keep it from them, and something others don't see except when it's "clean."

These elementary school lessons about groups and about writing are deeply imbedded, so much so that you may react with suspicion or even hostility now when your writing class—a freshman composition course or some other—encourages group work. Your past experience with group work in reading hasn't led you to feel that it will do much more than put you in some category you'd rather not be in, and past experience with writing suggests that sharing your work with someone else is foolish or illegal. Your college, after all, probably has an honor code that says something about giving and receiving help. Why should a composition teacher force the connection between writing and the small group, asking you to come up with ideas together, make plans together, read and revise together, and, strangest of all, write together?

I try to answer that question here. One of the reasons that group work fails in the classroom is that neither our past experiences in the reading group nor those with the writing lesson have given us much of a rationale for working in groups. When a person doesn't know why she's doing something, doing it seems relatively useless. Working in small groups, even though it's an idea touted by theorists and teachers in composition, is limited in actual practice for just this reason: Students and sometimes their teachers don't know why they're doing what they're doing when they meet in the small group. Just as important, students and their teachers aren't aware of why they're often so disposed against working in groups. I describe what underlies these attitudes so that you can begin to understand why group work fails sometimes and why it's so potentially useful for your development as a writer.

# Why Group Work Fails

I asked a group of students who will be student teaching in high school English classrooms this semester to use their own past experiences and their developing ideas about teaching to speculate about what makes groups fail in the classroom. Their list may mesh with your own feelings about the small group in the classroom:

### Too Many Chefs; No Chefs; Untrustworthy Chefs

Students mentioned the possibility of the "one member who dominates," who "thinks he knows it all," who "can't let the group decide." Or the possibility of having several members who all wanted to lead. What some described as a domineering personality in the group, others saw as responsible. "Somebody always ends up doing the most work. And that's usually me," says Beth, one of my first-year students at the beginning of the semester. "When I was in high school there were always a few who didn't want to do the work and goofed off, and they left the rest of us poor slobs to do it." The fear that the work won't be shared but shuffled off to one wimpy or guilty person is echoed in comments about who's prepared, who volunteers, who shows up. A student teacher reports on her experience with being given too much responsibility for her group's operation: "My classmates saw me as one of the smart kids and so in groups I was always expected to emerge as a leader and to get things done. There were many times when I felt I was carrying the load."

An even bigger fear about responsibility and personality centers on trust. "I don't know the other people in my group. Why would I want to talk to them about how I feel about anything?" asks a student teacher. And one freshman writer writing in her journal before her group met for the first time writes about her fears that the group won't be responsible to her: "What if they think my ideas are terrible? What if they think I'm stupid?"

### Chaos Rules

At first, the fear of spinning out of control in the group may seem primarily to be a teacher complaint rather than a student one. And it's true that the fear that there will be too much talk or that the talk will quickly get "off task" does prevent teachers from using group work at all, or they use it only sparingly and with rigid guidelines to control it. But students fear loss of control as well. When students are conditioned to the quiet classroom where only one person has the right to talk (the teacher) and the rest have the right to remain silent (the students)—and this is the typical classroom—students aren't comfortable with a lot of noise and movement either. "It gets too disorganized," one student lamented. "I'm an organized person. And I don't like hearing what the other groups are saying."

*If You Want Something Done Well—*

One student teacher remembers her 101 class doing revision of essays in small groups:

> We had writing groups to comment on each other's papers. This was fine except that no one would make any comments about my papers. I guess because my grammar is sound they couldn't find anything to say because they didn't know what else to look for.

A typical group dialogue went something like this:

> *First person*: I don't see anything wrong with your paper.
> *Second person*: Me neither.
> *Third person*: Yeah, it's a good paper. You'll get an A.
> *Me*: Well, what did you think about it?
> *First person*: Everything. The whole paper is fine.
> *Second person*: I liked your topic. How did you think of such a good topic?
> *Third person*: Yeah. You'll get an A.

> Not only did this fail to give me any useful feedback, but it also put me in an awkward position when the time came for me to comment on others' papers. They were so full of admiration and praise for mine, how could I say anything negative about theirs? So a vicious cycle where no one benefited was created.

Related to this feeling of the group not helping because no one knows what to do within the group is the feeling that the work they do is not very important. "It's a waste of time. I think teachers have us get in groups when they don't have anything left to say and don't want to let the class go. We just read the paper in my last class. Or maybe talked for five minutes and then read the paper." Another writer says, "I kept changing what my group said or changing what I said to match them. It would have taken a lot less time and been better just to do it myself."

# Why—and How—a Group Works

These students tell the story of why group work fails in the classroom. The stories reveal deep and often unconscious beliefs about how the writing class is supposed to proceed, about how writers are supposed to work. The beliefs come from those old experiences with reading groups and with writing. But they also come from what we've all imagined about how people learn in school. School, we've determined, is competitive, not cooperative, and therefore it's the individual not the group effort that counts. And counting is what school is all about. Who has the most points, the most stars, the most A's?

Who's the bluebird? The fact is we assume that effort can only be measured by a grade and that a grade can't fairly be given to a group. So attempts to work as a group seem futile and unnecessary given what we've assumed school is all about—keeping not sharing, winning not collaborating, cupping the hand, not opening the palm.

If it were true that people learn to think and write primarily alone—in solitary confinement so to speak—it might also be true that group work is wasted effort, or unhelpful or too chaotic or too hard. But the truth is that people don't learn—in fact, can't learn much at all—in isolation. They learn *by engaging in the world.* They come to terms with what's around them, understand it, through sound and movement, through talk. A child who never hears talk, as tragic cases show, never talks or talks only very little. Talking presumes at least one listener or commenter. Group work, then, because it encourages engagement—talk and reflection and response—mirrors the way people learn things inside and outside the classroom, the ways in which they make sense out of the world.

So conversation, communication with others, is vital to our understanding of others and ourselves. And people can't communicate unless they listen—work toward a shared notion about how to proceed. Do you know the movie *Airplane*? It's actually one long joke about how communications gets muddled when that shared notion doesn't exist.

"These people need to be taken to a hospital," the doctor says.

Walking up, stewardess Julie looks at them. "What is it?" she asks.

The doctor is impatient. "It's a big white building with sick people in it.

But that's not important right now." Or:

"Surely you can't mean it," Julie says.

"I mean it," the doctor says. "And stop calling me Shirley."

Julie and the doctor don't communicate because they haven't decided on a shared basis for their talk. They mistake words and ideas and don't care enough (because then it wouldn't be funny) to get it right before they go on. In the classroom group, when shared work and talk do take place, real communication can occur. People learn to listen to one another and use one another's talk to test and explore their own talk more fully. This notion of learning and understanding as essentially shared rather than possessed by one individual can be tested using a little game I came up with called Trivial Literacy (after E. D. Hirsch's best-selling book *Cultural Literacy: What Every American Needs to Know*, 1987):

1.  Choose part of Hirsch's list (or any list of words). A part of one list might read something like *hambone, harridan, Holden Caulfield, Huguenot.*

2.  Mark every word you don't know or can't guess about.

3.  In your group, see how many marks you can eliminate by getting information from others.

4.  In class, see how many marks remain when the group pools all infor-
    mation.

5.  Are there any words left? Guess about them. Ask somebody outside class.

You know what will happen before you do the test. You find out more and
more by talking. You hear the contexts people have for knowing things like
*Harlem Globetrotters*, and you bring up the context you have for knowing
*Huguenot*. In other words, you'll illustrate how your knowledge gets stronger,
better developed, more insightful, and more complete the more you combine
your knowledge with others'. This combining always works better if it's informal, conversational, unpressured, in some way equal. That's why Trivial
Literacy usually teaches so much. Because it's a game—it's fun, and the stakes
aren't high. Group works need to be nurtured because it works, often playful-
ly, to encourage the development of individual thought.

All writers need to hear their own voices, but I think they can only hear
them clearly when they find them in the chorus of lots of other voices.
Otherwise, for many writers the writing is hollow, without a sense of commitment or *investment* that characterizes the voices of confident, effective writers.
Kenneth Bruffee (1984), who's a composition teacher and writer, makes this
connection between the social and the individual explicit. "Thought is an artifact created by social interaction," he says. "We can think because we can talk,
and we think in ways we have learned to talk" (640). We're stronger and better developed individual thinkers and writers because we interact with people
in groups.

Partially because so much of writing is done in silence and solitude, college writers often fear the investment required in writing. They don't trust their
voices; the only thing they do trust is the certain knowledge that they will be
graded on what that voice is able to produce. They want control, and so they
ask "How long does this have to be?" or "Can we use first person?" And they
want to minimize risk, so they count words and number of footnotes, use simple sentence and forms they've read, and write with passive verbs that take
them out of the writing. "It can be seen that Jane Austen was expressing feminist concerns," they might say, as a way of avoiding a declaration that *they've*
been the ones to see it. They avoid the personal commitment that writing
requires because it seems too dangerous to risk. It's as though you walked into
a dark auditorium to speak to a group, knowing they were out there waiting but
not knowing how many there were, how big the room was, or if you had a
microphone. You'd probably clear your throat a few times, and test the sound,
but if you could see nothing but your speech, and you knew you were being
judged each time you opened your mouth, you might likely be stunned into
silence.

Your small group functions as a visible audience, a literal sounding board
for your voice, and, as Bruffee (1984) and others suggest, a source of your

growing knowledge of the world. As such, the group alleviates the sense of powerlessness in writing (and thinking) that so many student writers feel and thus reduces the fear of commitment and investment by helping you to hear your voice clearly.

## The Group at Work:
## First-year Writers Writing Together

The group lessens writers' deep and real fear of taking responsibility for what's on the page in lots of ways—by supporting and strengthening individual writer's attempts, providing other perspectives on ideas, and sharing responsibility. All of these benefits for the writer occur when groups do all kinds of activities together—read, comment, discuss, plan, interpret—but they're most visible and dramatic when groups write together. That's why I'm using this example of the work of the group from my freshman writing course.

Students had been in their 101 class and in groups for five or six weeks when I gave the assignment. They were already comfortable talking about writing and ideas. But this task asked them to go a step farther, to write together a short (two- or three-page) collective response to Dorothy Parker's funny and bitter short story "You Were Perfectly Fine." The story is primarily a dialogue between a male and female character discussing the events at a party the night before. The man's guilt about getting drunk leads him to pretend he remembers a "promise" he's made to the woman, who pretends too in order to hold him to it. After reading the story and doing some quick in-class writing, groups met to begin to decide how they felt about the hungover, guilty man, the seemingly sympathetic woman, and the reasons for the dishonesty in the dialogue. As groups talked, they jotted down notes, often asking one another to repeat or clarify, often interrupting one another with revisions. Some groups talked mostly about the distinctions between social life in the twenties, when the story was written, and the present. Others concentrated on whether it was the man or the woman who was more to blame for the hypocrisy. In the next week and a half, groups argued about men and women and Dorothy Parker, and they worked out ways to allow for varying perspectives and to combine them. Everybody had to negotiate what to say and how to say it, who would write the final copy, where they would revise. All the talk and writing helped them find new ways to make points and gave them finally the new voices they needed to write together.

Here's the first paragraph of one of the papers:

Dorothy Parker's negative view of relationships between men and women is obvious in "You Were Perfectly Fine." We analyzed the story as readers and listeners. Reading it, we felt that the woman was basically honest and the man without credibility. Then listening to it our ideas changed. We got more of a sense of the female being manipulative, romantic and lovesick, but dishonest and deceitful. Peter, the man, seems sensitive and witty, although he ends up being weak and panic-stricken. They seem like real people. Between reading and listening, we've learned that both these characters are dishonest and the relationship probably doesn't stand a chance.

This group ends their piece with a modern tale of deceit that connects romance in Parker's time and in their own, using one of the group member's own experience with deceit in relationships: "It's hard for men and women to be honest with each other whether they live in the Roaring Twenties or right now. Nobody wants to hurt somebody or get hurt themselves."

Notice that the voice in this excerpt is strong. It's controlled; that is, students talk both about the story and the relationships within it, but they feel free enough to be personal too, using the personal pronoun "we" and including a real-life example. There's a clear sense of commitment, interest, and investment in the task.

Collabortation in the group removed or alleviated some of the most debilitating fears about writing for the freshman writers in my class, and this ability of the group to nurture confidence proves how useful the group can be in strengthening the writing process in individual writers. I bet that these fears about writing hit close to your own.

## Fear of Starting

Many writers find a blank page of paper so intimidating that they delay beginning as long as possible, searching for the perfect sentence opening, the right title, the best word. But because in the group there were four or five sets of ideas about a particular sentence or a way to open or a character, no writer stared at her paper waiting for inspiration. Inspiration, in fact, came from the talk that went on in the group. "Wait a minute," a group writer would say. "Is this what you said?" And she'd read it back. Another member would say, "It sounds better like this." "And why don't we add something about his past?" another would add. Writing happened so fast that nobody had time to dread not being able to find the idea or the word they wanted to begin.

## Fear of Stopping

One first-year writer told me once that her writing was like a faucet with no water pressure—"it won't turn on hard—it just dribbles till it stops." Lots of writers fear that once they get the one good thought said, or the two points down, they'll be left with nothing but dead air time, and that they'll have to fill it with what one of my students calls "marshmallow fluff." But none of the groups had difficulty maintaining writing after they began. The group kept ideas flowing, and changing, and if one person was losing momentum, another would be gathering it. Ken Kesey, the author of *One Flew over the Cuckoo's*

*Nest* (1962) and a teacher, comments on this effect as he describes a collaborative project—an entire novel—that his creative writing class worked on in one group: "Some days you just don't have any new sparkling stuff. But when you got thirteen people, somebody always has something neat and it's as though somebody on your team is on and you're off" (Knox-Quinn 1990, 315).

### *Fear of Flying*

When you have a personal stake in your writing, a belief in your voice and in what you're saying, and a trust in your reader to hear you out, your writing soars. "Everyone can, under certain conditions, speak with clarity and power," composition teacher Peter Elbow says. "These conditions usually involve a topic of personal importance and an urgent occasion." The group helped make the topic personally important since each writer had to justify decisions and ideas to the others, and the occasion was urgent since talk, writing, and real communication were necessary to make decisions in a limited time.

## The Group and Changing the World

So what does this long example from my first-year class prove? First, the group validates rather than hurts or lessens the individual voice. The group reinforces the effort involved in writing, talking, by the energy and specificity with which they both support and challenge the writer's thinking. Ken Kesey watched larger perspectives get developed on character and plot in the novel his class wrote: "When we would sit down around the table . . . and start writing our little section, boy you could hear the brain cells popping. They knew they had to write and had to fit in with the other stuff. You couldn't be too much yourself" (Knox-Quinn 1990, 310). But knowing that gives writers a clearer sense of self when they write individually. Not being "too much yourself" is a way of finding what your writing self really is.

"People think it's about competing with each other," Kesey says, speaking of writers and writing. "But the real things that you compete with are gravity and inertia—stagnation" (Knox-Quinn 1990, 315). Writing is not some sort of contest between you and everybody else in the class, with the one who has the best grade—the fewest red marks—winning at the end of it, and that's why the cupped hand is a poor metaphor for what happens when you produce writing in a classroom. The struggle, the contest, is internal, between your desire to talk on paper and your fear or distrust of it. The group helps us compete with the real opponent of creative, critical thought—inertia, the fear of making a move.

As Kesey's work with his creative writers and my work with my first-year writers suggest, the group gives writers the strategies for winning that contest. I remember a few years ago, a freshman writer was writing an essay whose topic turned out to be something about the advantages of watching TV. She was bored with it, but chose it quickly as she was casting about for anything to do. The essay began, "There are many disadvantages to sitting in front of a TV. But there are some positive things about TV." Well, you get the idea. It was uncommitted, with no sense of the personal investment I've been describing, and a feeling in the writing of inertia. The writer wasn't just writing about couch potatoes; she was writing couch potato prose. When she read aloud her opening to her group the next day, she became aware that the group was growing glassy-eyed. She finally gave up. "It's bad, huh?" They laughed. Then she started talking. All of a sudden the couch potato had stood up. She was exploring an idea she was creating for and with her group.

Look back at the idealistic subheading that began this last section. Changing the world seems a pretty grandiose goal for group work, doesn't it? "Freshman Arrive But Not to Change the World" read the headline in an article this fall in the *Greensboro News and Record* that described how first-year students in colleges across the country didn't believe they would make real changes in the world outside themselves. I think the article was wrong. I think people want to change the worlds they live in, but they feel increasingly powerless to do it. And here's the last and best reason for the group. Because they force writers and thinkers to consciousness, groups foster action and change.

Deciding on what's significant about what you're reading, what you're writing, what you're listening to, what you're writing in a group, is the beginning of an understanding that you make knowledge in the classroom. You don't just find it in a book, and you don't just apply it from a lecture. You *create* it. That's a potentially powerful piece of information. Once you realize that you make knowledge, you see that you can act to change the knowledge that's there. As students of writing, your work in the group can help you become aware that the knowledge of the subject matter you work with, of voice, of forms and styles can be determined by you and those around you. The more your group meets and talks about reading, writing, and ideas, the more your group collaborates, the more *authoring* you do. What seat work and the bluebirds taught you to see as private and unique the group can help you recognize as also shared and social. And that realization really can help you make a difference in the world around you and within you.

## Works Cited

Bruffee, Kenneth (1984). "Collaborative Learning and the Conversation of Mankind." *College English, 46,* 635–652.

Hirsh, E. D. (1987). *Cultural Literacy: What Every American Needs to Know.* Boston: Houghton Mifflin, 1987.

Kesey, Ken (1962). *One Flew over the Cuckoo's Nest.* New York: New American Library.

Knox-Quinn, Carolyn (1990). "Collaboration in the Writing Classroom: An Interview with Ken Kesey." *College Composition and Communication, 41,* 309–317.

Parker, Dorothy (1942). "You Were Perfectly Fine." *Collected Stories of Dorothy Parker.* New York: Modern Library.

## Sharing Ideas

- As a writing student, I've experienced positive and negative writing groups; Hephzibah's essay helps me understand why this is so. And, she explains that group work actually doesn't take place all that often. Is that true to your life in school?

- Imagine that you're in a writing group and it's spinning out of control: One member is talking too much, or one member is never prepared, or two members are ignoring you and stranding you with that fourth person who never talks. Still, you believe in groups because last week even your struggling group gave you a great idea for revising your paper. How might you cope with each of these scenarios (and any other nonworking scenarios you can dream up)?

- For you, what is at stake in your classroom groups?

- Hephzibah claims that groups help writers by giving them voice. Is that true for you and to what degree?

- Can groups be useful even if not every member agrees? In fact, how effective are groups when every member does agree?

- Say that it's Christmas break. You're going home and telling your parents or a good friend about your writing class and writing groups because they've never experienced this method for learning to write.

- Share some tips for sorting out the different advice you receive from peers when sharing ideas or writing in a group.

- If you were able to form a writing group composed of your favorite authors, who would the members be, and how might they get along?

- Before this class, did you align yourself with the cupped hand or the open palm model? Tell some stories.

# 14

# Responding—Really Responding—to Other Students' Writing

## Richard Straub

---

Richard Straub lives on the borders of Tallahassee and teaches
courses in writing, rhetoric, and literature at Florida State
University. The focus of much of his work is on reading, evaluating,
and responding to student writing. He is from Dunmore,
Pennsylvania.

---

Okay. You've got a student paper you have to read and make comments on for
Thursday. It's not something you're looking forward to. But that's alright, you
think. There isn't really all that much to it. Just keep it simple. Read it quickly and mark whatever you see. Say something about the introduction.
Something about details and examples. Ideas you can say you like. Mark any
typos and spelling errors. Make your comments brief. Abbreviate where possible: *awk, good intro, give ex, frag.* Try to imitate the teacher. Mark what he'd
mark and sound like he'd sound. But be cool about it. Don't praise anything
really, but no need to get harsh or cut throat either. Get in and get out. You're
okay, I'm okay. Everybody's happy. What's the problem?

This is, no doubt, a way of getting through the assignment. Satisfy the
teacher and no surprises for the writer. It might just do the trick. But say you
want to do a *good* job. Say you're willing to put in the time and effort—though
time is tight and you know it's not going to be easy—and help the writer look
back on the paper and revise it. And maybe in the process learn something

136

more yourself about writing. What do you look for? How do you sound? How much do you take up? What exactly are you trying to accomplish? Here are some ideas.

## How Should You Look at Yourself as a Responder?

Consider yourself a friendly reader. A test pilot. A roommate who's been asked to look over the paper and tell the writer what you think. Except you don't just take on the role of The Nice Roommate or The Ever-faithful Friend and tell her what she wants to hear. *This all looks good. I wouldn't change a thing. There are a couple places that I think he might not like, but I can see what you're doing there. I'd go with it. Good stuff.* You're supportive. You give her the benefit of the doubt and look to see the good in her writing. But friends don't let friends think their writing is the best thing since *The Great Gatsby* and they don't lead them to think that all is fine and well when it's not. Look to help this friend, this roommate writer—okay, this person in your class—to get a better piece of writing. Point to problems and areas for improvement but do it in a constructive way. See what you can do to push her to do even more than she's done and stretch herself as a writer.

## What Are Your Goals?

First, don't set out to seek and destroy all errors and problems in the writing. You're not an editor. You're not a teacher. You're not a cruise missile. And don't rewrite any parts of the paper. You're not the writer; you're a reader. One of many. The paper is not yours; it's the writer's. She writes. You read. She is in charge of what she does to her writing. That doesn't mean you can't make suggestions. It doesn't mean you can't offer a few sample rewrites here and there, as models. But make it clear they're samples, models. Not rewrites. Not edits. Not corrections. Be reluctant at first even to say what you would do if the paper were yours. It's not yours. Again: Writers write, readers read and show what they're understanding and maybe make suggestions. What to do instead: Look at your task as a simple one. You're there to play back to the writer how you read the paper: what you got from it; what you found interesting; where you were confused; where you wanted more. With this done, you can go on to point out problems, ask questions, offer advice, and wonder out loud with the writer about her ideas. Look to help her improve the writing or encourage her to work on some things as a writer.

## How Do You Get Started?

Before you up and start reading the paper, take a minute (alright, thirty seconds) to make a mental checklist about the circumstances of the writing, the context. You're not going to just read a text. You're going to read a text within a certain context, a set of circumstances that accompany the writing and that you bring to your reading. It's one kind of writing or another, designed for one audience and purpose or another. It's a rough draft or a final draft. The writer is trying to be serious or casual, straight or ironic. Ideally, you'll read the paper with an eye to the circumstances that it was written in and the situation it is looking to create. That means looking at the writing in terms of the assignment, the writer's particular interests and aims, the work you've been doing in class, and the stage of drafting.

- *The assignment:* What kind of writing does the assignment call (or allow) for? Is the paper supposed to be a personal essay? A report? An analysis? An argument? Consider how well the paper before you meets the demands of the kind of writing the writer is taking up.

- *The writer's interests and aims:* What does the writer want to accomplish? If she's writing a personal narrative, say, is she trying to simply recount a past experience? Is she trying to recount a past experience and at the same time amuse her readers? Is she trying to show a pleasant experience on the surface, yet suggest underneath that everything was not as pleasant as it seems? Hone in on the writer's particular aims in the writing.

- *The work of the class:* Try to tie your comments to the concepts and strategies you've been studying in class. If you've been doing a lot of work on using detail, be sure to point to places in the writing where the writer uses detail effectively or where she might provide richer detail. If you've been working on developing arguments through examples and sample cases, indicate where the writer might use such methods to strengthen her arguments. If you've been considering various ways to sharpen the style of your sentences, offer places where the writer can clarify her sentence structure or arrange a sentence for maximum impact. The best comments will ring familiar even as they lead the writer to try to do something she hasn't quite done before, or done in quite the same way. They'll be comforting and understandable even as they create some need to do more, a need to figure out some better way.

- *The stage of drafting:* Is it an early draft? A full but incomplete draft? A nearly final draft? Pay attention to the stage of drafting. Don't try to deal with everything all at once if it's a first, rough draft. Concentrate on the large picture: the paper's focus; the content; the writer's voice. Don't worry about errors and punctuation problems yet. There'll be time for them later. If it's closer to a full draft, go ahead and talk, in addition to the overall content, about arrangement, pacing, and sentence style. Wait till the final draft to give much attention to fine-tuning sentences and dealing in detail with proofreading. Remember: You're not an editor. Leave these sentence revisions and corrections for the writer. It's her paper. And she's going to learn best by detecting problems and making her own changes.

## What to Address in Your Comments?

Try to focus your comments on a couple of areas of writing. Glance through the paper quickly first. Get an idea whether you'll deal mostly with the overall content and purpose of the writing, its shape and flow, or (if these are more or less in order) with local matters of paragraph structure, sentence style, and correctness. Don't try to cover everything that comes up or even all instances of a given problem. Address issues that are most important to address in this paper, at this time.

## Where to Put Your Comments?

Some teachers like to have students write comments in the margins right next to the passage. Some like to have students write out their comments in an end note or in a separate letter to the writer. I like to recommend using both marginal comments and a note or letter at the end. The best of both worlds. Marginal comments allow you to give a quick moment-by-moment reading of the paper. They make it easy to give immediate and specific feedback. You still have to make sure you specify what you're talking about and what you have to say, but they save you some work telling the writer what you're addressing and allow you to focus your end note on things that are most important. Comments at the end allow you to provide some perspective on your response. This doesn't mean that you have to size up the paper and give it a thumbs up or a thumbs down. You can use the end comment to emphasize the key points of your response, explain and elaborate on issues you want to deal with more fully, and mention additional points that you don't want to address in detail. One thing to avoid: plastering comments all over the writing; in between and over the lines of the other person's writing—up, down, and across the page. Write in your space, and let the writer keep hers.

## How to Sound?

Not like a teacher. Not like a judge. Not like an editor or critic or shotgun. (Wouldn't you want someone who was giving you comments not to sound like a teacher's red pen, a judge's ruling, an editor's impatience, a critic's wrath, a shotgun's blast?) Sound like you normally sound when you're speaking with a friend or acquaintance. Talk to the writer. You're not just marking up a text; you're responding to the writer. You're a reader, a helper, a colleague. Try to sound like someone who's a reader, who's helpful, and who's collegial. Supportive. And remember: Even when you're tough and demanding you can still be supportive.

# How Much to Comment?

Don't be stingy. Write most of your comments out in full statements. Instead of writing two or three words, write seven or eight. Instead of making only one brief comment and moving on, say what you have to say and then go back over the statement and explain what you mean or why you said it or note other alternatives. Let the writer know again and again how you are understanding her paper, what you take her to be saying. And elaborate on your key comments. Explain your interpretations, problems, questions, and advice.

# Is It Okay to Be Short and Sweet?

No. At least not most of the time. Get specific. Don't rely on general statements alone. How much have generic comments helped you as a writer? "Add detail." "Needs better structure." "Unclear." Try to let the writer know what exactly the problem is. Refer specifically to the writer's words and make them a part of your comments. "Add some detail on what it was like working at the beach." "I think we'll need to know more about your high school crowd before we can understand the way you've changed." "This sentence is not clear. Were *you* disappointed or were *they* disappointed?" This way the writer will see what you're talking about, and she'll have a better idea what to work on.

# Do You Praise or Criticize or What?

Be always of two (or three) minds about your response to the paper. You like the paper, but it could use some more interesting detail. You found this statement interesting, but these ideas in the second paragraph are not so hot. It's an alright paper, but it could be outstanding if the writer said what was really bothering her. Always be ready to praise. But always look to point to places that are not working well or that are not yet working as well as they might. Always be ready to expect more from the writer.

# How to Present Your Comments?

Don't steer away from being critical. Feel free—in fact, feel obliged—to tell the writer what you like and don't like, what is and is not working, and where you think it can be made to work better. But use some other strategies, too. Try to engage the writer in considering her choices and thinking about possible ways to improve the paper. Make it a goal to write two or three comments that look to summarize or paraphrase what the writer is saying. Instead of *telling* the reader what to do, *suggest* what she might do. Identify the questions that are raised for you as you reader:

- Play back your way of understanding the writing:
    This seems to be the real focus of the paper, the issue you seem
        most interested in.
    So you're saying that you really weren't interested in her
        romantically?
- Temper your criticisms:
    This sentence is a bit hard to follow.
    I'm not sure this paragraph is necessary.
- Offer advice:
    It might help to add an example here.
    Maybe save this sentence for the end of the paper.
- Ask questions, especially real questions:
    What else were you feeling at the time?
    What kind of friend? Would it help to say?
    Do you need this opening sentence?
    In what ways were you "a daddy's little girl"?
- Explain and follow up on your initial comments:
    You might present this episode first. This way we can see what you
        mean when you say that he was always too busy.
    How did you react? Did you cry or yell? Did you walk away?
    This makes her sound cold and calculating. Is that what you want?
- Offer some praise, and then explain to the writer why the writing works:
    Good opening paragraph. You've got my attention.
    Good detail. It tells me a lot about the place.
    I like the descriptions you provide—for instance, about your
        grandmother cooking, at the bottom of page 1; about her house,
        in the middle of page 2; and about how she said her rosary at
        night: "quick but almost pleading, like crying without tears."

## How Much Criticism? How Much Praise?

Challenge yourself to write as many praise comments as criticisms. When you praise, praise well. Think about it. Sincerity and specificity are everything when it comes to a compliment.

## How Much Should You Be Influenced by What You Know About the Writer?

Consider the person behind the writer when you make your comments. If she's not done so well in class lately, maybe you can give her a pick-me-up in your comments. If she's shy and seems reluctant to go into the kind of personal detail the paper seems to need, encourage her. Make some suggestions or tell her what you would do. If she's confident and going on arrogant, see what you can do to challenge her with the ideas she presents in the paper. Look for other views she may not have thought about, and find ways to lead her to consider them. Always be ready to look at the text in terms of the writer behind the text.

Good comments, this listing shows, require a lot from a reader. But you don't have to make a checklist out of these suggestions and go through each one methodically as you read. It's amazing how they all start coming together when you look at your response as a way of talking with the writer seriously about the writing, recording how you experience the words on the page and giving the writer something to think about for revision. The more you see examples of thoughtful commentary and the more you try to do it yourself, the more you'll get a feel for how it's done.

Here's a set of student comments on a student paper. They were done in the last third of a course that focused on the personal essay and concentrated on helping students develop the content and thought of their writing. The class had been working on finding ways to develop and extend the key statements of their essays (by using short, representative details, full-blown examples, dialogue, and multiple perspectives) and getting more careful about selecting and shaping parts of their writing. The assignment called on students to write an essay or an autobiographical story where they looked to capture how they see (or have seen) something about one or both of their parents—some habits, attitudes, or traits their parents have taken on. They were encouraged to give shape to their ideas and experiences in ways that went beyond their previous understandings and try things they hadn't tried in their writing. More a personal narrative than an essay, Todd's paper looks to capture one distinct difference in the way his mother and father disciplined their children. It is a rough draft that will be taken through one or possibly two more revisions. Readers were asked to offer whatever feedback they could that might help the writer with the next stage of writing (Figure 14–1).

This is a full and thoughtful set of comments. The responder, Jeremy, creates himself not as a teacher or critic but first of all as a reader, one who is intent on saying how he takes the writing and what he'd like to hear more about:

> Good point. Makes it more unlikely that you should be the one to get caught.
> Great passage. Really lets the reader know what you were thinking.
> Was there a reason you were first or did it just happen that way?
> Would he punish you anyway or could you just get away with things?

He makes twenty-two comments on the paper—seventeen statements in the margins and five more in the end note. The comments are written out in full statements, and they are detailed and specific. They make his response into a lively exchange with the writer, one person talking with another about what he's said. Well over half of the comments are follow-up comments that explain, illustrate, or qualify other responses.

## Figure 14–1

*Jeremy·*

Todd
ENG 1
Rick Straub
Assignment 8b

"Uh, oh"

When I called home from the police station I was praying *I like this paragraph. It immediately* that my father would answer the phone. He would listen to what I *lets the reader* had to say and would react comely, logical, and in a manner that *relate to you and* would keep my mother from screaming her head off. If my Mother *also pulling* was to answer the phone I would have to explain myself quickly in *the reader in.* order to keep her from having a heart attack.

When I was eleven years old I hung out with a group of boys that were almost three years older than me. The five of us did all the things that young energetic kids did playing ball, riding bikes, and getting in to trouble. [Because they were older they worried less about getting in trouble and the consequences of there actions than I did.] *Good point, makes it more unlikely that you should be the one to get caught*

*what other things did you do to get into trouble? Bio or is it irrevalent?* My friends and I would always come home from school, drop our backpacks off and head out in the neighborhood to find something to do.✓ Our favorite thing to do was to find construction cites and steal wood to make tree forts in the woods or skateboard ramps. So one day, coming home from school, we noticed a couple new houses being built near our neighborhood. It was a prime cite for wood, nails, and anything else we could get our hands on. We discussed our plan on the bus and decided that we would all meet there after dropping our stuff off at home. [I remember being a little at hesitant first because it was close to my house but beyond the boundaries my parents had set *great passage really lets the reader know what you were thinking* for me.✓ Of course I went because I didn't want to be the odd man out and have to put up with all the name calling.] I dropped my bag off and I headed to the construction cite.

I meet my friends there and we began to search the different houses for wood and what not. We all picked up a couple of things and were about to leave when one of my friends noticed a what looked to be a big tool shed off behind one of the houses. It looked promising so we decided that we should check it out. Two of the boys in the group said that they had all the wood they could carry and said they were going home. The rest of us headed down to the shed to take a look.

Once there we noticed that the shed had been broken in to previously. The lock on it had been busted on the hinges were *was there anyone you were first* bent.✓ I opened the door to the shed and stepped inside to take a look around while my friends waited outside. It was dark inside but I could tell the place had been ransacked, there was nothing *or did it just* to take so I decided to leave. I heard my to friends say some *happen that* thing so turned back around to site of them running away. I *way* thought that they were playing a joke on me so I casually walked

*continues*

The comments focus on the content and development of the writing, in line with the assignment, the stage of drafting, and the work of the course. They also view the writing rhetorically, in terms of how the text has certain effects on readers. Although there are over two dozen wording or sentence-level errors in the paper, he decides, wisely, to stick with the larger matters of writing. Yet even as he offers a pretty full set of comments he doesn't ever take control over the text. His comments are placed unobtrusively on the page, and he doesn't try to close things down or decide things for the writer. He offers praise, encouragement, and direction. What's more, he pushes the writer to do

*continued*                                                    *Figure 14–1*

out only to see a cop car parked near one of the houses under construction. As soon as I saw that cop car I took off but was stopped when a big hand pulled at that back of my shirt. I watched my friends run until they were out of cite and then I turned around.

The cop had me sit in the squad car while he asked me questions. He asked me if I knew those kids that ran off and I said "Nnnnnoooooooo". He asked me if I had broken in to that shed and I said "Nnnnnoooooo". The cop wrote down what I was saying all the while shaking his head. Then he told me that I wasn't being arrested but I would have to go down to the station to call parents and have them pick me up. Upon hearing that I nearly soiled my undershorts. "My God, I'm dead. My mom is going to kill me".

*[handwritten margin note: what else happened at the police station? How long were you there?]*

At the station the officer showed me the whole station, jail cells and everything. An obvious tactic to try and scare me, which worked. That plus the thought of my mom answering the phone and me trying to explain what happened nearly made me sick.

"Wwwwhhhaatttt! You're where?" She would say.

"The police station mom," uh oh, hear it comes.

"Ooooohhhh my God, my son is criminal," so loud I would have to pull the phone away from my ear.

*[handwritten margin note: maybe you could say more as to why you think your mom is like this.]*

She had this uncanny ability to blow things out of proportion right from the start. She would assume the worse and then go from there. This was a classic example of why I could never go to her if I had any bad news. She would start screaming, get upset, and then go bitch at my father. My father is a pretty laid back but when ever my mother started yelling at him about me, he would get angry and come chew me out worse than if I had just gone to him in the first place.

If my father were to answer the phone he would respond with out raising his voice. He would examine the situation in a logical manner and make a decision form there.

"Uhhmmm(long pause). You're at the police station."

"Yeah dad, I didn't get arrested they just had me come down here so I had to tell you."

"Uhm, so you didn't get arrested(long pause). Well(long pause), I'll come pick you up and will talk about then".

*[handwritten margin note: Did your Dad get into trouble as a kid? So he knows what it's like? Explain why he reacts as he does.]*

I feel like I can relate to my father much better then I can to my mother. He has a cool and collective voice that can take command of any situation. I always feel like he understands me, like he knows what I'm thinking all the time. This comes in real handy when I get in trouble.

*[handwritten margin note: would he punish you anyway or could you just get away with things?]*

*[handwritten right-margin note: I like the way you use dialogue in this section to illustrate how each of your parents would react and then explain to the reader what each of them are like. It works well.]*

*continues*

more than he has already done, to extend the boundaries of his examination. In keeping with the assignment and the larger goals of the course, he calls on Todd in several comments to explore the motivations and personalities behind his parents' different ways of disciplining:

> Maybe you could say more as to why you think your mom is like this.
> Did your dad get into trouble as a kid so he know what it's like? Explain why he reacts as he does.

He is careful, though, not to get presumptuous and make decisions for the writer. Instead, he offers options and points to possibilities:

> Perhaps more on your understanding of why your parents react as they do.
> What other things did you do to get into trouble? Or is it irrelevant?

*continued*                                                    *Figure 14–1*

```
     I called home.  Sweet beading on my lip.

     "Hello", my mom said.  Oh geez, I'm dead.

     "Mom can I talk to dad?"

     "Why, what's wrong?"

      "Oh, nothing, I just need talk to him," yes, this is going
to work!

     "Hold on," she said.

     "Hello," my father said.

      "Dad, I'm at the police station,"  I told him the whole
story of what happened.  He reacted exactly as I expect he would.

     "Uhhmmm(long pause).  You're at the police station..........
```

*I really like the ending, it tells the reader what is going to happen without having to explain it step by step. Good paper, I like the use of dialogue. Perhaps more on your understanding of why your parents react as they do.*

From start to finish he takes on the task of reading and responding and leaves the work of writing and revising to Todd.

Jeremy's response is not in a class by itself. A set of comments to end all commentary on Todd's paper. He might have done well, for instance, to recognize how much this paper works because of the way Todd arranges the story. He could have done more to point to what's not working in the writing or what could be made to work better. He might have asked Todd for more details about his state of mind when he got caught by the policeman and while he was being held at the police station. He might have urged him more to make certain changes. He might even have said, if only in a brief warning, something about the number of errors across the writing. But this is moot and just. Different readers are always going to pick up on different things and respond in different ways, and no one reading or response is going to address everything that might well be addressed, in the way it might best be addressed. All responses are incomplete and provisional—one reader's way of reading and reacting to the text in front of him. And any number of other responses, presented in any number of different ways, might be as useful or maybe even more useful to Todd as he takes up his work with the writing.

All this notwithstanding, Jeremy's comments are solid. They are full. They are thoughtful. And they are respectful. They take the writing and the writer seriously and address the issues that are raised responsibly. His comments do what commentary on student writing should optimally do. They turn the writer back into his writing and lead him to reflect on his choices and aims, to consider and reconsider his intentions as a writer and the effects the words on the page will have on readers. They help him see what he can work on in revision and what he might deal with in his ongoing work as a writer.

## Sharing Ideas

- What are your experiences with responding to other students' writing? Have you done so in other classes? How did that work out? Were you able to discuss your responses? In small groups or large groups? Which situation did you like best?

- Do you have any papers where others have responded to your writing? Collect one or more and see how the responses stack up against Rick's guidelines. Having read his essay, what would you say your respondent did well and needs to learn to do better?

- In the same way, after everyone in your small group responds to a first paper, go over those papers/responses together in a group and look at what was done and what could be done to improve the quality of responses. In addition, you might try to characterize each of you as a responder: What are your habits? What character/persona do you take on? Would you like to be responded to by the responder you find you are through this group analysis?

- Look at Hint Sheet I in this collection. How do my suggestions for response to student writers sound the same or different from Rick's suggestions? Do we come from the same "school" of responding or do we suggest different approaches? Characterize the differences or similarities you find.

- Rick shows you a responder—Jeremy—and the comments he wrote on Todd's paper. If you were Todd, how would you feel about Jeremy's responses? Do you agree with Rick's analysis of Jeremy's comments? What three or four additional things would you tell Todd about his paper?

- What are your insights into responding? What has worked for you? What do you wish people would do or not do when they respond to your writing? What would make you most inclined to listen to responses and use them to change your work?

# 15

# What Is a Grade?

## Pat Belanoff

---

Pat Belanoff is the Director of Undergraduate Studies (and former director of the Writing Program) at the State University of New York at Stony Brook, which is on the north shore of Long Island, a little more than an hour from New York City. She has coauthored two textbooks, one a freshman composition book with Peter Elbow called *A Community of Writers* and a somewhat off-beat grammar book with Betsy Rorschach and Mia Oberlink called *The Right Handbook*. She has also coedited a collection of essays (*Portfolios: Process and Product*) with Marcia Dickson. Pat also writes about the women of Old English poetry and spends more time than she should doing crossword puzzles.

---

Grades and school seem synonymous. Grades are the evidence educators, parents, politicians, and other citizens cite to demonstrate that students have (or have not) learned what they should learn. Such reliance on grades presumes that the student who gets an A has learned more than the student who gets a B, who in turn has learned more than the student who gets a C and so on down the line to an F: the student who gets one of those has obviously not learned much. Many in our society and in the schools accept without question these connections between grades and the quality of student learning.

But those who accept these connections argue for their validity within some fields far more strongly than within other fields. For example, most people are more willing to credit a ninety on a math or physics test than on a composition or on a paper responding to some piece of literature. Students, reflecting this societal attitude, often complain to me about the nature of

English studies—both literature and composition. It is the objectivity–subjectivity contrast that they usually bring up, lamenting that they wish grades on compositions could be objective like their math and physics grades. In those classes, they tell me, you know for sure what's right and what's wrong. In a writing class though, these same students say, everything is subjective: how well one does depends on what the teacher likes and dislikes—there's nothing substantial to guide one to better grades. Students come into my office to complain that a paper they got a poor mark on would have gotten an A or B from a previous teacher. And I suspect that among themselves they confess to the opposite: that some paper they just got an A or B on would never have gotten such a good grade from a previous teacher. They know from personal experience how greatly grading standards differ from teacher to teacher. Reacting to this, some students tell me that it isn't possible to get grades that mean anything in English classes and that they've come to hate English as a result.

Teachers of other subjects sometimes express similar judgments. I remember well, as a beginning faculty member, attending an interdepartmental meeting at which a member of the history faculty said that he envied English teachers because they didn't have to be bothered with "covering" a set range of materials every semester. When he was pressed to explain himself, he continued by saying that there was no "real" subject matter in English classes, only opinions and subjective ideas, no "facts." "How do you decide what grade to give?" he asked me. "It's all so subjective!"

How do I respond to these charges of subjectivity? First, I agree. I know, even better than they, that teachers do not give the same grades to the same pieces—particularly when these teachers work in unlike schools. But, rather than apologize for this lack of conformity, I actually celebrate it. I'll get back to why later in this essay.

After conceding the truth of these charges of subjectivity, I encourage those who make them to consider whether other subjects are as "objective" as they appear. Not all biology teachers cover the same material; not all of them focus on the same subjects when they make up their tests, and not all of them weigh answers in the same way. Biology teachers differ not only about what to teach but also about what's most important in the classroom. Some teachers think that how we discover information is more important than the information itself. They will teach and test quite differently from teachers who see their main goal as transferring information into the heads of their students. Furthermore, the deeper one goes into any subject, the less objective issues become. Astrophysicists look at the same data, but some posit a "big bang" theory for creation and others do not. Paleontologists study the same geology and the same bones and disagree about why dinosaurs disappeared from the earth. Newcomers in these fields gradually join these debates and earn the right to interpret data in their own ways.

Literature classes sometimes mimic the sequence I've just set forth for physical science: less and less agreement or objectivity as one moves deeper into the subject. Perhaps the teacher will give a test on the facts of a piece of literature: who wrote it, when, which character does what, where the figures of speech are, and so forth. Even literature teachers who approach their subject this way, however, move fairly quickly to interpretation, to an assessment of what the piece "means," which is equivalent to what the geologist does as he "reads" old bones and old geological formations. English teachers do seem to move to the level of interpretation more quickly than mathematicians do; but both fields deal with facts *and* interpretations. Both fields, that is, are objective *and* subjective.

I'm mainly a writing teacher, not a literature teacher, and must acknowledge that the objectivity–subjectivity issue is even more pronounced in a writing class than in a literature class. In the latter, there's at least some secure basis in that students are responding to published, established texts. But, in a writing class, there's a felt sense that the texts being produced are totally personal in a way nothing else in school is. We know, of course, that they're not totally personal: what we write is always partially determined by our backgrounds, our culture, our prior educational experiences, our past reading and writing activities. But all that is filtered through our sense of ourselves. Mikhail Bakhtin, a well-regarded Russian language scholar, once wrote that any word we use is only half ours, but that we can make words our own by saturating them with our own intentions and purposes. The more we're able to do that, the more individualized what we say and write becomes and the less likely it is to be like anything else a teacher has ever read. No A paper is exactly like another A paper in the same was as 2 + 2 is always 4. Thus, the grades of English teachers can never be based on exact correspondences between papers.

I celebrate and encourage this diversity. A major goal of the humanities is to guide students—not just while they're acquiring facts, but also while they're learning to interpret them. As a writing teacher, my task is to help students gain control *through words* over their developing interpretations. All of us struggle with language when we need to express ideas new to us. My particular students struggle as their already established ideas and thoughts interact with the new ideas and thoughts a new world (college) presents to them. As they react, they will agree with some of their classmates in one way, with others in some different ways and perhaps stand alone on still another issue. No one's ideas, opinions, and reactions are exactly like anyone else's. As a teacher I'm in the business of getting students to think, not of getting them to think like everyone else or even like me. Teachers who can get students to spit back information on tests will never know what these students are really thinking—or if they're thinking at all about what they're supposedly learning.

For the same reasons we do not react exactly like anyone else, none of us reads exactly like anyone else either. Thus possibilities multiply for diverse judgments—not only am I reading something I've never read before, I'm also reading in a way unique to me. It seems like common sense to see meaning as existing in the words on the page, but black marks on paper mean nothing until someone reads them. Meaning can only develop as a human mind interacts and inevitably interprets those black marks—and human minds come in all varieties. Quite simply, I never react to a student text exactly like any other teacher any more than I react exactly like anyone else when I read *Hamlet* or *The Color Purple*. And when the issue shifts to what these texts mean, differences multiply even more.

Many students do not like to hear this; it turns a world of seeming certainty into formless mush. It may be easier to have a teacher who tells you exactly how to write a paper. But once you realize that no teacher (because she is human) reads like any other teacher, you also realize that those directions for an A paper are valid only for that class. You don't learn much to carry to the next class if the teacher does not explain her standards for that A.

So far, I've written of the subjectivity resulting from the necessarily subjective acts of writing and reading. But subjectivity has other causes, one of which is the school setting. Because I've taught at a number of institutions of various kinds I've been forced to realize that grades are always relative to the institution where they're given. An A at one school isn't the same as an A at another school. What that means is that I'm judging each paper I read against other papers I've read at the particular school I'm teaching at. It also means that if that same paper were given to me at a different time at a different school, it would receive a different grade. And even within a department or program, grades are relative to the class in which they're assigned. A paper that earns a B in a developmental class will not be likely to get a B in freshman composition. And a B paper in freshman composition will not be likely to get a B in an advanced or upper-level writing class.

What's the alternative to the seeming unfairness or inconsistency? The alternative is to believe that somewhere out in the clouds is a model A paper, B paper, and so forth and that every paper I read (even though it is unique) can be graded relative to that model. Or, even more preposterous, that I was somehow born knowing what an A paper is. There are teachers who act as though they believe this is true, as though there is some absolute measure against which all student papers can be measured and that they know with absolute certainty what that measure is. Unfortunately for them no one seems to agree on any real, not-in-the-clouds paper which should serve as that model A paper. No sooner does a teacher offer one, than some other teacher finds fault with it and offers a different one. Usually teachers can only agree on the traits of good writing *in the abstract*. As soon as they start looking at individual papers, agreement disintegrates.

But even if we could get writing teachers together from all over the country and agree on a paper to which we would all give an A, we would not agree on how closely other papers approached our model, nor would we necessarily agree on what made that model A paper a model A paper. Some of us would cite its content first, some of us its organization, some of us its language, some of us the relevance of its arguments, some of us its originality, creativity, and imaginative power.

What I'm saying is that I inevitably judge the paper in front of me in terms of all other papers I've read. I make no apologies for that. That's the only way any of us ever judge anything: persons are beautiful in relation to others, movies are acclaimed or not in relation to other movies, scenery is lovely in relation to other scenes the observer has seen. I cannot know beauty, perfection, or loveliness apart from specific examples. It is hardly to be expected that decisions on the quality of writing could be made any differently. Thus the model of an A I have in my head is a product of all the papers I have read as well as of my own individual way of reading.

To be honest, I hate grading. I love teaching; I love talking to students about their writing, sharing my responses with them, discussing their subjects, listening and reacting to their ideas. But I hate grading papers. Most students work hard on their papers; many of them dig deep into themselves to express ideas and opinions important to them. It isn't easy to put "C" or "D" on such endeavors. It may be easy (I'm not really sure about this) for students and teachers in other classes to distance themselves a bit from the grades. A physics teacher gives problems to be worked out, formulas to be decoded and solved, and so forth. If a student does poorly, the teacher concludes that he didn't study or he's just not destined to be a physics student. The student can console himself by acknowledging that he should have studied more or that physics is just not his subject.

Somehow it's different when one writes a paper. It's hard to keep oneself out of it. The assumption—contrary to that about physics—is that everyone *can* "do" English. Everyone is assumed to have opinions and responses to events, to pieces of writing, to ideas presented by others; everyone is *not* expected to understand or master physics. Having an opinion on personal, social, and political issues or a reaction to a poem or an editorial is within the capabilities of all of us. We can't escape by saying that this isn't our subject. Thus we feel judged by grades on papers in ways we don't feel judged by a grade on a physics test. What we write (that is, if we genuinely commit ourselves to the writing) feels as though it comes from somewhere inside us; the answer to a physics problem feels like it comes from inside our heads only.

Perhaps the solution would be to abandon grading altogether in writing classes. I confess that this is a solution that appeals to me greatly. Instead of putting grades on a paper, I could simply respond to it: let the writer know my reactions to what it says and how it says it. If a student did all the assignments, met my attendance requirements, participated in class, and mostly got papers in on time, she would get a "Satisfactory" for the semester. There are colleges, universities, and even some high schools that have grading systems like this. Perhaps some of you reading this article may even attend such a school; if you do, you undoubtedly have an opinion about the value of it.

Unfortunately (for me, at any rate), most colleges and universities require grades. Mine does. Therefore, I've been forced to do a lot of thinking about what grades are and how to make them as fair as possible. Almost every time I sit down to grade papers, I ask myself: "What *are* grades; what do they measure?"

Despite my questions and doubts (or perhaps because of them), I argue for the validity of two kinds of grading in writing classes: grading by groups of teachers and grading by individual teachers who have worked through standards with their students. I am not going to argue that such grades are *not* subjective, but I will argue that they can be meaningful within the environment in which they're given.

If grades are only meaningful within limited environments, it's logical to argue for the joint awarding of grades by those within the environment. Gymnastics competitions come to mind as a possible model. For each performance of each gymnast, six or seven people give independent scores, and these are averaged or added up in some way. (It's interesting to consider that in gymnastics scoring the highest and the lowest scores are eliminated before the averaging is done.) In such situations, I don't have to convince anyone of my opinions; I just vote. Perhaps students' papers ought to be judged like gymnastics contests: six or seven teachers would give each paper a grade, and the actual grade would be an average or total of those given, after discounting both the best and the worst grade. The problem with such a scheme, as far as I'm concerned, is that I would be spending all my time grading papers! Since I hate grading, my enthusiasm for teaching might be considerably dampened. Although it isn't feasible to have every student's paper graded by six or seven other teachers, it *is* feasible for teachers to share grading once or twice during a semester. If two or three teachers jointly grade a set of each other's papers during the semester, both they and their students will develop a sense of community judgment.

Even teachers within an isolated classroom can make grades useful for themselves and their students. A teacher can, of course, simply put grades on papers and leave it up to the students to figure out what she rewards and punishes. Some students are quite good at this. Quite a few are not. I believe that if students are going to get better, I have to explain the standards I use to arrive at grades. I consider this part of my responsibility.

I sometimes ask college freshmen to bring to class a graded paper they wrote in high school, especially if the paper has some comments on it in addition to the grade. Then the class and I together analyze the paper and draw some conclusions about what the teacher who graded it valued. I may also give my students some papers from other years and ask them to arrange them in order from the one they consider the most effective to the one they consider least effective. We then talk about our personal standards, where we agree and disagree and why. Often I do need to introduce some standards into the grading process that may not grow out of our discussions simply because freshmen are new to the academic community. At the same time, I aim to help them understand how the standards I introduce may be different from the standards of other writing teachers. I cannot do this honestly unless I make it my business to be more familiar with the standards of those with whom I work most closely: my colleagues in the department who are teaching the same courses I am and my colleagues who are assigning writing in other subject areas.

On the basis of all these discussions, my students and I strive to reach some conclusions on standards without privileging any particular set of standards: mine, theirs, their former teachers. I then give them some papers to judge on the basis of the standards we've developed together. And, finally, I give them several assignments that will be graded on the basis of these standards. In the process, I am teaching what may be the most important lesson of all: the ability to write for a particular audience. If I can help students understand how to get an A or B in my class, I will be helping them learn to figure out how to analyze and impress other audiences too, both in and out of school. When I give assignments that will be judged by different standards, the class and I again discuss these fully.

No matter whether I grade individually or as a member of a group of teachers, putting one grade on one paper can be misleading because others (including the student who writes the paper) may deduce more from the grade than is warranted. Since neither I nor the student author can know whether she can write with equal skill on a different task, a grade can be meaningful only as a judgment of a particular paper, not as a judgment of a writer's overall skills. For this reason, I prefer to give a grade to two or more papers at a time. In fact, I prefer to grade a portfolio of a student's work at mid- and end-semester and give one grade for all the work with commentary explaining the strengths and weaknesses of the whole portfolio. Students can then get some sense of how I assess their overall skill in terms of what I, their classmates, my program, and my particular school value.

I recognize that not all teachers have either the time or the desire to discuss standards with students. If you have such a teacher, you can find ways to get at these standards. You can analyze graded papers and draw conclusions about what the teacher likes and dislikes and then make an appointment with the teacher to test these conclusions. (You'll learn more if you do some analysis too rather than just taking a paper in and asking for an explanation of the grade or for advice on getting a better grade.) Or you can ask a teacher if she is willing to read a draft of a paper several days before it's due. The worst she can do is say no. But most teachers are gratified to talk to a student who's willing to put in the time to improve his writing. My final suggestion in such situations is that you form study groups (research has shown that such groups result in better grades for participants) in which you share papers with one another before they're submitted for grading.

When I have this discussion with students in my classes, there's always more than one student who interprets me as saying that only conformity will lead to a good grade. My answer to that is not usually what they want to hear, for I tell them that language use always involves conformity. Speaking words others can understand means conforming to built-in rules of language. I can't give words my own meaning and adjust grammatical rules to my own liking. Creativity and originality can only develop *within* established meanings and rules. But that doesn't mean a language user cannot use the meanings and the rules in new, exciting ways—writers have been doing this for centuries. Taking into consideration a teacher's or class standards is the same as being tuned in to your audience. Once tuned in, you can decide whether to play to it or whether to try to influence these standards themselves—but, at least, you have a choice. And if you do strive to persuade your teacher and classmates of the validity of somewhat different standards and are able to meet them and thus demonstrate that validity, you may succeed in altering classroom standards. I've had students who could do that.

Frankly, I would be frightened about the future of our culture if we ever arrived at a point where I was sure that the grades I gave were the same as those all other teachers would give. This would suggest some rather unpleasant things about the future of discussion in the world. Not all of us think Shakespeare was the greatest writer the world has ever produced; not all of us think Jacqueline Suzanne is the worst writer the world has ever produced. Most of us fall somewhere in between on both these points. And most of us like it that way; but that means we have to accept and learn to value varying evaluations of student texts also.

Most decisions we make in our personal and professional lives are more like the problematic ones we wrestle with in English and writing classes; they're not usually as clear-cut as the answers on math tests. I'd like to think that coming to terms with the subjectivity of grades is good training for living with the subjectivity inherent in the world around us. But perhaps that's stretching my point too far. What is important within the world of the individual classroom is that grades can be useful and meaningful to students who understand the basis for them and who recognize that one grade on one paper can never be a judgment on all their writing.

---

## Shared Ideas

- Tell some stories of you, your writing, and grades.

- Have you encountered the subjectivity–objectivity problem before? What do you think about Pat's analogy to paper grading and gymnastics competitions?

- Are you "graded" in other (nonacademic) areas of your life? List the ways this happens. For instance, we may feel we receive grades in the workplace, on a date, when we go hunting and fishing, within our relationships, and so on.

- Are you willing to abolish grades and just get on with learning? What, for you, is at stake in earning grades in school?
- Have you ever learned in a nongraded and noncompetitive situation? Describe how that felt.
- How do you know when writing is "good"?
- Have you ever had to grade someone else? What did you do and what did it feel like?
- Using Pat's discussion, design your ideal writing class—how would grades work, matter, be assigned?
- If writing is a way of thinking, if writing is a recursive ongoing activity, leading to more and more revision and discovery through revision, what does it mean to stop the process and grade a paper?

# 16

# Resisting Writing/Resisting Writing Teachers

## Beth Daniell and Art Young

---

A former high school teacher, Beth Daniell now writes about literacy and teaches composition, literature, and women's studies courses at Clemson University. Her idea of fun and relaxation is to read murder mysteries and spy novels and to write in her journal. As a native of Georgia who has lived in Texas, West Virginia, and Illinois, she is happy to be back in the South. In upstate South Carolina, she explains, the dirt is red, the pine trees are tall, when it snows there's a holiday, and you can play tennis outdoors in February.

Art Young holds a unique appointment at Clemson University in South Carolina, where he is Campbell Professor of English and Engineering. In addition to teaching English courses, he works with engineering students and faculty in the Effective Technical Communication Program. When he is not involved with school work (and sometimes when he is), he enjoys traveling, sports, hiking, and fishing.

---

Last year Steve sat in the back row of Art Young's English 102 class. Steve was about twenty years old, a couple of years older than most students in the class, and when he volunteered in discussions, it was usually with a cryptic or sarcastic remark that elicited a few chuckles from his classmates and teacher. At

Clemson University, where we teach, English 102 is the second in the required first-year sequence in composition; its purpose is to develop students' abilities in argumentive writing, library research, and the academic essay. In such essays, students write about academic rather than personal subjects, develop an original thesis or perspective on a course subject, and integrate appropriate sources from their research to provide a knowledgeable context for their own contribution to the issue at hand. The first academic essay assigned in Art's class that semester was to be on the topic of civil disobedience. The class had read and discussed several articles on the subject in their textbook. In this persuasive essay students were to use these sources as background for developing an informed opinion about civil disobedience. A traditional assignment, to be sure.

The students read and critiqued each other's rough drafts in small groups; after they revised these drafts, they submitted them for Art's feedback before the final copy was due. When he returned their drafts with his comments, he asked the students to take a few moments of class time to reread their essays and consider his comments. He then asked them to write a brief response on how useful his comments were to them. Art had hoped such responses would give him constructive feedback, open communication between him and the students early in the course, and enable him to see each of his twenty-two students as individual writers. Steve wrote:

> I don't know what I am supposed to be writing to you. I read your critique and I think I disagree with 95% of them. It seems to me you want us to be robots and make the same argument. I can care less whether I'm right or wrong for two reasons. One I don't care about this topic. There is no relevence to real life. I came to college to learn about finance not English, History, and Biology. Yet I've spend my money taking an entire year of these bullshit courses. That money comes out of my pocket and I shouldn't have to pay an entire year's tuition for useless info that I learned in high school. Secondly, I got plenty of other classes and don't have 3 or 4 hours a night wasting time on this. Give me a damn D or F I don't care, and neither will my employer who's already offered me a job. This is my essay, and not going to do anymore than I have to. If you don't like it then give me a bad grade. If you don't like this response, well tough luck!!

Steve's response to Art is behavior that we would call resistance. Resistance can be defined as those games or strategies, ranging from fun to deadly serious, played by those with little or no power against those with power; the point of resistance is to diffuse authority, to thwart the plans of the bosses. Resistance can be as simple as a joke about an authority figure, or it can be, as in Nazi-occupied France, an act of violence like blowing up a munitions train. Resistance also can be an act of civil disobedience, as in Alabama in 1956 when Rosa Parks decided to face arrest and sit in front of the bus. History tells us that students have always resisted the authority of teachers.

And in one sense they should. How can students learn to think for themselves if they don't resist the authority of teachers and other powerful figures in their lives like parents and government officials? Sometimes students need to resist to protect themselves from dishonest or oppressive teachers or administrators. An example occurs at the end of *Dead Poets' Society*, when the boys stand on their desks as a salute to the teacher, played by Robin Williams, who had been fired because he tried to instill in his students a sense of individualism. The teacher in *Dead Poets' Society* wanted the boys he taught to resist the unthinking conformity he saw both in the school and in American society, but in this scene they do even more: They resist the headmaster's lies. If we study acts of resistance, we may come to understand a particular situation better than we did before. That is, resistance can offer a critique. An act of resistance may not be malicious disobedience but rather a criticism of injustice or protest of events that are unfolding in a way the resistor does not endorse.

Students often resist writing and writing teachers, and such resistance can be either healthy or unhealthy. As part of the classroom dynamic, resistance can play a role in promoting learning and critical thinking or it can be a way to refuse to learn or to become critically engaged. For example, with hours of drill on *lie/lay* and *sit/set*, tests on the eight comma rules, fill-in-the-blank questions about the ways to develop a paragraph, five points off for every misspelled word, students are probably right to resist such mindless "drill and kill" exercises often associated with being taught to write. Of course, usage, punctuation, paragraph development, and spelling are important in writing well, but we think that students realize that heavy emphasis on these issues by teachers often deflects attention from what students are thinking and saying. Unfortunately, schooling sometimes teaches students that the teacher is the enemy and that school work is irrelevant and alien to their concerns.

But not all resistance in school provides a critical examination of abusive situations. Some resistance is habit: resist the teacher, any teacher; resist the work, any work. As writing teachers, we are frustrated when students resist for the sake of resisting. After all, we are teachers who try, admittedly not always successfully, to make our classes and our assignments fulfill institutional goals and also be relevant to our students' lives. But sometimes, despite our good intentions, students—like Steve—resist our teaching. In this essay, we speculate about why Steve and other students resist writing and writing teachers. Further, we suggest that sometimes students who resist our approach to teaching writing don't realize that they are resisting a kind of teaching that is also critical of the traditional "drill and kill" approach to teaching writing.

But perhaps an instructive way to continue our discussion of student resistance is to focus on teacher perception, to explore Art's reaction to Steve and his writing.

When Art read Steve's response, his first reaction was defensive. What had he done to create such hostility? What could he have done to avoid it? Although none of the other students wrote a similar response, was it because they were too timid to do so? Did Steve speak for many students who dared not speak for themselves? Next, Art realized that Steve was making this a personal matter, as if Art were forcing him to do something that was against his best interests. Steve may have targeted Art's writing course as symbolic of a more pervasive problem created by an educational system with its "useless" general education courses. For neither Art nor the English Department required that Steve take this course; Steve's major department required it. Art might explain that to Steve, refer him to the Head of the Finance Department for answers on why they required useless courses, and thus deflect responsibility from his own teaching.

Art's third reaction was anger. He was working hard to provide Steve and his classmates with a meaningful educational experience, and this was the thanks he got. He had taken the time and trouble to provide constructive feedback on Steve's essay, while many of his colleagues skipped this step and saved themselves several hours of effort and the hassles of dealing with unappreciative students like Steve. Who did Steve think he was anyway—to speak to a teacher that way? This student seemed to delight in challenging the teacher's authority; he had passed around his response so that several classmates could read it before he turned it in. He flouted the power Art held over his grades. Maybe that was the best response—take him up on his offer to receive an F. Steve already implied the course was a waste of his time—which meant any time Art spent reading and thinking about Steve's writing was a waste of both their time. Hadn't Steve said that neither he nor his employer would care if he received an F in the course? So Art could give him an F on this essay and promise him further F's unless his attitude changed. Or Steve could drop the course. If he didn't like this response, "well tough luck!!"

As his anger continued to grow, Art's next reaction was to use Steve's own writing to refute his argument, a very clever and academic thing to do. Did he learn in high school to make pronoun reference errors (critique/them) or misspell "relevence"? Do his employers really want his writing to be full of errors? So civil disobedience has no relevance to real life? Who says? Can he prove this claim? Maybe faculty in the Finance Department believe students like Steve harbor misconceptions about real life, which is why they require courses in English, history, and biology, or why they require students to think and write about academic topics as well as immediately personal ones. Maybe Steve's next essay could be a definition of "real life" that Art and the rest of the class could examine critically?

Eventually, Art's anger abated, and he reassessed the situation. Art realized he had initiated Steve's response by asking him for an "honest" reaction to the commentary, and from one perspective, Steve had given Art just that. In his first sentence, Steve said he didn't know what he was supposed to be writing, and it is true that Art did not provide further directions, preferring to leave the assignment open-ended to provide the freedom necessary to encourage a wide range of responses. Indeed, Steve may not have been asked previously by a teacher to write this kind of response, and so he may not have known the pro-tocol apparently familiar to the rest of his classmates. Art had asked for these reponses hoping to create a dialogue about their mutual enterprise, and Steve had obliged.

And so Art reread Steve's writing from a sympathetic perspective, trying to understand Steve's viewpoint, his experience, and his apparent anger, and this was the perspective Art communicated to Steve. We can't be sure how appropriate Art's response was nor how Steve actually received it. We do know that the relationship between Art and Steve settled into a civil give-and-take in which Steve revised his essays and modified his attitude somewhat, and Art often took note in class discussions of the reasons for Steve's original protest.

Reflecting on this incident, we now see both Art and Steve as part of the "paradigm shift" that Maxine Hairston (1982), who teaches writing at the University of Texas at Austin, says is taking place in the teaching of composi-tion. A paradigm is a model, a pattern, a set of forms to follow. Philosopher of science Thomas Kuhn has used the term *paradigm shift* to describe a major change in theoretical orientation; it was a paradigm shift, for example, when people began to believe that the world was round and not flat, because that new belief, that new set of "forms" for the mind, changed not only how people thought about the world and the universe but also how they did things like sail boats and build buildings. The theory of relativity has changed the model of matter and energy, initiating another paradigm shift. Professor Hairston bor-rows Kuhn's term to explain what has happened with composition teaching over the last three decades.

In the 1960s, many teachers of writing became dissatisfied with the way composition was being taught on their campuses. They argued that composi-tion classes often seemed concerned more about following rules than about writing. Some of those teachers, especially those who taught in open enroll-ment colleges, saw that the traditional ways of teaching writing really didn't work with students described as "under-prepared." Nowadays, the name given to the old way of teaching writing that those teachers were rebelling against is "current-traditional." Here's basically how it worked: You thought of a topic; then you wrote an outline, often a Roman numeral outline; then you wrote the paper; next you proofread, paying a lot of attention to commas, spelling, and usage (that is, things like *lie* and *lay*); you handed the paper in; and a few days (or weeks) later you got it back with a grade and with all your errors in punc-tuation, spelling, and usage marked, usually in red. Sometimes there was a comment in the margin like "awk" or "frag" or even "good," but usually you didn't know what those abbreviations meant or what was good in the para-graph. Then you did the same thing over again, often eight times in one semes-ter. Class was devoted to lectures on commas, sentence structure, and syn-onyms and to the analysis of essays by great writers.

In the current-traditional paradigm, what was important was the student's essay, the product. Under the new model, the process of writing became as important as the product. Sometimes called the "process method," it works like this: you spend a lot of time in class on prewriting activities—journal entries, making lists, freewriting, journalist's questions (who? what? where? when? why?), small-group discussion; then you write; you revise; you bring your paper to class for workshops or peer-editing sessions; you write another draft; you might go for a conference with your teacher; the teacher reads a draft and comments on the strengths and weaknesses of your paper, paying particular attention to purpose, audience, and organizational strategies; you might write still another draft; you may or may not get a traditional grade; and you might even revise again.

One problem with the process method is that it keeps changing. In the 1960s, writing teachers wanted to help students find authentic voices and so spent a lot of time on prewriting activities. In the 1970s, composition teachers began studying the process of writing more systematically than they had before. As they observed successful adult writers, they began to emphasize setting goals, making plans, organizing, revising drafts, and editing; they recognized that good writers can and do move back and forth among these activities. In the 1980s, scholars began to look at writing not just as an individual act, but as a social act as well. These teachers argued that what we write is a social artifact and that how we write results from the social situation we are in. They began to pay attention to both the product—that is, the text, its genre, and its conventions—and to collaborative learning—that is, the ways writers and readers work together to create a text. To sum up, there are lots of different ways to teach the process of writing, probably as many different ways as there are teachers who say they teach it.

With this background in mind, we now see Steve's resistance to writing and to Art a little differently. First, if Steve's high school teachers were old paradigm teachers, then he may have been expecting a class where he could get by just following orders. Many students figure out rather quickly that a current-traditional teacher may lose enthusiasm for students' ideas under the time-consuming obligation to find all surface errors. Such teachers often become so bored marking errors that they forget that students do have important things to say, and they don't remember that helping writers state their messages appropriately is more important than telling them one more time that they misspelled *relevance*. If Steve has had enough old paradigm teachers, then he may know that what he has to say will be of little interest. In such a case, writing multiple drafts is not just a chore but in truth a waste of time.

Furthermore, students trained under the old paradigm often learn to manipulate the system to get by with a minimal amount of work and mental engagement. Since Steve believes that English doesn't matter to him personally or to his employer, perhaps this is what he wanted: a course that would make few demands on his time or energy. But here he is in Art Young's class, where Art asks him to write a draft, then another draft, then still another draft, all the while paying attention to what the other students and Art have to say.

Art asks Steve to look at his own writing process, to change his text in response to comments and suggestions, and to make decisions about what to keep and what to leave out, about what to add and what to change to a different place. Art is asking Steve to do more work and more thinking than in the old way.

The heart of the clash between Steve and Art may be a student trained in the old paradigm resisting a new paradigm teacher. Steve may be thinking, Why spend all this time trying to write an effective essay on civil disobedience when no one cares what I think anyway? Since it is not an important or relevant topic to me, I'm not even sure I know what I think about civil disobedience. He may deduce that, to take the process of learning to write seriously, he will have to take ideas (his own and those of interest to others) seriously. Perhaps this class, full of unfamiliar tasks, interferes with Steve's plans for his semester or triggers his insecurities about English or about school.

Indeed, many students resist the new paradigm simply because it is unfamiliar. The old way carries with it a lot of certainty—"two fragments and you flunk," for example—and certainty makes all of us feel secure. "The devil you know is better than the devil you don't," according to folk wisdom. In other words, some students may resist simply because this new teacher does it differently from the way other teachers have done it. Perhaps the rules for getting a good grade don't seem as clear as they were before. Perhaps because Art's class doesn't fit familiar patterns, Steve becomes defensive. Perhaps Steve prefers a class in which he writes a paper, the teacher grades it, and then it is forgotten—filed or thrown away.

Let us suppose, on the other hand, that Steve has had a process teacher before. In such a case, he may not recognize the familiar in another process teacher's classroom. This is because those of us who claim to teach process don't all teach it the same way. One teacher may hold conferences with individuals or with small groups; another may use collaborative learning techniques for editing workshops; one process teacher may give grades on the third draft; and another may give no grades at all until the end of the semester when she grades students' portfolios.

Maybe Steve's teacher in English 101 was a new paradigm teacher. Maybe he or she also required drafts, group work, conferences, journals, freewriting. Maybe Steve did all that and still got a C. Even if he got a grade better than C, perhaps he did all this work but never felt that he learned anything new. Maybe it all felt like "busy work" to him. So perhaps when Steve gets to Art's class and realizes what is required, his reaction is, Oh no, not more revising. I learned that in 101. Maybe the other teacher's comments on drafts were not suggestions but orders. And so perhaps Steve sees feedback from his audience, whether peers' responses or Art's, not as help in clarifying his thinking for this specific audience (his teacher and his peers) but as an infringement on his freedom to say what he thinks in any way he wants.

One thing that undoubtedly makes composition confusing for students is that their teachers are themselves caught in the transition period of this paradigm shift. Many teachers prefer the process approach to the traditional approach, but there is no general consensus among these teachers on how most effectively to use the writing process in support of teaching students to think and write clearly. In other words, it isn't just students like Steve who are caught in the paradigm shift, but teachers as well. Some teachers proclaim process but give objective tests on how to write a paper, or they count off a letter grade for every comma splice, or they use peer-editing groups but fail to help students know how to be effective editors. Some talk a lot about the process but consider only products in grading.

But the shift to process is not just a change in classroom practices. The paradigm shift in composition is part of a larger shift in looking at knowledge. In many fields, from literature to physics, knowledge is no longer regarded as something that exists separately from human beings. This shift has been described by Paulo Freire, a professor of education in Brazil in his book *Pedagogy of the Oppressed* (1970). Freire believes that knowledge is not a *thing* that teachers possess that they can just pass on unchanged to students. Instead, according to Freire, knowledge is what we—teacher and students—make together as we talk to each other, as we ask questions, and put into our own words our experiences with the world. Freire believes that together we can use language and literacy to "rename" our world, to change the world, to make it more equitable and more humane for everyone. For Freire, the purpose of education is to help students (and teachers) develop "critical consciousness"—that is, an attitude of questioning and analyzing the world as it has been given to us.

The old way of teaching writing, the current-traditional approach, resembled what Freire has called the banking concept of education. In the banking model, the teacher makes deposits of knowledge into the pupil's mind; the student only receives this knowledge but doesn't do anything with it. The student is required, in fact, to be a passive learner, not an active one. When the student has accumulated enough deposits, he or she can cash them in on a grade or a degree. In America, we expect to trade the degree in on a "good" job. The university is often seen as merely a hoop to jump through on the way to economic security, not as a place to learn to use both spoken and written language to engage in dialogue about how the world is and how it ought to be. Steve appears to accept the banking concept of education. He seems to have been convinced long ago that English as well as history and biology has little relevance to finance or business or to his life. For Steve, the purpose of higher education is to prepare students for jobs, not to get them to think about and discuss such concepts as civil disobedience.

If in fact this is how Steve views education, he has lots of company. Historically and statistically, in the United States the level of education correlates highly with income. Although there are exceptions, the general rule in our economic system is that without an education there is little if any economic security. So Steve's point of view has validity, and we are not so naive as to try to ignore that fact. But we—and faculty in the Finance Department—also believe that Steve should know that important decisions even in the business world are rarely made on only the "bottom line"; the equations also include human values. And human beings are the subjects of such courses in English, history, and biology. Coming to decisions in the "real" world that Steve wants to be a part of requires conversation, argument, dialogue, language—the traditional concerns of rhetoric, which is what we are trying to teach in our writing courses.

In addition, although we may not initially like Steve's resistance to the way we teach writing, we believe his resistance to authority is valuable, and we want to help him learn to resist effectively. We see a connection between some forms of resistance and the ability to think critically. Learning to resist effectively includes creating a context for critically reexamining generally accepted ideas and practices. Such resistance is based on courage, self-respect, and respect for others. These attributes cannot be measured in dollars and cents but instead often require difficult and even unpopular actions. Our country has a long tradition of civil disobedience, of resisting government policies that people consider immoral, unjust, or unfair. We honor individuals like Rosa Parks who have the courage to nonviolently disobey laws with which they disagree and thereby challenge governments to change laws in order to create a more just society. But this concept is not limited only to laws; sometimes it is necessary to resist at work. Sometimes individuals in business and technology have to say no to company policy. The tragic example of the NASA spacecraft Challenger comes to mind. Some of the engineers and scientists resisted and some of them succumbed to company pressure to change the temperature safety rating of the O-rings that were used on that fatal flight. While it is true that Americans expect education to serve economic ends, we also expect it to serve a higher purpose: Education should help students learn how to make moral decisions and how to argue for them.

As teachers of rhetoric, we hope that we can contribute to this purpose by helping our students learn to read carefully, write effectively, and think critically. Ideally, the new way of teaching writing, the process approach, requires that students and teachers work together. Through questions, feedback, answers, and suggestions, both texts and ideas are revised. This process creates knowledge. The new paradigm asks students not to be passive writers, saying only what they are told to say the way someone else wants them to say it but active writers, making decision about what they want to say and the most effective way to say it to a particular audience, learning to construct through conversations with others their own interpretations of the world.

The new pedagogy, or way of teaching, makes all of us—students and teachers—uncomfortable because it critiques schooling as it has usually been carried out. The new paradigm resists the old model that has taught us that knowledge is a set of facts that we have no influence over. It resists teaching that implies that obeying a set of rules is more important than questioning, thinking, seeing inconsistencies, or speaking in one's own voice. Because many students who come to college have been successful with the old methods, with Freire's banking concept, they don't want to question familiar methods and standards or their own success. The new pedagogy asks students to take charge of their own writing and their own learning. In addition, the new paradigm asks teachers to reconsider their role, to look at students not as empty vessels into which knowledge is poured, but as persons who also help create knowledge and whose view of reality must be taken seriously. It is easier for teachers to slip into their old role as authorities than to share power with students. It is easier for students to resist participating actively in their own learning. Sometimes we all resist the responsibility for creating our world. It is easier to accept someone else's view of it.

In a writing class, the new pedagogy asks students not only to think and question but to take risks and to live with some uncertainty, all activities that create anxiety. Maybe it will help our students—Steve, for example—to know that the new paradigm requires us teachers to question tradition, to think critically about our roles in educating students, to take risks, and to tolerate uncertainty. We are all—students and teachers—caught up in this paradigm shift. The changing view of knowledge and of the world is scary, but at the same time exciting, for we can contribute to it. In this new paradigm, Steve's resistance in Art's class last year is no longer a disrespectful gesture but an opportunity to analyze the circumstances in which teachers and students now find themselves. We think our consideration of Steve's resistance has helped us better understand both our students' situation and our own profession. We hope it has proved enlightening for our readers who may resist both writing and writing teachers.

## Works Cited

Freire, Paulo (1970). *Pedagogy of the Oppressed.* New York: Seabury.

Hairston, Maxine (1982). "The Winds of Change: Thomas Kuhn and the Revolution in Teaching Writing. *College Composition and Communication, 33,* 78–86.

---

## Sharing Ideas

- Pretend you were in Steve's writing group all semester as he wrote in Art's class. Then try to add to Beth and Art's analysis.

- Share a story of a time you resisted a teacher. If you've never resisted, explore why that is so.

- Have you ever seen a teacher go through some or all of the stages Art and Beth describe—anger at student behaviors, refuting a student with the student's own arguments, reassessing and changing the classroom in response to student comments, then giving the resisting student a more sympathetic reading?

- What are your thoughts on the Freirian model of education and the banking model of education? Consider whether they are at work in your own classes.
- Do you think there is a connection between resistance in the writing classroom and the tradition of civil disobedience?
- Share ways you have worked to change institutions or institutional practices.
- What are your feelings on the possibility of students sharing educational power and authority?
- Describe what you view as ideal roles for teachers and for students in writing classrooms.
- Have you ever been in a class where a student seems to be resisting the teacher for reasons you don't understand? In light of Beth and Art's essay, try to describe what that student's reasons might have been; also, detail the impact that student's resistance had on you and your classmates' learning.
- You might read this essay alongside Lizanne Minerva and Melanie A. Rowls' essay, Chapter 19. How does each comment on student resistance and connect to your own classroom experiences?

———————————

# Part V

# Writing to Figure out the World and to Figure in the World

/The essay seems to have originated with Montaigne, a kind of adult French Bart Simpson, who seemed to hate the schools, school masters, and school writing of that time, but who wrote for his own purposes, in his own way. Montaigne wrote very untraditional little sets of explorations, of tentative wonderings, about himself and his world that he called essays. Writers would do well to recover Montaigne's sense of essaying. Writing is a dialogue with one's world, open, unfinished, not always pretty, but often ongoing.
—James Zebroski, writing teacher

At times when Kevin wrote faster or stopped thinking aloud, she was "brainstorming." She would feel a rush of things she wanted to say and could not write or say them fast enough before she wanted to say and could not write or say them fast enough before she lost the thought(s) altogether. This caused her to reread what she began to write in order to recall what she was trying to say.
—Stephany Loban on observing a fellow student's, Kevin Jackson's, writing process

As I read, I find clues that help me to write my paper. I measure my ideas against the ideas of people who are considered experts. Their ideas force me to rethink my own. I conduct a dialogue between the author and me that sometimes causes me to change my mind and sometimes merely reconfirms my original ideas. But a book or article seldom leaves my thinking unchanged, and it always helps me put new words on the page.

—Marcia Dickson, writing teacher

Our texts are "safe" when we do what we know we've gotta do to get a good grade, rather than approaching a paper creatively. Regardless, you must make your point, but a safe paper is one you write, stylistically, for others, not yourself. I hate safe. . . . I feel safe squashes innovation, and as in each new generation, innovation should be nurtured more than ever. . . . Freshman English teachers try to "unteach" this [safe] style, yet freshmen must stick to it in history classes and humanities (sometimes).

—Anonymous in-class freewrite

# 17

# Style: The Hidden Agenda in Composition Classes or One Reader's Confession

## Kate Ronald

Kate Ronald is the Roger and Joyce L. Howe Professor in English at Miami University. She teaches writing and rhetoric courses at all levels from first-year to graduate courses, and she works with faculty across the curriculum on ways to teach writing effectively. She has just published a new book, coauthored with Hephzibah Roskelly, called *Reason to Believe: Romanticism, Pragmatism, and the Teaching of Writing*, whose title comes from a Bruce Springsteen song.

In some ways I see this essay as a confession. I have been teaching writing and theorizing about how it should be taught for almost fifteen years now. During those fifteen years, you, the students reading this essay, have been in school, taking English classes and writing compositions. I have been teaching those classes and reading those compositions; plus I've been teaching some of your teachers for the past ten years, and so I feel responsible to you even though I've never had you in one of my classes. Now I'm going to tell you something you might already know. Since you started school in the first grade, there's been a revolution in the way you've been "taught" to write. It used to be that teachers focused on and evaluated your writing according to two main things: its structure and its correctness. Those were the days of diagramming sentences and imitating types of organization. In the 1960s and '70s, however,

169

many people who studied writing began to talk about teaching the "process" of writing rather than the "products" of writing. In other words, the focus has shifted in the 1980s from organization and correctness to generating ideas, appealing to audiences, and developing a "voice" in writing.

Composition or "rhetoric" as it used to be called, is an ancient discipline going all the way back at least to Plato and Aristotle in the third century BCE. You are the most recent in a long, long line of students sitting in classes where teachers assign writing tasks and evaluate your ability. In ancient times, the art of writing was divided into five steps: invention (coming up with ideas), arrangement (organizing them), style (making them sound right), memory (remembering speeches), and delivery (oratorical ability). One way to think about the history of writing instruction is to look at the different emphases that different eras have put on these five steps. Today, with computers and photo-copy machines, we don't worry much anymore about memory, for example, but it was terribly important in the time before the printing press. And we don't "deliver" what we write orally very much anymore, although the kind of font you choose from your word-processing program might be considered a matter of delivery. Of course all writers have to think about invention, arrangement, and style, no matter what age they work in. However, different eras have emphasized different parts of composition. Plato and Aristotle were upset by what they saw as an enchantment with style; they worried that writers could dazzle audiences without caring much about telling them the truth. And so they focused on invention, on figuring out issues by thinking and writing. By the sixteenth and seventeenth centuries, the focus had shifted back to style, going so far as giving students manuals that provided hundreds of ways to say "I enjoyed your letter very much." How a person sounded was more important than what a person had to say.

I see the shift from "product" to "process" while you've been in school as a reaction to that overemphasis on style. Once again, the focus has changed back to make *invention* the most important step in composition. Writing teach-ers who are up-to-date these days (including me) tell you (our students) not to worry, for example, about grammar or spelling or organization as you write .your early drafts. We invite you to choose your own topics for writing and to get feedback from responsive small groups in your classes. We don't grade individual papers, but instead ask you to write multiple drafts and submit for final evaluation the ones you think best represent you as a writer. We don't lec-ture on punctuation or topic sentences. It's what you say, not how you say it, that counts. No doubt you all are familiar with this kind of teaching—I doubt you'd be reading this essay right now if you weren't in a class with a thor-oughly "new rhetoric" teacher. Obviously this whole collection is focused on the *processes* of writing, the main theme of writing instruction in the 1980s.

But here comes my confession. Your teacher, and I, and all the others who were part of this latest revolution in rhetoric, haven't been exactly honest with you about the matter of style. We say we aren't overly interested in style, that your ideas and your growth as writers is uppermost in our minds, but we are still influenced by your writing style more than we admit, or perhaps know. In other words, despite all the research and writing I've done in the past ten years about composing, revising, responding, contexts for writing, personal voice, and all I know about the new rhetoric, I'm still rewarding and punishing my students for their writing styles. And here's the worst part of my confession: I'm not sure that I'm teaching them style. Of course any teacher quickly realizes that she can't teach everything in one semester, but I worry that I'm responding to something in my students' writing that I'm not telling them about—their style, the sound of their voices on paper. This essay is my attempt to atone for that omission in my own teaching. Despite that selfish motive, I also want to suggest to you ways in which you might become aware of your own writing styles and your teachers' agendas about style, as well as show you some strategies for studying and improving your own style in writing.

Let me stop to define what I mean and what I don't mean by "style." I don't mean spelling, grammar, punctuation, or usage, although if I'm going to be completely honest, I'd have to tell you that mistakes along those lines do get in my way when I'm reading. But those can be fixed, easily, by editing and copyreading. By style, I mean what my student, Margaret, said last semester after another student, Paul, had read a paper out loud for the whole class. She got this longing look on her face and cried, "I want to write the way Paul does!" You know students like Paul. He's clever, he surprises with his different perspectives on his topics, and he has a distinctive voice. I call this "writing where somebody's home," as opposed to writing that's technically correct but where there's "nobody home," no life, no voice. Let me give you some examples of these two kinds of voices.

### Much Too Young to Be So Old

The neighborhood itself was old. Larger than most side streets, 31st Street had huge cracks that ran continuously from one end to the other of this gray track that led nowhere special. Of the large, lonely looking houses, there were only six left whose original structures hadn't been tampered with in order to make way for inexpensive apartments. Why would a real family continue to live in this place was a question we often asked and none of us could answer. Each stretch of the run-down rickety houses had an alley behind them. These alleys became homes, playgrounds, and learning areas for us children. We treasured these places. They were overgrown with weeds and filled with years of garbage, but we didn't seem to care. Then again, we didn't seem to care about much. (Amy)

### The Dog

In 1980 I lived in a green split level house. It was a really ugly green but that is beside the point. The neighborhood was really rather pretty, with trees all over the place and not just little trees. They were huge. My friends and I played football in my backyard right after school every day. The neighbors had a white toy poodle that barked forever. You would walk by the fence and it would bark at you. I had no idea whatsoever that the dog was mean. (Corey)

Even though both these writers begin these essays by describing the settings of their stories, and both end with a suggestion of what's coming next, Amy's opening paragraph appeals to me much more than Corey's. I could point out "flaws" in both openings: I think Corey's suffers from lack of concrete detail, and he takes a pretty long time telling us only that the trees were "huge." Amy uses too much passive voice ("hadn't been tampered with"). However, I'm much more drawn into the world of 31st Street than I am to the neighborhood with huge trees. And I think that's because I know more about Amy from this opening—her words and her rhythm evoke a bittersweet expectation in me—whereas I'm not sure what Corey's up to. In other words, I get the distinct feeling that Amy really wants to tell her readers about her childhood. I don't see that kind of commitment in Corey. I know Corey's going to write a dog story, and usually those are my favorites, but somehow I don't very much want to read on.

But teachers have to read on, and on and on, through hundreds and hundreds of drafts a semester. So I can't just say to Corey, "This is boring." And, being a believer in the "new rhetoric," I'm interested in the process that leads to these two different styles. How does Amy come up with this voice? Was she born clever? And why does Corey make the decision to take himself out of his writing? I can think of many reasons why he would choose to be safe; in fact, he admitted to me later in that course that he had "copped out," choosing to write in what he called his "safe, public style" rather than take chances with what he thought was a more risky, personal style. That makes sense, if you consider the history of writing instruction up until the last fifteen to twenty years. Certainly it's been better to get it right, to avoid mistakes, than to get it good, to try for a voice. And it makes sense that Corey wouldn't want to expose his personal style—writing classrooms traditionally have not been places where students have felt safe. Writing and then showing that writing to someone else for evaluation and response is risky, a lot like asking "Am I OK? Am I a person you want to listen to?"

And so, to play it safe in a risky environment, it's tempting to take on a voice that isn't yours, to try to sound like you know what you're talking about, to sound "collegiate," to be acceptable and accepted. There's also a sort of mystique about "college writing," both in composition courses and in other disciplines. To write in college, this thinking goes, means to be "objective," to make your own opinions, your own stake in the subject, completely out of your writing. That's why people write, "It is to be hoped that" rather than, "I hope" or, "There are many aspects involved" rather than, "This is complicated." And then there's also a real fear of writing badly, of being thought stupid, and so it's tempting simply to be bland and safe and not call too much attention to yourself.

And teachers have encouraged you, I think, to remain hidden behind your own prose. Remember when you got a "split grade" like this: "C+/B"? One grade for content and another for style. That sends a clear message, I think, that what you say and how you say it can be separated and analyzed differently. That's crazy—we can't split form and content. But teachers tend to encourage you to do that when they ask you to read an essay by Virginia Woolf or E. B. White from an anthology and then tell you to "write like that." Or, we teachers have been so concerned with form that we've discouraged you from real communication with another person. One of my students just yesterday described her English classes this way: "I wanted to learn how to write and they were trying to teach me what my writing should look like." Preoccupation with correctness, with organization, and with format (margins, typing, neatness, etc.), all get in the way of style and voice. So, too, do prearranged assignments, where each student in the class writes the same essay on the same subject ("Compare high school to college," "Discuss the narrator's attitude in this short story," "My most embarrassing moment"). Such assignments become exercises in competition, in one sense, because you've got somehow to set yourself apart from the rest of the essays your teacher will be reading. But they are also exercises in becoming invisible, for while you want to be noticed, you don't want to be too terribly different, to stick out like a sore thumb. And so you write safely, not revealing too much or taking many chances.

I used to teach that way, giving assignments, comparing one student with another and everyone with the "ideal" paper I imagined in my head (although I never tried writing with my students in those days) correcting mistakes and arriving at a grade for each paper. The new rhetoric classes I teach now have eliminated many of these traps for students, but I've also opened up new ones, I'm afraid. Now my students choose their own topics, writing whatever they want to write. And sometimes I'm simply not interested in their choices. In the old days, when I gave the assignment, naturally I was interested in the topic— it was, after all, *my* idea. Now I read about all sorts of things every week—my students' families, their cars, the joys and sorrows in their love lives, their athletic victories and defeats, their opinions on the latest upcoming election, their thoughts about the future, etc. Frankly, I don't approach each of these topics in the same way. For example, a dog story almost always interests me, while a car story might not. Or, a liberal reading of the latest campus debate on women's issues will grab my attention much more quickly than a fundamentalist interpretation. That's simply the truth. But, as a teacher of "process," I try my best to get interested in whatever my students are writing. And, I'm usually delighted by how much my students can move me with their ideas. So what makes me interested? I'm convinced it has to do with their style. And here I'm defining style not simply as word choice or sentence structure, but as a kind of "presence" on the page, the feeling I get as a reader that, indeed, somebody's home in this paper, somebody wants to say something—to me, to herself, to the class, to the community.

Mine is not the only response students receive in this kind of classroom. Each day, students bring copies of their work-in-progress to their small groups. They read their papers out loud to each other, and we practice ways of responding to each writer that will keep him or her writing, for starts, and that will help the writer see what needs to be added, changed, or cut from the draft. This can get pretty tricky. It's been my experience that showing your writing to another student, to a peer, can be much more risky than showing it to a teacher. We've all had the experience of handing in something we knew was terrible to a teacher, and it's not so painful. People will give writing to teachers that they'd never show to someone whose opinion they valued. But sitting down in a small group with three of four classmates and saying, "I wrote this. What do you think?" is, again, like asking "Do you like me? Am I an interesting person?" And so my classes practice ways of responding to one another's writing without being overly critical, without taking control of the writing out of the writer's hands, and without damaging egos. And they become quite sophisticated as the semester goes along. Still, one of the worst moments in a small group comes when someone reads a draft and the rest of the group responds like this: "It's OK. I don't see anything wrong with it. It seems pretty good." And then silence. In other words, the writer hasn't grabbed their attention, hasn't engaged the readers, hasn't communicated in any meaningful way. What's the difference between this scenario and one where the group comes back with responses like "Where did you get that idea? I really like the way you describe the old man. This reminds me of my grandfather. I think you're right to notice his hands"? I think the difference is in *style*, in the presence of a writer in a group who is honestly trying to communicate to his or her readers.

But I know I still haven't been exactly clear about what I mean by style. That's part of my dilemma, my reason for wanting to write this essay. All of us, teachers and students, recognize good style when we hear it, but I don't know what we do to foster it. And so for the rest of this essay I want to talk to you about how to work on your own writing styles, to recognize and develop your own individual voice in writing, and how to listen for your teachers' agendas in style. Because, despite our very natural desires to remain invisible in academic settings, you *want* to be noticed; you want to be the voice that your teacher becomes interested in. I think I'm telling you that your style ultimately makes the difference. And here I'm talking about not only your writing styles, but the reading styles of your audiences, the agendas operating in the contexts in which you write.

I'll start backward with agendas first. There are several main issues that I think influence English teachers when they are reading students' writing. First, we have a real bent for the literary element, the metaphor, the clever turn of phrase, the rhythm of prose that comes close to the rhythm of poetry. That's why I like sentences like these: "As the big night approached I could feel my stomach gradually easing its way up to my throat. I was as nervous as a young foal experiencing its first thunderstorm" (from an essay about barrel racing) and "Suddenly the University of Nebraska Cornhusker Marching Band takes the field for another exciting half-time performance, and the Sea of Red stands up *en masse* and goes to the concession stand" (from an essay about being in the band). I like the surprise in this last sentence, the unexpectedness of every-one leaving the performance, and I like the comparison to a young foal in the first one, especially since the essay is about horses. I till my students to "take chances" in their writing. I think these two writers were trying to do just that. And I liked them for taking that chance.

But you don't want to take chances everywhere. Of course this kind of writing won't work in a biology lab report or a history exam, which brings me to another troublesome issue when we talk about style in college writing. You move among what composition researchers call "discourse communities" every day—from English to Biology to Sociology to Music to the dorm to fam-ily dinners to friends at bars—you don't talk or write the same way, or in the same voice to each of these groups. You adjust. And yet many professors still believe that you should be learning to write one certain kind of style in college, one that's objective, impersonal, formal, explicit, and organized around asser-tions, claims, and reasons that illustrate or defend those claims. You know this kind of writing. You produce it in response to questions like "Discuss the caus-es of the Civil War," or "Do you think that 'nature' or 'nurture' plays the most important role in a child's development?" Here's a student trying out this kind of "academic discourse" in an essay where he discusses what worries him:

> Another outlet for violence in our society is video games. They have renewed
> the popularity that they had earlier in the 1980's and have taken our country
> by storm. There is not one child in the country who doesn't know what a
> Nintendo is. So, instead of running around outside getting fresh air and exer-
> cise, most children are sitting in front of the television playing video games.
> This is affecting their minds and their bodies.

Why wouldn't Jeff just say "Video games are popular again" instead of saying that "they have renewed their popularity" or "Kids are getting fat and lazy" rather than "This is affecting their minds and bodies?" Besides using big words here, Jeff is also trying to sound absolutely knowledgeable: he states that every child in this country knows Nintendo, they are all playing it, when if he thought about that for a minute, he'd know it wasn't true. I don't like this kind of writing very much myself. Jeff is trying so hard to sound academic that "there's nobody home," no authentic voice left, no sense of a real human being trying to say something to somebody. I prefer discourse that "renders experi-ence," as Peter Elbow (1991) puts it, rather than discourse that tries to explain it. He describes this kind of language (or style) as writing where a writer "con-veys to others a sense of experience—or indeed, that mirrors back to themselves a sense of their own experience, from a little distance, once it's out there on paper" (137). Here's an example of that kind of "rendering" from Paul's essay about a first date:

> Her mother answers the door. My brain says all kinds of witty and charming things which my larynx translates in a sort of amphibious croak. (Ribbitt, Ribbitt. I can't remember what it was I actually attempted to say.) She materializes at the top of the stairs, cast in a celestial glow. A choir of chubby cherubim, voices lifted into a heavenly chorus, drape her devine body with a thin film of gossamer. (No, not really. She did look pretty lovely, though. I tried to tell her as much. Ribbitt. Ribbitt.)

Now, perhaps Paul goes too far here, trying a little too hard to be clever, but I like this better than the discussion of video games. (And not just because I like the topic of dating better—since I've gotten married, I don't date anymore and I confess I'm addicted to Mario Brothers 3). Paul here is conveying the *feeling* of the moment, the sense of the experience, and he's complicating the memory by moving back and forth between the moment and his interpretation of it. In other words, he's letting me into the story, not explaining something to me. Paul is involved in what he's writing while Jeff is detached. And Paul's funny. Besides dog stories, I like humor in my students' writing.

Now, this brings me to another issue in the matter of style. I prefer the rendering style over the explanatory style, perhaps because I'm an English major and an English teacher, and therefore I like the allusion over the direct reference, description over analysis, narrative over exposition. But perhaps there's another reason I like the more personal style: I'm a woman. There's a whole body of recent research which suggests that men and women have different writing styles, among all sorts of other differences. Theorists such as Pamela Annas and Elizabeth Flynn suggest that women writers in academic situations often are forced to translate their experiences into the foreign language of objectivity, detachment, and authority that the male-dominated school system values. Women strive for connection, this thinking argues, while men value individual power. Feminist theory values writing that "brings together the personal and the political, the private and the public, into writing which is committed and powerful because it takes risks, because it speaks up clearly in their own voices and from their own experiences" (Annas 1985, 370; see also Flynn 1988). Here's an example of that kind of writing, an excerpt from an essay titled, "Grandma, You're Not So Young Anymore":

> My grandma was always so particular about everything. Everything had to be just so. The walls and curtains had to be spotless, the garden couldn't have a weed, the kolaches had to be baked, and the car had to be washed. . . . Each spring she was always the first to have her flowers and garden planted. She could remember the littlest details about our family history and ancestors. . . . There were always kolaches in the oven and cookies in the refrigerator. . . .

I really didn't notice the aging so much at first. . . . When I would come home from college Mom would always say, "Grandma's really lonely now. Grandpa was her company, and now he's gone. You should really go and visit her more often. She won't be around forever."

I had to admit I didn't visit her all that often. . . . I didn't notice how much slower she'd gotten until Thanksgiving Day. Grandma took us to Bonanza because she didn't want to cook that much. I noticed the slower, more crippled steps she took, the larger amount of wrinkles on her face, and most of all, her slowed mental abilities. She sometimes had trouble getting words out as if she couldn't remember what she wanted to say. She couldn't decide what foods she wanted to eat, and when she did eat, she hardly touched a thing. I didn't think my grandma would ever get old. Now I don't think she will last forever anymore.

Here, Deanna uses her own experience and observations to go on and talk about how the elderly are treated in our culture. She could have written a statistical report on nursing homes or a more formal argument about how Americans don't value their old people. But she chose instead to draw from her own life and therefore she draws me into her argument about the "frustration" of getting old. I like old people, and I can identify this woman's deterioration with my own mother's several years ago. But I still think it's more than my personal history that draws me to this essay. I suspect it's Deanna's willingness to explore her own experience on paper. Deanna definitely needs to work on editing this draft to improve her style (something more specific, for example, than "larger amounts of wrinkles" and "slowed mental abilities"). But she doesn't need to work to improve her style in the sense of her commitment to this topic, her presence on the page, or her desire to figure out and to explain her reaction to her grandmother's aging.

Each of these three issues might lead me to advise you that you should write metaphors for English teachers, formal explanations for male teachers in other disciplines, and personal narratives for your women professors. But you know that would be silly, simplistic advice about style. You have to maneuver every day through a complex set of expectations, some of which aren't made explicit, and the whole idea of teacher-as-audience is much more complex that simply psyching out a teacher's background or political agenda. "Style" in writing means different things to different people. I have to be honest and admit that my definition of style as presence on paper is simply my own definition. I hope this essay will lead you to your own thinking about what style means, in all contexts. But I am going to end by giving you some advice about your own style in writing anyway—the teacher in me can't resist. That advice is: Work on your style without thinking about school too much. Here are five suggestions to help you do this.

*In School or Out, Write as if You're Actually Saying Something to Somebody.*
Even if you're not exactly sure who your audience is, try to imagine a real

person who's interested in what you have to say. Probably the most important thing I can tell you about working on your style is: Think of your writing as actually saying something to somebody real. Too often in academics we can imagine no audience at all, or at the most an audience with evaluation on its mind, not real interest or response. When I'm able to get interested in my students' writing, no matter what the topic, it's because I hear someone talking to me. My colleague Rick Evans calls this kind of writing "talking on paper," and if you keep that metaphor in mind, I think you'll more often avoid the kind of "academese" or formal language that signals you're hiding or you've disappeared.

I can illustrate the difference in style I'm talking about through two journals that Angie gave me at the beginning and the end of a composition and literature course last year. All through the course, I asked students to write about how the novels we were reading connected to their own lives:

> January 24: Well, I'm confused. I haven't written a paper for an English class that wasn't a formal literary analysis since 8th grade. Now, all of a sudden, the kind of writing my teachers always said would be of no use in college *is*, and what they said *would* be, *isn't*. Go figure. Now, if Kate had asked me to churn out a paper on some passage or symbol in *Beloved*—even one of my own choosing—I could get out 5–8 (handwritten) pages easy. But this life stuff? Who wants to know about that anyway?

> May 1: This portfolio represents the work closest to my guts. It's *my* story, not *Beloved*'s or Carlos Rueda's. I hasten to point out that this may not be my best work or even my favorite work, but it's the work that sings my song. My goal was to communicate a set of ideas, to spark a dialogue with *you*, as my reader, to inspire you to think about *what* I have written, not *how* I have written it. So here it is, bound in plastic, unified, in a manner, ready for reading. I hope you like what I have woven.

Notice how Angie's attitude toward me as her reader changed from January to May. At first she referred to "Kate" as if I wouldn't be reading what she had written, even though this was a journal handed in to me; later I become someone she wants to engage in a dialogue. (She had expected the kind of writing class I described at the beginning of this essay, but she found herself writing for a new rhetoric teacher.) Notice, too, how at first she talks about how she could write five to eight pages *even if she had to choose her own topic*. The implication is clear—that it's easier to write when someone else tells her what to do, what to write about. In other words, it's easier to perform rather than to communicate. Notice, finally, Angie's relationship to the literature we were reading in these two journals. At first she wants only to write about the symbols in Toni Morrison's (1987) novel, *Beloved*, focusing all her attention on the literary work and not on herself. At the end off the course, she subordinates the novels almost completely to her own stories. This is an engaged writer, one with a clear sense of her own style, her own presence.

*Write Outside of School.*       Play with writing outside of school. You'll need to write much more than just what's assigned in your classes to develop a beautiful writing style. (Sorry, but it's true.) One of the truisms about good writers is that they are good readers; in other words, they read a lot. (And they were probably read to as kids, but we can't go into that right now.) So, here's an exercise in style that I recommend to my students. Find an author whose writing you admire. Copy out a particular, favorite passage. Then imitate that style, word for word, part-of-speech for part-of-speech. Here's an example from one of my students last semester. We were reading *Beloved*, and Sarah used its opening passage to talk about the first day of class. I'll show you Morrison's passage and then Sarah's:

> 124 was spiteful. Full of a baby's venom. The women in the house knew it and so did the children. For years each put up with the spite in his own way, but by 1873, Sethe and her daughter Denver were its only victims. The grandmother, Baby Suggs, was dead, and the sons, Howard and Buglar, had run away by the time they were thirteen years old—as soon as merely looking in a mirror shattered it (that was the signal for Buglar); as soon as two tiny hand prints appeared in the cake (that was it for Howard). Neither boy waited to see more. (3)

> Andrews 33 was quiet. Full of a new semester's uneasiness. The students in the room knew it and so did the teacher. For a few minutes, everyone took in the tension in their own way, but by 12:45 the roll call and Kate's lame jokes broke the ice a little bit. The course, a new program, was explained, and the syllabus, papers and papers, looked simple enough by the time Kate explained her marvelous approach—as soon as really deciding on a topic excited us (that was the reason for the authority list); as soon as four friendly voices read to each other (that was the reason for small groups). No students lingered too write more. (Sarah)

Sarah told me later that doing this imitation surprised her—she had never written with parentheses before, nor had she stopped sentences in the middle this way ("the syllabus, papers and papers"). She wasn't sure she liked this imitation, but it showed her she could write in different ways. And playing with different voices on paper will help you make choices about your own style in different situations.

*Read Your Work-in-progress out Loud, Preferably to a Real Person.* Looking back over this essay, I realize that so much of what I've said about style revolves around the sense of sound. Teachers have good ears, and so do you. Listen to your own voice as you read out loud. Do you sound like a person talking to someone? Or a student performing for a grade?

*Practice Cutting All the Words You Can out of Your Drafts and Starting from There.*       This is one of the hardest things for any writer to do, and yet I think it's one of the most effective ways to make your writing more interesting. Most of the time there are simply too many words getting in the way of your meaning, making too much noise for you to be heard. Look closely at your drafts and be hard on yourself. Let me give you a few quick examples:

> The first thing that really upsets me is the destruction of our environment due to ignorance, capitalism, and blindness in the world. The attitude that most people take is that by ignoring the problem it will go away. An example of this attitude is the turnout for elections in America.

> Revision: Ignorance, capitalism, and blindness destroy our environment. Most people look the other way. Many don't even vote.

Once Jim revised this opening sentence from an essay on what worries him, he realized that he hadn't said much yet and that he was moving way too quickly. He learned that he had several ideas he felt strongly about, ideas worth slowing down to develop. Here are two more examples:

> I also think that we need to provide more opportunities for the homeless to receive an education so they can compete in today's job market. Another reason for educating these people is because the increasing numbers of unemployed persons is a factor that is contributing to homelessness in our country. There are declining employment opportunities for unskilled labor in todays job market, and since many homeless are unskilled laborers, they are not able to acquire a decent job. Therefore they cannot afford to buy a home. I think it is critical that these people be educated if the homeless problem in our country is going to be resolved.

> Revision: We need to educate the homeless so they can compete in a market where jobs are becoming more scarce.

> There are so many things that a person can fill their mind with. I find that when talking with friends the majority of their thoughts are filled with worries. I don't really believe that it is all negative to worry unless it becomes an obsession. So many people are worried about so many different things. Some of which are personal while others are more societal. When I try to figure out what worries me most I find it to be on a more personal level.

> Revision: I'm sort of worried that I worry so much about myself.

Each of these last two writers realized that they hadn't said much of anything yet in their initial drafts. Going back to cut words, asking themselves questions about what they meant to say to a reader, allowed them to start over with a different, clearer perspective. I know this isn't easy, especially in school, where you've been trained to "write 1000 words" and, by God, you'll writer 1000 words whether you have one or 1000 words to say on the subject. Try to stop padding and counting words in the margins. Cut words. This is probably the most practical piece of advice I have.

*Finally, Write About Your Own Writing Style.*        Keep a record of your reactions to what you write, a list of your favorite sentences, and a reaction to the reactions you get from readers. Most of all, forgive yourself for writing badly from time to time. One of my professors in graduate school told me that I was capable of writing "awkward word piles," and here I am with the nerve to be writing an essay to you about style. I've tried to practice what I preach, and now I'm suggesting that you throw out more than you keep and to notice and remember what works for you. Writing about your own writing is another piece of practical advice.

This is really my last word: don't let *me* fool you here. Even though I understand what Angie meant in her last journal to me about my being more interested in what she has to say than *how* she said it, I'm still very in tune with the how, with her style, I'm happy that her focus has moved away from me as evaluator toward herself as a creator. But I'm still influenced by her style. Don't forget that. And I'm happy that the emphasis in composition has shifted from style back to invention. But I still reward and punish style in my reactions to students' writings. Yes, I try to be an interested reader, but my agendas also include listening for the sound of prose I like.

I suppose what I'm really confessing to you all in this essay is that I am not only a teacher, but I'm also a reader, with her own tastes, preferences, and phobias about what I like to read. And, as a reader, I look for style. There's a play that I love that I think can show you what I mean by style, by presence in writing. *The Real Thing*, by Tom Stoppard (1983) is about real love and real life, but it's also about real writing. At about the end of Act One, Henry, the playwright/hero, talks about good writing. He's picked up a cricket bat (could be a Louisville slugger, but this play is set in London) to make his point. (Read this out loud and listen to the sound):

> This thing here, which looks like a wooden club, is actually several pieces of particular wood cunningly put together in a certain way so that the whole thing is sprung, like a dance floor. It's for hitting cricket balls with. If you get it right, the cricket ball will travel two hundred yards in four seconds, and all you've done is give it a knock like knocking the top off a bottle of stout, and it makes a noise like a trout taking a fly. What we're trying to do is write cricket bats, so then when we throw up an idea and give it a little knock, it might . . . *travel.* (22)

This image has stayed with me for seven years, ever since I first saw and read Stoppard's play, and it's an idea that I think all writers and readers understand. "Ideas traveling"—surely that's what I want for myself as a writer and for my students. I love the image of the dance floor too—the idea of a piece of writing as an invitation to movement, a place to join with others, a site of communal passion and joy. But I don't think people in school always think of writing as something that travels, or as a dance floor, and I would like somehow to help you a little toward Henry's vision. Later in the same speech he picks up a badly written play that he's been asked to "fix" and describes it:

Now, what we've got here is a lump of wood of roughly the same shape trying to be a cricket bat, and if you hit a ball with it, the ball will travel about
ten feet and you will drop the bat and dance about shouting "Ouch!" with
your hands stuck in your armpits (23).

I've read writing, my own and my students' and professionals', that makes me
want to do this different kind of dancing. Many of your textbooks read like
"lumps of wood," yes? Henry tells us that no amount of simple editing will fix
something that has no life or passion to begin with. But how to transform
lumps of wood into cricket bats? It seems to me the key lies in this play's other
theme—the "real thing," meaning real love and real passion. When I encourage you to develop your style in writing, I'm inviting you into the game, onto
the dance floor, encouraging you to commit yourself to your ideas and to your
readers. That's the essence of *style*, which, without knowledge and passion,
amounts only to a performance that dazzles without touching its readers, and
which, without practice, amounts to very little. In that sense, Plato and
Aristotle were right to say that we shouldn't emphasize style over invention,
ideas, and voice. And in another sense, my last piece of advice would apply to
students in ancient Greece as well as modern America: write about something
you care about to someone you care about. Even if you are writing in school,
try to have a presence—show them that somebody's home, working. Writers
must know and love not only their subjects but their audiences as well, so that
ideas will dance, so that ideas will travel.

## Works Cited

Annas, Pamela. (1985). "Style as Politics." *College English, 4,* 370.

Elbow, Peter (1991). "Reflections on Academic Discourse." *College English, 2,* 137.

Flynn, Elizabeth (1988). "Composing as Woman." *College Composition and
Communication, 39,* 423–435.

Morrison, Toni (1987). *Beloved.* New York: Knopf.

Stoppard, Tom (1983). *The Real Thing.* London: Faber & Faber.

## Sharing Ideas

- In different eras writers have been encouraged to pay more or less attention to style. In fact, style doesn't just manifest itself in our writing but in
  our living, also. We often talk about lifestyle and style of dress. Do you
  see any connections between your writing style (or the style you'd like to
  attain) and your lifestyle and style of dress?

- Don, Ellie, and Kate all talk about a shift from product to process. But
  Kate's article indicates such shifting can be problematic. She reminds you

that "mistakes along those lines [spelling, grammar, punctuation, or usage] do get in my way when I'm reading" and then she suggests that writing teachers tend to listen for certain types of difficult-to-describe writing voices. What do you think of her discussion?

- Looking through some of your writing, find samples of pieces where you, the writer, are "not at home" and where you, the writer are clearly "at home." Do Kate's discussions of style and voice explain differences in voice in your own writing?

- Have you ever taken a piece of writing to class to share and had it flop? Why do you think that happened? Did you ever take a piece to share that you felt lukewarm about and it was a hit? Again, what do you think was going on, what were readers responding to in that piece of writing?

- Kate tells you that English teachers tend to like certain types of writing— writing that renders, writing that uses allusion, narrative, and (particularly for women teachers perhaps) personal style—do these attributes help you understand past teachers' responses to your writing? Explain by using examples of your own writing with the teacher's response if you still have them.

- Do you think it's silly to think that you might write "metaphors for English teachers, formal explanations for male teachers in other disciplines, and personal narratives for your women professors," or do you find yourself already making some of these shifts?

- How do you learn what type of writing a professor expects from you? How able or willing are you to deliver writing in that style? Are you comfortable or uncomfortable when meeting teachers' demands?

- Look at Kate's five writing suggestions, offered at the end of her essay. What in your own writing practices would you have to change to follow her advice?

---

# 18

# The Values(s) of Style, the Style of Value(s)

Lizanne Minerva and Melanie A. Rawls

Melanie A. Rawls teaches composition at Florida A & M
University, writes poetry, short fiction, and essays. Lizanne
Minerva, fiction writer, teaches creative writing and composition at
Southwest Missouri State University.

Racial difference is almost impossible to talk about honestly in a class—or in any public place, for that matter. We often recognize stereotypes for what they are, but we're not sure how to address other differences productively as teachers and students. Many of us hurry to define ourselves as color-blind or, at least, just nicely color-aware. Others of us turn away. Some of us seethe. Very little true dialogue occurs when the topic is raised.

Differences exist among us as racial groups, because we're positioned to see the world from separate vantage points; and to deny these diverse perspectives is to deny our history. As teachers and coauthors, we—Melanie A. Rawls and Lizanne Minerva—want to take a look at how one difference manifests itself in academe: the value of style in writing classes where the students are predominantly African American.

*Mel:* When I accepted a position as a composition instructor at Florida A & M University (an HBCU or Historically Black College or University), after having been a composition teaching assistant and receiving my graduate degree from Florida State University (a BWI or Big White

184

Institution), people, black and white, would ask me if teaching at an HBCU was different from teaching at a BWI.

I remain intrigued by the manner in which the question was asked. Something about the facial expression and the intonation, as if I had taken a job in, say, the Galapagos Islands or at the Arctic Circle. Real change of environment, people seemed to be implying, must be quite an adjustment.

*Lizanne:* For me, choosing to teach first-year writing for Horizons Unlimited, Florida State's minority retention program, drew polite surprise. Fellow teachers often responded with, "Oh. And why would you want to do that?"

You see, Horizons classes had a reputation as tough to handle: poorly prepared students; tense classroom dynamics. But I had taught in several predominantly African American writing classes before, and was looking forward to it, including the smaller, more intimate class. In short, I was ready to go, wherever the destination might be.

*Mel:* The more I think about the question, the odder it seems to me. After all, both universities are state universities that accept students from more or less integrated public and private American school systems and employ faculty, staff, and administrators from the same sources. Why the presumption of radically different environments?

Even odder, perhaps, is the implication that I, an African American woman, would find my transition to an HBCU some kind of radical change.

*Lizanne:* As unsettling to me as the baffled well-wishing friends were the white Horizons teachers who noted that they had achieved a kind of honorary black person status in their classes. They wore this badge with pride: I was one of them.

These two kinds of responses alerted me to approaches I wanted to avoid: first, the racial us/them dichotomy I would set up if I viewed this teaching assignment as proof of what a good liberal-minded person I was; second, the impulse to demonstrate to my Horizons students how Afrocentric I could be. I didn't expect students in my predominantly white classes to accept me as one of them (though, in terms of race, I already was), so why ask that of Horizons students?

*Mel:* That first-year, when I was asked how teaching at FAMU contrasted with teaching at FSU, I would answer, "Not much difference. Classes are bigger, there's a greater range of student writing abilities, and they use a different textbook, but other than that, it's pretty much the same."

I would tell inquiring minds that I have about the same percentage of students who come into my classes as competent writers, about the same percentage who don't seem to have a clue; about the same percentage who accept writing classes as merely part of the educational experience, and the same who really hate writing (and don't hesitate to tell me so!), seeming to view it as the educational equivalent of hiking across Death Valley in a snowsuit and sandals. Difficult, absurd, and scarcely necessary, you know?

But the longer I am at FAMU, the more I become aware of how the difference in textbooks represents a difference in program agendas for my former FSU and my current FAMU students; and that difference in agendas is reflective of a cultural difference that is facilely and superficially, I believe, embodied in the question, "How is it, you know, teaching at FAMU?"

Currently, my answer to the question, stated or unstated, about contrasts between the HBCU and the BWI is, "There are differences. I'm still thinking about it."

*Lizanne:* In a process-oriented, first-year writing class, you compose multiple drafts to be graded in a portfolio that often includes letters or memos about how you wrote the paper. Your writing textbook encourages you to question and explore, starting with your experience and views. You receive input from peer readers and the teacher, and revise your work in stages. The idea behind this method is that good writing occurs when the writer makes discoveries along the way rather than putting together a pre-fab essay; also, peer groups encourage you to become a more astute reader and critic rather than always looking to the teacher for advice.

When composing multiple drafts, coherence and correctness sometimes go out the window. To perfect sentences is a waste of time when any sentence may ultimately be deleted, so you must focus on major ideas rather than sentence structure in the drafting process.

One advantage of this approach for the teacher is not having to look at predictable, dead-end themes. Students derive the greater benefit, though: learning something rather than rehashing what they already know about the topic.

*Mel:* In terms of the freshman composition programs, the difference in the textbooks is the most noticeable dissimilarity between the goals for writing students attending FAMU and FSU. Florida A & M's English Department selects, for its students, textbooks that emphasize the product, that is, a finished essay. The department requires diagnostic tests for sentence structure, punctuation, and grammar, and the textbooks have chapters on the modes of writing: Description, Argument and Persuasion, Comparison and Contrast, and so on. There are discussions of thesis statements, topic sentences, and the five-paragraph essay (a species of writing that exists nowhere but in academia). Standardized tests, such as the College Preparatory Exit Examination, are used to measure competence. (Such tests, of course, whether essay or multiple choice, appeal to conformity and convention—after all, isn't that what "standardizing" means?) Such tests are also about correct results.

For our students, the Three *c*s of composition are emphasized: clarity, coherence, and correctness. The final draft—the end result—is what counts most at FAMU, because it is that final draft that earns the grade, passes the test, moves a student on. The composition textbooks used at FAMU aim for a clear, coherent, and correct final result.

*Lizanne:* Trying to isolate the differences between Horizons sections and my other first-year writing classes is tricky, as no Horizons student was typical, and each class had its own personality. Like Melanie, I noticed a wider range of abilities than in my other writing classes: some gifted students, others woefully unprepared.

A seemingly small difference between my classes caught my attention. I introduced myself as Lizanne Minerva to both my first-year writing classes, and said I preferred to go by Lizanne. In the Horizons sections, students called me Miz L or Miss Minerva, while most of my other first-year writing students addressed me by first name. These choices told me how each class constructed me, or wanted to: as the person in authority or as a potential ally in the writing process.

*Mel:* I started my teaching career at Florida A & M by attempting to graft the process approach to writing that I had learned about at Florida State (and which I practice myself, though I never learned it formally in any school) to the product-oriented approach of Florida A & M. I pushed prewriting and I required multiple drafts and peer reviews. I exasperated my students by answering questions with counter questions: When asked, "Ms. Rawls, is this right?" I would reply, "What makes you think there is a problem with what you've written?" Or when asked, "Ms. Rawls, if I did thus-and-such, would it be alright?" I would reply, "I haven't the slightest idea. Why don't you try it and see what happens?"

In grading, I assigned a portion of the credit—30 percent or 60 percent, depending on the project—to a written analysis of how the student wrote the paper and why he or she made the writing decisions that were made; and this analysis accompanied the paper. "*How* you do it and *why* you do it is, in the long run, more important," I promised. "The grade is a mere side effect."

"Uh huh," responded my students.

*Lizanne:* During the first week of the semester at FSU, I asked students to bring in examples of good writing. A woman read a poem supplied by a Horizons program coordinator called "Mountain Mover," an inspirational work about rising above difficulties.

I commented that the approach in first-year writing was probably closer to scaling a mountain than moving one. Growing flustered as faces closed to me, I kept crafting my awkward metaphor. Moving mountains implied a kind of omniscience we didn't often have in the middle of a project, and it was all right to explore. Writing was a process of straining to see through the trees, making mistakes and doubling back . . .

I've embarrassed myself in front of classes, rambling on too long, but this was no ordinary foolish moment. I had critiqued a poem that encouraged Horizons students to transcend the hardships they'd encountered at a BWI, like having one's teacher find fault with one's values. Not one student would look at me.

*Mel:* I have my arrogancies, but I'm not arrogant enough to assume that FSU's process-teaching style could or should be forced upon my FAMU students, or that my colleagues who are teaching the five-paragraph essay just haven't gotten the Good Word about process pedagogy. I started giving serious thought as to why FAMU values the product so highly, and a stylistically correct product at that.

I got a big clue the first day I saw business majors all dressed up.

There they were, striding back and forth across campus, clad in sharp black or navy blue suits. The young women, in their sheer dark stockings and heels, looked chic; and the young men, in crisp white shirts and marvelously polished dress shoes, looked, well, looked manly. They were such a contrast to the majority of the student body, clad in denim and funky T-shirts or tight, provocatively short flowery dresses and chunky, clunky shoes.

"What's going on?" I asked, and was told that the SBI (School of Business and Industry) students had Forum that day.

"Forum" is a series of seminars that business majors are required to attend dressed in business attire. FAMU's School of Business and Industry has an excellent reputation that translates into internships, regular six-figure corporate contributions to the program, and a strong sense of pride in its majors. After that display of sartorial style, I was not surprised to read an article wherein a corporate recruiter praised SBI students because "they are so prepared" and "already have the corporate attitude and style." Those navy blue suits and straight backs are most impressive. Style (so often viewed as an outward manifestation of ability and attitude) opens doors for these students.

*Lizanne:* My apparent lack of style—both in dress and manner—concerned Horizons students. I wore skirts and sandals most days, not jeans or shorts, but I did not look the part they'd envisioned for me. Horizons students preferred to see a recognizable authority figure standing at the front of the room.

Some comments on my appearance were in good humor. In final evaluations, one woman's sole suggestion was that I wear more cute outfits like the one I'd worn the day before. Then there were stinging remarks, like an anonymous evaluation that said simply, "Go back to Woodstock." This insult went deeper than appearance. It aligned me with lazy, sloppy, stupid hippies, an image of indolent white people who lacked purpose in life.

In similar fashion, my manner irritated these students. If I knew the answers, why didn't I act more authoritative and provide the answers? Why would I want to be called by my first name? Why didn't I give normal assignments like five-paragraph themes? What did any of this freewriting nonsense have to do with college-level writing, and wasn't freewriting some kind of hippy-dippy enterprise anyway?

And what if this all seems like a game? The five-paragraph theme was one game (and one they knew how to play), and the process paper another. Pleasing the teacher was the familiar way to win, but students could not figure out how to do so when I offered responses and strategies, but no formulas or promises, and no letter grades until a series of drafts had been completed.

We were trapped in conflicting ideas of how the world worked.

*Mel:* Another clue about the cultural difference came from an education major who wrote an essay exploring why his fellow students were so concerned about whether their responses were right or wrong. It's how they're raised, this student concluded. And their parents are concerned with right and wrong—making sure about the correctness—because in the black community, immediate correctness can be a matter of survival. Our history seems to indicate that black people don't always have the luxury of fooling around processing various possibilities, either.

And when I thought of how often the success of black students is not regarded as routine, even when it is routine for the individual in question; and when I considered how a lack of preparedness is so often regarded as genetically ordained, I had to ask myself if the FAMU agenda, among faculty and students, was not only eminently sensible but was clearly evolved from the needs of the community as the community itself perceived its needs: *to prepare for success* students in this world will rush to judgment—will evaluate by their style, allow less time for processing and exploring, and definitely permit less margin for error.

*Lizanne:* For more than three semesters teaching Horizons students, I struggled with the notion of diversity within the university—that is, trying to demonstrate that superficialities like appearance do not figure into college classrooms where content, the heart of the matter, is at stake. Our identities do not reside in our wardrobes.

But the appearance of things—of convention, of authority, of correctness—can make a huge difference in how these students are perceived by the outside world; many of them come to class already conscious of how their style helps or hurts them at a BWI and beyond. For me to preach the value of "alternate" style while looking like their idea of a '60s icon exasperated students for whom exploration may have seemed a luxury.

The value of style became more clear to me as I sat down to talk with Melanie about our teaching experiences. It became more clear to me how students could have a similar response to our teaching styles. A few years after the Horizons classes, when I taught other predominantly African American classes, I dressed up every day and introduced myself as Dr. Minerva.

*Mel:* I know students have heard the saying, "You have to know the rules before you break them." This adage fits product pedagogy well, since attention to the rules and conventions allows anyone to construct an acceptable, useful essay; and we can leave it to the truly committed and creative—to our Ishmael Reeds and Toni Morrisons—to break the rules and break them well.

Among the Murphy's Laws of the world is the one that states, "As soon as you learn the rules, somebody changes them." I worry that my students, appropriately and understandably concerned with correctness, may find themselves armed with a set of conventions that will have limited usefulness in a number of situations they may encounter. I worry that correctness may not be enough. Then what?

So the two of us, Lizanne Minerva and Melanie A. Rawls, are left questioning the effectiveness of both product and process pedagogy in predominantly African American writing classrooms and the connection of both to style. We are wondering how to address students' preferences for authority and convention as well as their need for experimentation and options. There's no denying that convention is powerful: What is the message and the power of a well-cut suit? But exploration opens new worlds: our identities, after all, do not reside in our "wardrobes."

And what does this issue of style say about the styles we value? Or, to present an even more vexed question, the values of our styles?

We're still thinking about it . . .

## Sharing Ideas

- What do these teachers' narratives say about differences between teacher and student expectations in writing classes? What do your experiences tell you about these differences?

- What advantages and disadvantages do you see in a product-oriented approach to writing? A process-oriented approach to writing?

- What effect does the format of the article have on you as a reader? Why do you think the authors chose to set the article up this way, that is, using both personal and academic voices, in alternating voices?

- Read Kate Ronald's essay and this essay together. What issues do they raise when read that way? What do you think Kate would say to Lizanne and Melanie and vice versa? What would you like to say to any of these authors?

- Do this again by reading this essay together with Hans Ostrom's essay. Does a paired reading complicate and/or explain some of the issues of value and style raised in this essay?

- Did you want to argue, agree, protest, explain, correct, emphasize your (similar or different) point of view at any time when you were reading this essay? Go ahead—do it by writing your own interruptions, just as if you interrupted the conversation they're holding. Share the "interruption" paragraphs you'd like to insert with your writing group.

# 19

# When All Writing Is Creative and Student Writing Is Literature

## Wendy Bishop

---

Wendy Bishop works with writers and writing teachers at Florida State University. She arrived in Tallahassee after some years living and teaching in Alaska, Arizona, Nigeria, and California. She writes about the connection between composition and creative writing; she writes poems, stories, and essays. And she enjoys seeing her children—Morgan and Tait—grow into writing and reading. They take particular pleasure when her books include their names, which they always do.

---

Here are journal excerpts from two writing students:

### June

If we are to accept the definition of a writer as one who writes, we must accept the fact that writers are not a special type of person. Those who write might be of any age, shape, background or interest. They may produce a technical manual or a provocative essay or a piece of artistic prose. The one thing they hold in common is the use of language.

If I write a letter to my friend, I am a writer. If I submit a term paper of the same caliber of technique to a committee judging a dissertation, they might dispute whether or not I am a writer! Perhaps writing, like beauty, is in the eye of the beholder.

On the other hand, I can consider myself a writer if no one beholds that I write. Emily Dickinson certainly was a writer during her lifetime, not just after the discovery of her wealth of poetry. The first grader who tells in scrawled words and pictures of the arrival of a baby sister should be encouraged to call herself and be called the writer of that piece.

Perhaps by widening the definition of writer and dissolving the aura of specialness as a prerequisite, we might better encourage possible writing artists to give it a try. Ah-ha! Now there is another category—the writing artist. All writers won't enter that category, due to lack of talent, or dedication, or luck or some mysterious something that can't be pinned down. But with a recognition of a larger pool of writers as those who write, we are more likely to find among us those who write well.

### Chris

The suggestions about how "art" writing may be similar or different from regular writing particularly intrigues me. After spending this school semester learning about composing as a process, I am more apt to see similarities between "art" and regular writing. Similarities exist in the process itself. The stages are the same whether you are wring a sonnet or an essay, pre-writing, writing, and revision. It happens over and over no matter what the outlet. The stages may vary slightly but by and large they remain similar. By learning about the composing process a writer can become more fluent in the language of writing.

In journal entries like these, collected for several years, my writing students often voice strong ideas about what constitutes good and bad writing. Many feel, or have learned to feel, that a writer either has *it* or hasn't got *it*. Sometimes, students enter my composition classroom remarking on differences between essay writing and "literary writing." Sometimes, they don't see differences, easily calling their essays "stories" and their stories "essays." Equally, many student writers are confused about the distinctions between types of writing classes they may enroll in—creative writing or composition. Is a composition class a place where they won't be allowed to be "creative"? Or a place where they just can't write poetry and fiction? And, when they move from composition to creative writing, will they be asked to put away all their compositional skills and never again write essays?

### Fran

Is creative writing stuff that is done for fun, and composition stuff that the teacher makes you do? That's what it meant in elementary school, and later. Composition was writing about a specific topic, picked out by the teacher and had to be a certain length and certain form. Creative writing was anything you felt like putting down on paper.

As someone who teaches both kinds of classes and does both kinds of writing, I know that in the past composition was often taught as a skills class. Students were asked to write in particular essay forms (narration, description, exposition, argumentation) and to bring in a finished essay each week for grading. Such classes are now labeled current-traditional. Being product-oriented, those classes resulted in formulaic writing and rarely offered students glimpses into the messy, generative, exciting process of writing. Creative writing classes, too, for many years were taught in predictable ways; master poets or fiction writers asked students to share and critique a story or poem each week (again, almost always this writing represented a "finished" product). Workshops were stimulating in that twenty or more writers examined a single work. They were also frightening since a traditional creative writing workshop could feel like a performance, making new writers eager to conform to what they assumed were the expectations of their teachers or the models of "excellent" literature found in their particular class anthology.

But I don't believe either of those teaching approaches serves the writer in you very well, and my teaching strategies for both classrooms have become increasingly similar and more process-oriented. I aim to let writers see how writing is put together and to explore the necessary risks of sharing multiple drafts. I think a well taught composition or creative writing class should allow you to explore writing beliefs, writing types (genres) and their attributes, and your own writing process. You will be successful to the degree that you become invested in your work. And you need to be willing to experiment and to study your own progress.

I realize not everyone feels this way, and I believe I know why. In some classrooms, teachers encourage writing students to believe that literature consists only of famous (old) examples of poetry, fiction, and drama.

### Robbie

Student 'lit' is not old enough. Student writing can be literature, if it's published and recognized, and read by a lot of people. If it's just in the classroom, then it's a bill and not a law. Literature is Shakespeare, Chaucer, Coleridge, Shelly, Joyce.

But in other classrooms, teachers broaden the definition of literature to include more than texts in the traditional categories of poetry, fiction, and drama; they include nonfiction and the writings of many modern experimental writers. Students then learn to broaden their definitions, too.

### David

Literature, to me, is just about anything that has been published. There are, of course, different levels of literature ranging from journals to novels, comics to compilations.

And in still other writing classrooms, teachers expand categories to include student writing as literature, encouraging writers to consider how their work functions in a universe of texts and text categories.

**Karen**

Student writing can be literature—it just may not necessarily be 'good' literature.

**Sean**

There's not a reason why a student can't do it [write literature]. In fact, judging from what I've read of the students here over the last couple of semesters, they are pumping out literature.

If, during the course of your college career, you encounter two or even three writing teachers who make you feel strongly but differently about these issues, you may reasonably be confused. This essay won't resolve your confusion, but it will begin to talk about these points by letting you hear some student writers, and teachers who are writers, voicing their opinions.

## Risk Taking, Creativity, Engagement

Creativity involves risk taking. It's likely that in your writing past, you were not praised for taking risks. Rather, you were told that you had to follow the conventions for the type of writing focused on in that class, writing an academic essay, a short story, or a research report. You were rarely asked to "publish" several drafts of your creative writing in workshop; instead, you were asked to produce a polished research paper and a finished story.

When writing classes don't highlight risk taking, it's hard to see the complicated ways authors go about their work. Sometimes it's difficult to realize that the "finished products" you read in anthologies often went through days, weeks, months, and years of change, alterations, false starts, and even sometimes temporary abandonment. For most of us, risk taking in writing spells disaster and failure rather than excitement and discovery. We haven't often been graded A on our outrageously playful parodies or our intelligent-but-still-problematic third drafts.

Since you generally write within classrooms and under the direction of teachers who value particular models of excellent writing, it's no wonder that you want always to present your best, most polished, most finished work to peers and your teachers. In doing this, it's natural to play it safe, but safe work is often conventional and derivative.

All this is understandable, too, since the penalty for risk taking in the traditional writing class is failure if your work is judged ineffective, unfinished, inexpert. And no one wants to fail in a writing class. Most of us remember too many past failures. We all have stories of teachers correcting our grammar and marking in red ink across every white and open space in our texts. As we grew up as school writers, there was so much to learn about spelling and sentences and paragraphs and citation systems that trying and failing in order to find a new, better, more original way of saying something would have sounded like a recipe for academic suicide. Yet without risk and experimentation, most writers remain disengaged with their work.

### Fran

Then I wrote a paper that was required, and it turned out to be fun. What??!? Yes, and it was an English (ugh! don't say it!) *term* paper. I chose my own topic, so I wouldn't get bored with it. Something *totally* off the wall, so fascinating that its appeal overwhelmed my intense hatred of term papers. It was on parapsychology.

Another writer found that writing expository prose and creative prose was not a matter of inspirational difference; rather, it was a matter of cognitive difference, thinking in somewhat different ways for different purposes.

### Juan

I don't find a difference when writing expository prose and when doing "creative writing." To me, it's all essentially writing. To me, they're very similar, just the writing research comes from two different areas: internal source or external source.

For Juan, the creative writer conducts mainly "inner" research while the expository essayist conducts mainly "outer" research to support his text-in-progress.

Writing teacher Stephen Tchudi (1991) also feels that his experience writing in several genres—children's fiction to essays on teaching writing—have shown him fewer differences than similarities: "It's okay to put a little jelly on your bread-and-butter writing. My nonfiction prose style has been greatly aided by my ventures in imaginative writing" (105).

I'm suggesting then that writers need classes that allow them to take risks and experiment with prose, and they need to see similarities between the types of composing they do, adding a little jelly to their bread-and-butter writing (and I might guess that sometimes their jelly writing would benefit if it grew from the solid base of bread-and-butter prose).

## Genre, Subgenres, Popular Genres, and Literary Genres

None of these suggestions mean, however, that in writing classes you should stop valuing the work of professional writers or fail to study the forms their writings take. Traditionally, a great deal of student time in English classes has been spent acquiring genre knowledge, examining strategies for making poems seem like poems, stories like stories, and essays like essays. So part of the writing classroom, too, always involves the study of exemplary or expert writing in the forms you hope to learn. But you also always need the opportunity to write against and experiment with those forms. *You have to try it to do it,* whether bread-and-butter *or* jelly writing.

All of us can learn to value literary forms just as all of us value nonliterary forms or literary subgenres. My own not-so-hidden secret is that I love the writing of women detective novelists as well as the finest, most famous academic poetry I've ever read (and I've read a lot of both). Within her genre, for my money, Agatha Christie is still tops. Just as within his genre of lyric English verse, Gerard Manley Hopkins produced writing of incredible power.

Further, I've seen that my students have the same ability to perform well in many types of writing—many genres—if they choose and therefore value those forms. Over several years of writing and publishing student work in books about writing, I've come to like the works of Ken Wademan, Pam Miller, and Sean Carswell—who were writing essays, journal entries, in-class writing experiments, nonfiction, and parody—as well as any writing I've ever read. And these writers have strong feelings about their work because they are involved with it; they take risks, but also they take writing seriously.

### Sean

I like to think all of my expository prose is creative. I like to think that the only difference is that it's focused on something that bores the hell out of most people. Also, my expository prose generally doesn't have characters, a plot, or foul language. Not that the language in my "creative" writing is foul, just a bit more vulgar.

Everything I write is literature and I'm offended that you'd doubt me. Sure student writing is literature. F. Scott Fitzgerald wrote the first half of *This Side of Paradise* while he was at Princeton. I've seen pieces go through the workshops here that are better than any John Updike I've read. Langston Hughes poem "Poem for English B" or something like that was written in college, and that's a great poem. I think Kerouac started his first novel at Columbia. I guess all that literature is taking on a theme worth reading about, writing well, i.e., good images, powerful language, different levels of meaning, none of the shit that's in Danielle Steel. There's no reason why a student can't do it.

You can see from Sean's remarks that widening what we define as creative and literary and viewing student writing as literature doesn't prevent us from categorizing and judging writing; humans understand their world through categories and judgments. I would simply argue that we shouldn't assume that there is only one way to categorize or that those categories should (or could) hold fast for all people, in all cultures, in all historical times.

Current theories of reading and writing suggest that there is no ideal, exemplary "best poem" or "great American novel" out there, waiting to be written. Rather, once texts are composed, we find them more or less like other texts that we have already sorted by general categories, *and* we do this sorting by community agreement: We do it within the worlds of literary critics, the worlds of English departments, the worlds of writing classrooms, the worlds of independent reading groups, and so on.

### Karen

> Literature to me can be just about anything. The word "literature" is kind of lofty and snobbish to me. The distinction I'd make is between "good" literature and "bad" literature. I don't have any rules for that—I think for example, that something like an article in the *Enquirer* is bad literature compared to maybe *Moby Dick*—then, again, if an *Enquirer* article was taken from its context and issued as a satire of comedy piece, it might be good (author's intent can be important in *some* instances. . . . ).

Karen is grappling with a category system here than says *Moby Dick* is better than an article in the *National Enquirer* just as I for many years felt a bit silly that I enjoyed Agatha Christie (and the subgenre of detective novels) as well as the work of Gerard Manley Hopkins (academic poetry).

Of course, most writers aim for a genre at some point in their drafting process. These days, we know writers can incorporate a lot of what they hope to share, but not all that they wish to share; they are unable to *fix* a text so that each reader will read it in exactly the same way because readers bring themselves, their backgrounds, associations, experience with texts, and so on, to each reading occasion.

Since a text can never be completely fixed, it is open to interpretation. Readers can offer several possible readings of your text without doing the work a disservice, although certainly some readings appear more "sophisticated" or may turn out to be closer to your original intention than others. At the same time, often you fail in your intentions and are unable to incorporate some of the genre characteristics you had hoped to incorporate, leading to a less than successful text.

For instance, your argument may be based on shaky facts, your "serious" story may be sewn together from absurd and unbelievable events, your *free* verse may go "Ta-dum, Ta-dum, Ta-dum" with constrained regularity, or your informal journal may be knotted up with self-consciousness. It takes study and time and practice to turn out a "traditional" piece of work in an accepted form and style (essay or novel or newspaper article) just as it takes study and time and practice to loosen the bounds of accepted conventions to write an exciting, experimental, or exploratory piece.

Equally, readers depend on the conventions they have learned to understand your work, yet they also need to be willing to suspend their judgments in order to understand *each* new work they encounter. A reader has to identify the genre you are attempting as well as decide to what degree *you intended to deviate* from the standards of that genre.

Reading and writing are *both* interpretive acts, then, requiring intricate intellectual negotiations from all parties concerned. And literature, traditionally, has been a set of texts, all having features that a group of readers and writers have agreed upon. This set of texts changes as the community changes, for, over time, agreement about common features of those texts changes. It's always been that way, even though English teachers often prefer their set—called a canon—of texts fixed, and therefore easier to "cover."

But sermons and letters have gone "out" of the set and stories and poems *of certain agreed upon quality* have been put "in." Women and racial, ethnic, and class minorities have often been out but nowadays many are arguing for including them as in. Students have often been out, but they know better, seeing themselves as in. After all, *someone* has to write literature before it can be classified as such.

### Charles

Student writing is definitely literature; Literature is not only found in textbooks, it has to start somewhere.

### Gordon

Student writing is always literature, however, the quality of that literature is never determined by the writer, but by the readers of that work.

### Bill

To me, if a piece of written work is read by even a few people and enjoyed by at least one—then it was worth writing. The amount of popularity a piece gets is not NECESSARILY how good a piece of writing is, but what is most readily accepted at that time. What I'm writing now is not literature, but it could be if I spent a lot of time editing, and rewriting it would probably sound a whole lot different. I think that student literature can be considered literature if the student perfects the piece through revision. Many students disbelieve this because a lot of work is involved and many papers turned in are not up to literary standards are discouraged.

I believe student writing is literature, too.

I understand that conventional standards for judging writing always affect us.

At the same time, we, in our classroom communities, always affect those standards when we discuss together what we know about and appreciate in the writing we review.

That's how writing and reading work.

I hope you can see how certain questions about texts—When should writers obey or break writing conventions? What is successful work and unsuccessful work? What makes a poem a poem, a story a story, and an essay and essay?—have always interested those who write and study writing. Such questions are perhaps answered best by the nonanswer of overlapping genre categories; that is, categories don't start and stop but shade into each other. You can learn to write a traditional poem, and you can take risks with that form, exploring prose poems and short fiction along the way. You can learn to write the traditional first-year writing essay, and you can enliven that form by taking risks with your voice and your style as you adopt first person (I), add some unexpected narration, and/or use logic lightly. Sometimes you'll fail, but you'll always find that you learn from exploring conventions, sometimes—often—you learn as much by breaking those conventions.

## Literature in the Writing Student

The questions and voices I've shared here suggest that you should approach composition classes and creative writing classes in pretty similar ways. Overall, both types of classrooms need to encourage *and reward* risk taking and experimentation as you learn to conform to and break genre conventions. Mimi Schwartz (1989) writes:

> To value self-investment, to avoid premature closure, to see revision and discovery, to go beyond the predictable, to risk experimentation, and above all, to trust your own creative powers are necessary for all good writing, whether it is a freshman theme, a poem, a term paper. . . . Few of us reward risk taking that fails with a better grade than polished but pedestrian texts. We are more product-oriented, judging assignments as independent of one another rather than as part of a collective and ongoing body of work. No wonder that students interpret our message as "Be careful, not creative!" (204)

If you are creative before you are careful, you will be more likely to gain an understanding of the writing process of professionals. This will happen when your workshops focus on drafting (being creative), revision, style experiments, editing (being careful), and use of portfolio evaluation (which allows you to share both experiments and final products). And being part of such a classroom doesn't mean that you won't still have to examine and explore some of these issues for yourself.

### Anji

> Of course student writing can be literature. If critics consider some of the trash out today to be literature, you better believe that students can writer litererature too. The ability to write something that is considered literature is not only a God-given talent. Most people can do it if they just make the time and collect their thoughts.

Like Anji, most of us are given to grand pronouncements about the quality of this or that piece of writing, but we need to temper our value judgments with an understanding of genre conventions, how they developed, and how they have gained value in particular communities.

**Summer**

*Literature* what is canonized by the unknown people who create anthologies and textbooks, is a formal definition. In an informal definition, literature is a completed piece which has been published or disseminated to an audience, and has been read by a number of persons (which would include everything, even graffiti and advertisements). To narrow the definition, it is not intended for business or propaganda purposes, is received in a "legal" form (NO graffiti, etc.) and is meant to be enjoyed by readers and meets cultural standards of literature (circular argument). Unpublished works can never be literature, no matter how worthy.

You start acquiring this knowledge as you learn about category systems and how texts work in the classroom community; you also learn that it is possible for you to become part of that writing community. These questions you have, the beliefs you hold, the worries you may feel, can all be explored. Remember, risk taking and experimentation results in knowledge, not in anarchy. At the same time, if your writing goal is, ultimately, to become a mystery novelist, you won't be tempted completely to ignore the requirements and limitations of that type of writing. A consummate mystery writer, Agatha Christie (1977) once wrote:

> If you were a carpenter, it would be no good making a chair, the seat of which was five feet up from the floor. It wouldn't be what anyone wanted to sit on. It is no good saying that you think the chair looks handsome that way. If you want to write a book, study what sizes books are, and write within the limits of that size. If you want to write a certain type of short story for a certain type of magazine you have to make it the length and it has to be the type of story that is printed in the magazine. If you like to write for yourself only, that is a different manner—you can make it any length, and write it in any way you wish; but then you will probably have to be content with the pleasure alone of having written it. (334–335)

When you view your writing as literature—through a broad definition and understanding of that word—you allow yourself to share a supremely satisfying human activity. For most of us, writing is never easy, but it is made worthwhile when we "publish" in the writing classroom and when we are "read by even a few people and enjoyed by at least one."

# Works Cited

Christie, Agatha (1977). *An Autobiography*. Great Britain: Collins

Schwartz, Mimi (1989). "Wearing the Shoe on the Other Foot" in Joseph Moxley (Ed.), *Creative Writing in America*. Urbana, IL: National Council of Teachers of English.

Tchudi, Stephen (1991). "Confession of a Failed Bookmaker" in Mimi Schwartz (Ed.), *Writer's Craft, Teachers Art.* Portsmouth, NH: Boynton/Cook.

## Sharing Ideas

- Since it's hard to be objective and to maintain distance from my own writing, I'll ask you to play editor here. Make up five questions about this essay and/or relate it to other essays in the book. Then work with other writers to explore these questions.

- Choose any quote in my essay and write your own informal response to the issues the writer raises. Put yourself in dialogue with the essay and these writers; add to our conversation.

# 20

# I Am Not a Writer,
# I Am a Good Writer

## Joe Quatrone

---

Joe Quatrone was a student at Boise State University when he wrote
this end-of-term analysis of his writing.

---

I am not a writer. I don't do writer-type things. I don't drink coffee. I've never
read Keroak. I don't even know how to spell Keroak. I don't enjoy lurking in
second-hand book stores, pretending I'm waiting desperately for delivery of
one of my top-ten favorite writer's long-lost out-of-print fifth editions that will
finally complete my vast comprehensive home collection. I don't have an
opinion. I prefer ads to articles. I don't know what hyperbole really means. I
like pictures. I have no interest in writing the great American novel. I don't
"get" Hemingway. I think poetry is bunk. I've got bad grammar. And, I happen to believe a burp *is* an answer.

I am a good writer. I like to write what comes out of my head. I like to
write about things that are goofed up in the world (not wrong, nor tragic, nor
sad, nor socially unacceptable—just goofed up). I like writing with my pen on
a legal pad. I like bad grammar. I like to write like I'm a camera. I like to write
like I'm a Mac truck. I like to write like I'm not a writer. I like observing
things. I like being a sniper. And, I like a warm, cuddly blanket with a book on
a couch on a rainy day although I've never done it.

I think before I started this class, I always had this kind of defensive attitude about college writing that made me hate the prospect of it. I have always had a sort of laisez-faire attitude about grammar and style that I enjoy on a personal level, but that didn't usually go over well with my former professors. It's been refreshing to be able to write like I want to and not have to worry about comments like, "what do you reeeeeeeeely mean . . . ?????" I tend to just say stuff and not flower it up, and have comfort in knowing that anything written can be considered "interpretive." I've learned that it's okay to have a style and preference in my writing, and that I don't have to write like a secretary (not an administrative assistant—a secretary) to write successfully.

I think that one of my biggest weaknesses as a writer is my attention span. George Lucas has been quoted as saying that a motion picture is never really finished, it can only be improved upon. I think the same way about writing. However, I don't have the attention span to revise and revise. Granted, I know that revising is critical and I do it with everything (sometimes to a ridiculous degree), but often I lose interest in a piece soon before it's perfected. Excuse me: improved upon.

Another weakness I have is with what I call my hootie-tootie voice. It's the voice that sounds like I'm a motivational speaker and that I live in a transparency projector. It's that voice that you have to use when writing a formal document used in a big meeting with suit-types that say words like "kudos" and "Cool beans." Barf. It's the same voice you read in retirement home brochures and oral hygiene literature. I find myself using phrases like, "point-of-interest," "key to success," and "such as." Icch. I haven't any examples to illustrate my point, other than what's above.

Most of my peers and classmates say I have a pretty good grip on writing, with a fun and witty style. The really obvious critical comments tend to focus on confusing material or stuff that comes out of nowhere in a given piece of writing. While I'm happy to have my writing received optimistically, I fear that same witty, sarcastic voice that most people like, is getting a little "old hat" for me.

I frequently wonder whether I could be a beautiful writer. Write beautiful things that make people think deeper and more emotionally. I wonder if I could write about a walk down a dirt road and make it both interesting and beautiful. I know how the greats do it. I just wonder if I have what it takes to hit those things that everyone reads and goes, "Yea! I know exactly what he's talking about." It's that one thing that any reader can identify with and understand on an emotional level, exactly what I'm describing about that one rusted hinge. Or that leather boot that caressed the foot like a long-lost kitten. Hands touching cold, lifeless steel in the moonlight, burning like a hot iron in a calf's tender hide.

Hmm. That's not so bad. I guess I'm not that bad a writer. I guess I have a lot to learn, too, though.

## Sharing Ideas

- Read Joe's statement in light of my essay in the previous chapter. What assumptions does he seem to have about art and writing and himself as a writer? How do you think he'd respond to that essay?

- How do you think you've changed from the beginning of your writing class to the end? Do you hold contradictory opinions about your own work like Joe does? What do you think your classmates think about you as a writer? What do you think at this point in time?

- You might move from this essay to the questions in Hint Sheet L that encourage you to read your term's work and analyze it. I like to read writers' self-analyses because they can always tell me something about their work that I can't see from the products. What have you learned about writing this term that couldn't possibly (or just doesn't) show up in your written products?

- Now, read your products—what do you like best, want to celebrate, think you'll enjoy rereading in the future and why?

# Part VI

# Hint Sheets for Students and Teachers

My mother looked at fabric and imagined clothes she could make from it. I look at language and imagine essays I could write. Just as a piece of cloth can be fashioned into any number of garments, the essay I construct from language is not the only one I could have written.

—Linda Brodkey
"Writing on the Bias"

# Hint Sheet A:
# Inventing Inventions

Inventions are writing prompts in the form of a writing exercise that help you start and then continue writing. I invent inventions for myself to help me dig more deeply into a subject without wondering if what I'm producing is good or bad, or to simply get going when I don't have specific ideas but do have an urge/need to write. I also create them as a writing teacher for writing classes.

Originally, I figured out how to create these prompt sheets by working backward from a piece of writing I liked, asking: What effects were achieved and what directions would I need to give myself or another writer to achieve those same effects? I also developed inventions by reading other textbooks, other teachers' assignment sheets, and thinking about what worked and didn't work. Eventually, I started adding style prompts to encourage myself and other writers to try things they simply forget to try—to use metaphors, to use the five senses, to look at an idea or issue upside down and backward, to play.

Below, you'll find an invention sheet I just finished for my upcoming writing class. I'll put my voice in italics between some of the lines to explain why I thought some of these prompts might work to free up a writer to explore the issue at hand—in this case language + community. At the same time, I'm aware that I could pretty easily translate a lot of these prompts to other writing situations (I know that because I recycled some of them from other invention handouts). Inventions are what writers do naturally—invent interesting questions about the world and try to answer them.

## Prompts for Writing About Language Communities

1. What languages do you speak? When do you speak them and to whom?
   *I want to get you, the writer, thinking about what expertise you already have.*

2. Under what circumstances does your dialect (register, vocabulary) change? Tell a story about this.
   *Here I'm asking you to think about language choices.*

3. Have you ever traveled and not known the language? Where, when, how did you feel, what did you do? Did you try to learn the language? Did you enjoy not knowing it at all, why?
   *Again, I'm tapping on your past experiences.*

4. When do you feel silenced, without language?
   *Reversal is always a good trick—it gets you thinking about the other side of things, new angles.*

5. What do you think about (when do you think about) body language? Can you read it? When, under what circumstances?

6. Do you have a peer group that uses a certain language? Give examples.

7. Do you or someone you know work in a profession with its own language? For instance, what is the language of school? What is the language of therapy? What is advertising language?
   *This one connects to a course goal: to think about language communities.*

8. Do animals have languages? If they do, explain why you think so. If you don't think so, explain why you don't believe they do.

9. In either case, what animal language would you most like to speak and what would you ask that animal first?
   *These two questions connect with topics I know interest us all and also to try to get those discussions moved to a serious playful level.*

10. What—if anything—will be lost when we all speak the same language (as when Europe moves to the Eurodollar)? What gained?
    *Here I'm working on analogy, asking you to make connections.*

11. Tell a story about you and language.
    *Tried and true but important—we all love to tell stories and learn from them and from telling them.*

12. Have you lost a language? Where, how, why?

13. How important is a language to a culture?

14. Well into this century, some cultures had only spoken and not written languages—what would be the benefits of this? The drawbacks?
    *Here I'm trying to deepen the discussion, to move from personal to historical/cultural thinking.*

15. Read the essay by Marcus Laffey in "The Word on the Street" from *The New Yorker.* After you've finished, freewrite again about "language."
    *Now, of course, I'm being teacher and asking writers to connect to a text that I think will prompt more thinking and/or interesting writing.*

# Hint Sheet B:
# Reading Assignment Sheets

Assignment sheets—what does the teacher want? What do you have to do? How can you handle and approach this topic, assignment, course requirement? I don't have fixed answers but it does help to:

1. read the sheet carefully

2. ask questions of your teacher and your peers

3. look at key terms and be sure you understand them and, finally,

4. be willing to push against your own resistance and try (not say: It's unclear, it's too hard, it's dumb, and so on)

I include a short assignment sheet here for you to talk about. It might be useful to think of it in light of the Hint Sheet A on Inventions, too. Next, if you're lucky, you'll have one of your own teacher's sheets to look at; she may encourage you to bring in sheets from other/previous classes to discuss. Remember, it's not just teachers who set assignments, most working writers I know work to assignments—as large and vague as "I want to write a good poem" and as specific as, "I need to do x, y, and z to complete a revision for the second edition of *The Subject Is Writing* and I have to do it by this date under these space and style constraints."

## Exploratory Writing 1: How I Learned to Write

In class, we've been writing and talking about how you learned to write. You've read Audrey Brown's essay in *The Subject Is Writing*. Tell your "story" about learning to write; feel free to draw from any of your freewritings that we did in class the first day in response to invention prompts. (Remember these? They are: drawing our home at the time we learned to write and telling a story about writing in each room; listing any general writing memories; telling one school story about writing, or not writing; describing our writing processes at this point in time; describing our first memory of the "tools" of writing—what the pencil, paper, crayons felt and looked like; listing everything we can remember ever writing in elementary school, and so on.)

To tell your story, you'll want to *remember, in as much detail as possible* (this might be aided by a phone call to a parent, sibling, or friend). Then, you'll want to *explore and work to understand* why this experience/story came to the surface for you, *why is it important, what can you (and we as*

211

*readers) learn from the experience.* Even if you classify yourself as a non-writer, you have a relationship with learning to write.

Bring a copy of this exploratory writing for your group members and one for me. Your group will share these. Your job as discussants is to encourage the writer to explain and explore even further.

Remember, the exploratory writing must be typed, single-spaced, one page (not $\frac{1}{3}$ page)—that is, about 500–600 words, and must be labeled with our class number, section, date, and your name.

# Hint Sheet C: Getting Your Journal Going

*Names Include.*    learning logs; to-do lists; dialogue journals; day books; travel journals; double-entry journals; reading logs; diaries; collage journals; fieldnotes, daily planners; e-mail journals; letter correspondences; audit books; dialogue journals with teachers; letters as journals (please feel free to add to this list).

*Uses.*    to keep track and keep records; to keep in touch with yourself; catalog the world; make connections (between something being studied and seen and you); to create places to learn (to write, to read, to analyze, to speculate); to create places to play, to digress, to speculate; places to experiment, to take risks, to be excessive, to be safe, and to be personal (add to this list; try some new options).

*Useful Habits.*    use the first person; don't worry about looks or worry about looks only if it's fun to play with typography and mixed media; write regularly; write informally and explore leads and digressions; write in your own voice(s), that is, use slang, dialect, comfortable sayings and language; make use of chronology and explore time constraints; don't worry about correctness and grammar and punctuation and readers—you don't have readers unless you chose to share with someone (add to this list; make a version that is appropriate for you).

*People Who Journal.*    diarists and observers (Samuel Pepys, Anne Frank, Anais Nin, Anne Morrow Lindberg); record keepers and historical documentarians (early records of the Incas and Aztecs, the Babylonians and Egyptians to Richard Nixon's revealing White House tapes to formal presidential archives); artists, painters, photographers, musicians (Frida Kahlo, cave painters, Edward Weston, Paul Gaugin, Andy Warhol, Keith Haring, Ludwig von Beethoven); authors and poets (May Sarton, George Sand, Doris Lessing, John Cheever, Coleridge, Buddhist poets who captured their travels in mixed verse and prose, Leslie Silko and James Wright—who corresponded, ditto William Stafford and Marvin Bell—Mark Twain, Virginia Woolf, Ana Akhmatova, Charles W. Chestnutt, Audre Lourde, Mary Shelley, Sylvia Plath, John Steinbeck); spiritual travelers and philosophers (Thomas Merton, Joseph Smith, Emerson, Henry David Thoreau); earthly travelers, adventurers, explorers (Frederick Catherwood and J.L. Stevens, Lewis and Clark, Lewis

Henry Morgan, Robert Falcon Scott); soldiers, historians (Charles Kikuchi, Colonel Charles S. Wainwright, Emma Simpson); naturalists and scientists (Sigmund Freud, Glenn T. Seaborg, Hippolito Ruiz, Aldo Leopold, Edward Abbey, John James Audubon); writing teachers (Donald Murray, Toby Fulwiler, Chris Anson, Richard Beach, Wendy Bishop); writing students like you (add to this list; find samples and photocopy them and share them around; create new and different categories).

*What Not to Do.*     Don't grade them, correct them, or force writers to publicly share things meant to be private without warning or permission; don't let them turn into busywork; don't make boring catch-up entries or give up because a pattern is broken—just plunge in again; don't be pedantic, over-precise; don't pay more attention to form than content or forget to be playful (add to this list).

# Hint Sheet D: A Sampler of Creative Ways to Respond to a Literary Text

1. Choose a resonant phrase or crucial word and begin clustering in response.

2. Write a letter to a character or author—ask questions, give responses.

3. Write a reversal—change gender, actions, scene, or simply reverse language.

4. Write an extension—take the piece an hour, day, or week beyond its current ending.

5. Write a treatment—what contemporary movie stars would you have star in this text and why?

6. Explore the narrator or a character—use the following metaphoric prompts to add to your understanding of the narrator/character:

   - He/she is the kind of person who wears . . .
   - He/she is what color?
   - He/she is keeping what secret(s)?
   - He/she has this dream . . .
   - He/she would like to say but never says:
   - He/she is what kind of fruit? what kind of landscape? what kind of time of day?
   - What job should this person never have? what kind of a car does he/she drive?
   - This person is what kind of weather?
   - And so on

7. Choose five words from the text you're studying—words that resonate or have odd significance, interesting locations. Freewrite on each for one minute. Then choose one of the freewrites to continue into an initial response writing.

8. Recast an issue or scene

   - If the text talks about love and food, freewrite about love and food

- If a text talks about moral and ethical decisions/turning points, freewrite about those in your own life
- If the text has a lyrical description of *x* (summer, winter, the coast, and so on) freewrite about *x* in your own life
- Draft your own text in a situation contemporary to you (create a word meal for a current lover, describe a current living landscape for a distant friend, and so on)

9. Explore the texts' rhetoric and style.

10. Write a parody (new subject same linguistic style).

11. Change genre (turn a poem into a prose passage by filling in gaps and recreating sentence patterns; turn prose into a poem by lining out, cutting, repeating, altering the rhythm).

12. Write a reply to the text using the same style (or a reply for a character in the text).

13. Collage your text (any of the above exercises) with those of members of a group.

## Intentionally

Cluster from the same core word and then share the resulting freewrites by reading a sentence one at a time, around the group.

Let several of the created-from-text characters speak together—put them into a scene or dialog together after you flesh them out with metaphoric prompts.

Do a call and response—one person reads a passage and everyone writes a response (do this one time for each group member), then read the entire set in compositional order (or in a set alternation).

## Randomly

Cut and paste sentences together from individual writings or choose three or four phrases for the group to freewrite on and then share in a round-reading.

*This is not about competitive art-making, it's about understanding and experiencing.*

# Hint Sheet E:
# Partner Inventory for
# Working Together

Circle the right or left term on the following list to indicate where you rate yourself on what are obviously extremes. Look for a partner who 1) is someone you don't know terribly well, 2) interested in some of the same things as you, 3) has many of the same personality and learning traits as you, 4) is available to work out of class an hour or two a week until the project is complete. It would help if between the two of you, one person has easy access to a computer for drafting together. After circling which terms best suit you, share these with others in class and then choose your partner and set up your first meeting.

I (am a/an)

| | |
|---|---|
| introvert | extrovert |
| like working with others | dislike working with others |
| procrastinator | ALWAYS on time |
| like to read and talk about reading | don't like to read and talk about reading |
| feel lost in libraries | know my way around libraries |
| known for a good imagination | not known for a good imagination |
| not interested in editing | good editor |
| good sense of humor | take things pretty seriously |
| follower | leader |
| engaged with school | feeling lost or unengaged |
| get the point of this project | totally confused about this project |
| feeling worried this semester | things are going great this semester |
| good at time management | friends think I'm scattered |

(Note: these are class- and task-specific qualities—this type of sheet should be modified and adapted class by class.)

# Hint Sheet F: A Discussion of Drafting Levels

In workshop and process-oriented classrooms, you'll want to develop your own classroom language for revision—zero draft, rough draft, first draft (I call these full-breadth drafts nowadays; complete enough to merit discussion but really an initial trying on of ideas that will be revised after readers' responses), professional drafts, portfolio-quality draft, and so on—because so much writing classroom time these days is spent in drafting and response sessions.

*Early Revision.*    In early drafts, a writer is primarily involved with developing ideas although also making initial decisions about what form might best communicate those ideas. A writer tries out options, lots of them, options and ideas that are never seen by a reader. This happens because a writer at the beginning needs to look at the big picture and it takes some time to plot out that picture.

During early drafts, a writer is not very concerned with the fine details—mechanics, spelling, punctuation, and word choice. The writer pushes on to discover. The writer is not worried about perfection. To do this type of drafting, the writer must be flexible, try not to worry about the product, and learn to trust the process of setting out on a writing journey.

*Late Revision.*    Late revision is a relative concept. For some writers, late revision happens in the second draft and for others it happens during draft twenty-five. During late revision, a writer finalizes ideas, fits those ideas to the form the writer has chosen and becomes concerned with smaller style options, particularly at the paragraph and sentence level. After the big picture is blocked out, it's time to look at the nuances, the precise effects this text will have on an intended reader, asking, will he understand or enjoy this?

During later revisions, the writer starts looking seriously at audience issues but does not become overly concerned with the finest of details of mechanics, spelling, and punctuation; there is still time to move a paragraph or a sentence, to think up a more effective phrase. The writer is not yet concerned with perfection, but the writer is getting close to that point.

*Editing.*    It's most efficient—and generally most satisfying—to edit a piece of writing immediately before relinquishing it. When we give a text to a teacher or publisher, we must be concerned with perfection. This is, at least momentarily, a writer's best opportunity to focus on surface-level clarity.

Editing is the smallest picture of all; the writer is concerned with detail and mechanics—getting a dark print from the printer toner, setting standard margins, having a title, including a writer's name, proofreading for spelling errors, checking for unintentional punctuation and/or grammar errors.

A writer edits so as not to alienate a reader by making the reader do the writer's work. During editing, we strive toward some standard of perfection. Editing is not a time to remove paragraphs four through seven and rewrite them or to dramatically change the genre or focus of a piece or to add a new set of research issues.

# Hint Sheet G:
# Revising out—Expanding and Amplifying a Draft (Before Revising in)

My argument: We tend to stop down our texts too soon. To tire out, to play it safe, to not invest, to not develop enough text to truly revise. Thorough revision means to revise at the global level (paragraph to whole text) as well as the local level (word and sentence). These exercises (like the sequence outlined in Toby Fulwiler's essay "A Lesson in Revision"), allow you to generate more text before you close down and finalize your options. I ask writers I work with to choose one of these options after their first full-breadth draft has been shared in a small group response session.

*A Fat Draft.*    Arbitrarily double your text. Turn a one-page poem into a two- page poem. Turn a five-page essay into a ten-page essay. Turn a one-act play into a two-act play. It doesn't have to be "good" or "better" or "finished" it just has to be honestly twice as long.

*A Memory Draft.*    Read your text carefully. Say two times. Once silently. Once aloud. Then you put it away. Immediately (or if you prefer, after you've dreamed upon it), sit down and write another text of at least the same or longer length—you can try to "remember" your text, go off on a tangent, or do both. This is a memory draft; it may closely shadow the original or strike off in a new direction. Again, this does not have to be "good" or "better" or "finished" it just has to be as long or longer and written without a single turning back to the original, except for what you have retained in memory.

*Move from Participant to Spectator.*    Narrate an earlier memory, event, scene, and then move between that time and the present to turn an *event* into an *experience*. Variation 1. Set yourself at a certain age and remember beliefs, way of life, attitudes, scene and then move to the present and reflect on how those beliefs, actions, attitudes, scenes have shifted and why. Variation 2. Revisit an actual site. Tell a past story from that site while actually there. Look around and draw on the present physicality of your location which may require that you shuttle back and forth through time—how it was then, how it is now.

*Fragments and Extensions.*     Reread what you've written. Along the way, collect five words or phrases from your text and freewrite on each word. Let the word or phrase take you anywhere. See if any of this new material helps you open up the draft; can you insert the new material at the point you find the original word or phrase? Somewhere else?

*Burrow.*     Find a place where readers asked for more (or said they were confused). Imagine that every sentence contains its own next sentence. You can hear it if you listen. Begin with a single sentence, to which you add, by the sheer force of language itself, just another sentence, which adds a little bit to the first. Now in place of a single sentence, you have two, to which you add a third. Each time you increase your text, you are adding on to the whole that proceeds it, and each time the whole is transformed. Burrow into the sentences you write as if on an archeological dig. Turn your words and their sounds and their sentences over and over. Listen for the spark, for connections, for the force of your own desire. When the initial impulse of your sentence has exhausted itself, stop. Go to the next sentence marked by readers, proceed as described above, add a new sentence, and continue . . . for a while.

*Try Like an Essay Tries.*     Contradict, associate, use one or more voices, offer multiple truths, digress, argue, stay open, define, redefine, digress, imply, perform. You may want to try all these options on a single word (a core word) from your original text.

*Write Between the Lines.*     Begin with a text you have written. Begin by convincing yourself you have only just begun to know anything about what you have written. Now begin again by writing in between the lines of your text. Between every two lines, insert a new line that adds to, or deepens, or further explores what the lines on either side of it have started. Variation 1. Break each sentence into two sentences, adding to the middle to fill them out. Variation 2. Identify the basic organizing unit of the text—if you are writing prose, make it paragraphs; for poetry, stanzas. Open the text at the joints of each unit and write something new at each break. Add paragraphs, or stanzas. Repeat as necessary. Variation 2a. Add a different genre between each unit. Variation 3. Have someone make random slash marks on your text—at each slash mark, break open the text. Variation 3a. Proceed as in Variation 2a above, only at the slash marks.

# Hint Sheet H:
# Some Style Play

*In Praise of Punctuation.*     Author Pico Iyer claims, "the comma gets no respect." In fact, punctuation rules and regulations have nearly killed our enjoyment of the perfectly deployed exclamation point or the well-formed semicolon. Change that, by reveling in different punctuation marks the better to learn how to use them. Going by the theory that it takes excess to curb one's enthusiasm back to controlled usage, I'd like you individually (or with a group of writing friends) to assemble a collection of paragraphs on punctuation.

Write short paeans, praise paragraphs, or longer explorations devoted to the following marks (and, of course, utilize the mark strategically but also all over the place, to excess; you may choose to digress and wax philosophical about the uses of your punctuation mark of choice).

Write then, in praise of: ! ' __ . — ; : " ? ( ) [ ] , and so on. If you must, you could even write in praise of e-mail emoticons like sideways smiley faces: ;-).} Someone, too, might want to take on the powerful absence or quiet or purity or deviousness of the punctuating empty white space.

As a follow-up exercise, take a current paragraph from one of your class essays and load it up and down and sideways. Make it heavily exclamatory. Turn statements to questions. Join the several sentences into one long elegantly orchestrated snake of an exposition. Or, eliminate punctuation entirely and make line breaks and/or syntax shifts do the pausing and turn signaling for your wary or unwary reader. Read these versions aloud to better hear what you say in this way.

*Sentence (Non)sense.*     There are a lot of rules about sentence length and complexity, but the usual prescription is for sentences that are not too long, and not too short, and not too complex. Clear, concise, coherent. Okay, but sometimes we enjoy the reverse. The labyrinthine sentence, properly handled, can be elegantly elaborate. And it sounds quite different from the short, sharp sentences of the detective novel that seems to thrive on what can be damned as "primer prose"—short subject + verb + object sentences. And to prove that neither short nor long, simple or complex, can possibly be the rule, sentences can have complicated rhythms and balances, parallel structures, teetering and tottering digressions to create an effect.

In fact, in many sentences, you find curled up and waiting for you a sense of the persona the author is trying to create. This happens through repetition, alliteration, word play, punning—self-conscious, high-spirited writing. So, okay, professional writers in all venues, all genres, play with sentence variation. What happens when you do the same?

Try the following sentence exercise first by writing a new paragraph. Everyone writes (you write) about a beverage—milk, tea, coffee, coke—using only words of a single syllable and then try to rewrite the paragraph using the variations below. Sample paragraph on coffee:

> It's day. I drink. Warm. Brown. Milk, of course. Jolt takes me. Gives me time to take time. Cup of stain. Teeth. Brain. Eyes wide I look out. Type. Grind more beans. Drip. Perk. Perk up. I write. Type. Cold cup. Add more. Too much. Grind teeth. Drink day. Full up. Full up.

Now take your one syllable paragraph and do the following exercises:

1. Recast your paragraph using words of two or more syllables only.

2. Recast your paragraph into a single, labyrinthine sentence.

3. Recast your paragraph into a fragment, then a longer central sentence, then end again on a fragment.

4. Recast your paragraph into a series of balanced sentences—modifier, main clause, modifier—say; do the same for at least two other sentences in the paragraph.

5. Break your paragraph down into constituent parts by dismantling to smaller and smaller kernels. ["I went to the store to buy bread" becomes—"I went. I went to the store. I went to buy bread."]

6. Rebuild your paragraph from the dismantled parts, looking for different ways to combine and modify (called sentence-combining).

7. Recast your paragraph to use parentheticals, slang/conversation, and/or lots of repetition (choose your effect depending on your subject).

8. Look at all your experiments and write your final best paragraph and a note on why you chose the sentence structures, patterns you choose.

After you've completed the exercise with your play paragraph, try completing the exercise using a favorite opening paragraph from your own work (begin by recasting that paragraph in words of one syllable) to see how what you thought you already liked can take different tones and timbres. Then try the exercises with a paragraph that isn't working to see where simple experimentation can take you.

*About That Title.*      I think of titles as opportunities. I say this even though I know some writers agonize over them, avoid them, dread them. I've learned to use titles to help me find ways into a work, to collect ideas for other work. (I've spent years keeping titles to pieces I'd like to write, plan to write, might never write but like to think about.)

Titles can set the scene, color a reader's expectations, offer a key to your work: I think of them as reader aids, as a kind of hint sheet like this. They can be ads for your work, provoke a certain reader mind-set. In a short work like a poem, they're a real opportunity. For instance, the haiku is generally translated from the Japanese form into an English version consisting of five, seven, five syllables. But it's fun to force that form by adding a title, and the title can be as long as you want. Interestingly, works as long as a novel can have single word titles, just the reverse use of haiku with long-title experience.

Sam Myer, in an essay called "Prose by Any Other Name: A Context for Teaching the Rhetoric of Titles" analyzed, as you and your class might analyze, the titles used by authors in well-known fiction and nonfiction. He found authors labeling with noun or adjective/noun clusters; using imagistic or figurative titles (metaphors, symbols, irony, puns), or allusions (to other literary titles, events, connections—using a line from Shakespeare, for instance, to title your essay, as in "To Be or Not to Be"), and finally he grouped a lot into special effects titles (you'll find a lot of these in CD titles and *Rolling Stone*-style journalism). You'll also find you can make up your own category systems or that these categories shift according to types of writing. Contemporary poems are titled in certain ways as are contemporary songs. Modern essays are titled one way and contemporary journalism a little differently. Textbooks sure use predictable (sellable?) titles. Like this one, writing textbooks always try to work in pointers to their contents and their uses.

So the question remains: how to get titles going when you feel titleless. First, do some collecting of titles you like, analyze them, and then practice finding alternate titles for any and everything you write. You can practice too on your own exploratory or practice work—title your journal entries and your grocery lists and you'll learn a lot about abstracting, pointing to elements of, and calling attention in general to your writing.

Now, here's an exercise adapted from one by Richard Leahy ("Twenty Titles for the Writer,") that has worked for some writers in search of titles.

Reread your essay. While you do this, highlight ten words, phrases, or sentences that are: snappy; evocative; intriguing; mysterious; central to your paper. Copy these out and play with them—try to turn them into title-sounding words or phrases. Put the best one of these on a Title List for later consideration.

Write down the same number of words, phrases, or sentences that are not in your draft. Play with three of them and turn them into possible titles. Put the best one on your Title List.

Create five titles—each must use a different one of your five senses— taste, sight, feel, smell, sound. Chose the best of these for your Title List.

Write ten titles that derive from other arts—songs, movies, plays, well-known cultural artifacts. Best one, of course goes to your Title List.

Write a one-word, then a two-word, then a three-word, then a four-word title (continue on as far as you can, even to a twenty-word title). Chose the three best for your Title List.

Write a title beginning with the word "On . . ." Beginning with an –ing word, beginning with "In . . ." Chose one for your Title List.

Write three titles that play on 1) regional sayings, 2) clichés, 3) folk sayings. Put all of these on your Title List.

Write the most obvious title for your piece. A title that's a lie. A title for the essay you wish you had written instead of this one. A title that is absolutely visual and concrete. Chose one of these for the Title List.

Write a separate title using each of the following words: what, who, when, where, how, why, will, might, should, is/are, do/does, if. Chose the two best for your Title List.

Now.

Take your Title List and share it with other readers of your essay. Read them aloud. Let them write down/note the best, funniest, most strange, most provocative.

Play with the several you/they like the most: Hook two together with a dash or a colon. Twist them by sound so they're just a little different. Twist by punning or substituting a word.

Choose a title for your essay. From anywhere in this exercise. Enjoy.

# Hint Sheet I: Responding to Peer Writing Before a Full-class Workshop

Please respond to each essay with a letter (or paragraph, or note) from you to the author (suggestions for things you may want to discuss follow). Also, annotate the writer's text. Return the text and letter after each discussion.

1. Each writer will read a paragraph aloud.
2. All class members will share in the discussion.

   a. Try to offer the writer a sense of how you read the piece.
      Among many other things, you might tell her:
      - how you understood or enjoyed the text
      - what sentence or image seemed crucial to the text and your understanding of it (essentially, identify the center of gravity)
      - where your attention lagged (and perhaps picked up again)
      - how you felt as the audience for this piece (were you the right audience? do you need to know more about the writer's intended audience? and so on)
      - where you felt gaps, wished for more, felt something was being held back, and so on

   b. Try to offer the writer a sense of possible revision directions.
      Among other things, you might tell him:
      - how to lengthen or shorten the piece, if the beginning and ending are effective, and so on
      - how he could experiment in a way you'd find interesting
      - if you sense any risk taking going on and how to keep capturing that sense of working dangerously (but also productively)
      - where breaking the conventions works (usage, sentence structure, invented words, punctuation) and/or where you're worried by broken conventions (are they intentional/effective?)

   c. Try to offer the writer insight into her prose style.
      Among other things, you might tell her:
      - what you notice about word choice
      - which sentences are effective (and *why*) and which ones are choppy, tangled, confusing, or so on

- about the strategies you notice (metaphorical language, repetition, balance, circular movement, self-consciousness); suggest whether they should be used more or less often
- about style or technique by saying how the writer's prose differs or seems similar to your own

There is always something to say about a piece of writing. All writings can be studied and, through careful response, be strengthened. Your comments will help other writers challenge themselves.

# Hint Sheet J: The Executive Summary for Sorting out Full-class Responses

You go to the writing response workshop to share work and gain revision ideas. After the workshop, the formerly nervous writer returns to a text, needing to make decisions, to sort out emotional reactions, and to draw energy from what was said and suggested.

To get some needed distance from the workshop situation, try writing an executive summary and revision plan. Some writers need to do this just once, to internalize and formalize a process of sorting and weighing advice. Other writers will find this a useful sequence to follow after each workshop, particularly if the writer needs to delay revision to a later time—the executive summary can keep revision ideas fresh and well ordered.

Here's how the sequence could work for you, but remember, it's the thinking process that's important, the way you list and summarize will be the way that makes the most sense to you, the writer.

Do the following, before you forget what was said in the workshop.

1. Read all the written responses and write an executive summary by listing and tabulating comments and numbers of times you received them. (Remember—there are various ways to present these summary lists but it should be easy to skim to get a general impression of agreement and contradictions—you'll receive both.)

2. Write a short response to the workshop and then discuss what you think about contradictory suggestions.

3. Write a detailed one-page revision plan and revision timetable.

4. Revise (following your plan if it helps—remember, it's a plan, an aid, not a straightjacket. Like a diver who "imagines" a dive before executing the dive, you're "imagining" the revision in great detail before executing it. But when you dive [write] you work to do the best you can at that instant).

# Hint Sheet K: Radical Revision

Choose a class essay from early in the term that is already "retired"; it's easier to radically revise an essay you're at least temporarily finished with and/or don't feel close to.

1. You will revise this paper in a way that challenges you to take risks and try something you've never tried before.

2. The revision can end up less effective than the original (there's no real risk taking without the possibility of failure).

3. The core of the assignment is your process cover sheet where you recount what you chose to do, and why—why is this a risk/challenge for you as a writer, how it worked, and what you learned.

For next class, bring both your earlier essays and a freewrite exploration of what you could do with each one to create a radical revision. Share these with your group and decide where you'll go next.

To radically revise, try one or more of the following:

*Voice/Tone Changes.* Double, multiple, meta-voice, interrupting voice, change from first to third or try second singular or third plural; write as a character, change tone (serious to comic, for example), change point of view from conventional expectations, Socratic dialogue, change ethnicity, change perspective, use stream of consciousness, use point of view of something inanimate, use a voice to question authority of the text.

*Syntax Changes.* Alternate sentence length, in planned patterns; sentences in arbitrary lengths (all in seven words); use computer spell-check alternates to distort tone; use spell-check alternates to insert "nonsense" words; translate into another language (and maybe translate back again), double columns to highlight double voice.

*Genre Changes.* Nonfiction to poem to song to ad campaigns, bumper stickers, fables, letters, sermon, journal, fairy tale, recipe, prayer, cartoon, and nontext genres—dolls, origami, game.

*Audience Changes.* Change from adult to child to alien, fracture or change tone, try parody, imitation (sometimes, really, variations of tone/voice changes?).

*Time Changes.*    Future (flashforwards, flashbacks), continuous present, parallel times, simultaneity, tell backwards, situate in different era or point of time, change expected climax point of narrative.

*Typography/Physical Layout.*    Different fonts for speakers or emphasis, one sentence per page, large margins and illuminate, cyber text, lengthen, space differently, shorten/compress.

*Multimedia/Art Piece.*    Performance, play, audio and/or videotape, art installation, sing-along, write on unexpected objects (shirts, shoes, walls), choral performance, mime, push your text, fracture, bend, flip, break conventions to learn about them.

# Hint Sheet L: The Processes of Writing Portfolios

## Handout for Submitting Writing Portfolios

Your final portfolios should be in a plain, inexpensive, two-pocket folder. They're due at the beginning of our last class. *I will not be returning any material in the portfolio so please be sure to photocopy anything you want to keep or give me photocopies and keep the originals.*

1. In the left pocket of the portfolio, I'll expect to see your final course work. Each essay should have a process cover sheet attached to it (the story of how you wrote the essay—about a one-page narrative). Each essay should have your name, date, the course number, and the title on it, followed by the typed body of the text. I'll also want either the radical revision/or a "script" for the radical revision and the extended process cover sheet for the radical revision.

2. In the right side of the pocket, I'll expect to see, clipped together, early drafts and class materials for each essay. I'd like no more than two earlier drafts—first full-breadth draft and one professional quality workshop(ed) draft (shared with a small or large group) and copies of the most useful responses peers made. Essentially, this side represents the raw material of your drafting and process cover sheets. This is where you can store a copy of your executive summary for the essay you shared with us all.

3. In the right side of the pocket, I also require a final letter from you to me, maximum two, single-spaced pages. I would like your letter to address *all* of the following issues (in whatever order you like):

   • Read the final drafts of your essays and cover sheets. Take me through each of these essays pointing out what you learned, what worked and didn't work, where you think your writing and reading of writing (ability to improve your own texts) improved. If you didn't see much growth, tell me why that is and how the class could be changed to help future students improve as writers and readers of writing.

   • What were your favorite class activities? In what ways did they help you as a writer/reader?

   • Revisit some of your earliest class journal entries/exploratory writings about reading and your first essay, and discuss what—if any—has changed in your understanding of yourself as a reader of texts.

- What in the class activities and assignments would you urge me to keep and what should I change?

- How did this course meet or disappoint your expectations about what you'd accomplish?

- Think about your own participation in all the class elements—discussion, reading, writing, responding to peers' texts, reading group, researching, and so on. Talk about your strengths and your weaknesses in participation.

- Who in the class influenced you, helped you, taught you the most? What specifically did he/she do? In turn, who do you think you influenced, helped, interacted with most usefully?

- Reread the course information sheet. Given the class design and your own knowledge of your participation and progress in class, give yourself a grade using any scale you like: check, check minus, or check plus; 1–10 (ten is high); A, B, C, D, F—(you know how those work);and so on. Explain in some detail the basis for your decision.

- Tell me one or two things about the class that I should know but didn't ask about.

Think of this letter as a "user's guide" to your portfolio. Your answers will help me to read your work with more skill and appreciation and will help me improve the class for future students.

# Handout for a Portfolio Checklist

Evaluation for:  _____

*Please complete and put inside the front of your portfolio.*

Completeness—portfolio drafts:

_____  Paper 1 (title)  _____

_____  Paper 2 _____
         includes executive summary for full-class workshop

_____  Paper 3 _____

_____  Radical revision (and/or "script" describing project)

_____  Writing process cover sheets papers 1–3

_____  Extended process cover sheet for radical revision project

_____  Letter of self-evaluation

_____  Drafts for each paper

         It seems to me, I was absent on the following dates: _____

         I was late: seldom; often; never (circle one) or supply dates:_____

Final thoughts, if any, that might help a reader to read my portfolio:

_____

_____


For the teacher's use

Attendance/Participation (30%): _____

Portfolio/Writing (70%): _____    _____

                          Final Course Grade: _____

# Works Cited

Brodkey, Linda (1997). "Writing on the Bias." *College English.*

Myer, Sam (1988). "Prose by Any Other Name: A Context for Teaching the Rhetoric of Titles." *Rhetoric Review* 8, 71–81.

Leahy, Richard (1992). "Twenty Titles for the Writer." *College Composition and Communication,* 516–519.